Hand-Hewn in Old Vermont

by Ruth M. Rasey Simpson

Published by

CRANE HILL
P U B L I S H E R S
2923 Crescent Avenue
Birmingham, Alabama 35209

Illustrations by Burton Turner, except
cover illustration by Scott Fuller

Library of Congress Catalog Card Number: 93-71112

ISBN: 1-881548-05-8

For Ruby and Arthur,
with treasured memories of our own
hand-hewn days in our Vermont

Books by the author

ACKNOWLEDGMENTS

The main portion of the material for this book has come from the diaries, scrapbooks, notebooks, personal manuscripts, almanacs, newspapers, and letters which belonged to my ancestors, especially my Grandfather Seymour Harwood, his father, and his cousins. His 1860 editions of *The Geological Survey of Vermont* and of *The Statutes of Vermont*, his 1840 edition of the *Thomsonian Materia Medica*, and an oldtime cookbook have also provided much information.

My understanding of the contents of these books and papers has been greatly expanded and clarified by research-tours of the Museum at Shelburne, Vermont; the Hyde Log Cabin at Grand Isle, Vermont; Old Sturbridge Village in Massachusetts; the Farmers' Museum at Cooperstown, New York; the Gettysburg National Cemetery; the Arlington National Cemetery; many public buildings at Washington, D.C.; and numerous burial grounds in the states of Vermont and New York, as well as the Missionaries' House in Honolulu, Hawaii.

To my sister, Ruby (Mrs. J. Leslie Tyler), her son James, and my brother Arthur Rasey, I am indebted for further addition and clarification of historical and agricultural detail.

The late Bernis Kinnie, generally known as "D," supplied the main body of material pertaining to the marble industry. This was supplemented by the papers of the late Ernest West. Access to these was granted by the late Katherine E. Child, Dorset Librarian, and the late Anna Gilbert, Secretary of the Dorset Historical Society. To Dr. L.J. Whalon, I wish to express appreciation for permission to quote his father's poem, "Quarry Voice." Further details regarding "Dorset Marble" I secured from Roy Webster, Superintendent of the Danby Tunnel for many years, and from several desk clerks who searched out brochures at the New York Public Library.

ACKNOWLEDGEMENTS

I am especially grateful to Richard Carter Barrett, the former Director-Curator of Bennington Museum, to the late Allen D. Hill and to Charles G. Bennet, Genealogical Consultants at the same Museum, for access to early issues of newspapers and the other papers, now filed in the Museum Library.

I am equally grateful to Mr. and Mrs. Jay Beebe for access to the Rupert Town Records; to Mr. and Mrs. William Bahan for the Sunderland Records; and to "Desk Clerks" at the Bennington Town Clerk's Office for Records filed there.

My expression of thanks goes also to the late James McCabe for the data in the Dr. George Russell Library at Arlington, Vermont.

Others who have supplied me with most helpful information include: Duncan A. Campbell, Hugh T. Putnam Jr., William H. Meyer, Donald Lourie, and others of the Merck Forest Foundation staff; the late Mr. and Mrs. Gilbert Croff and Mrs. Wilma Batease regarding "Moore's Inn"; the Paul Bohnes of Bennington, owners of Apple Hill; the late John Spargo, Director-Curator of Bennington Museum and publisher of local history booklets, and Albertine Loomis of Honolulu, great-granddaughter of two of the first American Missionaries to Hawaii.

The Vermont Historical Society, National Life Insurance Company of Montpelier, and The Vermont Marble Company all provided photographs, which were most valuable aids in my research, as well as source material for the illustrations in this work.

Much gratitude goes also to my most understanding and helpful husband, E. Wilbur Simpson, whose photography likewise expanded my knowledge and provided further illustrative material. My appreciation includes, too, the host of others whose generous interest, criticism, and observations have been most stimulating throughout the years of my preparing this book.

All of these have, indeed, implemented *Hand-Hewn in Old Vermont*.

R. M. R. S.

Arlington, Vermont
August 29, 1978

SPECIAL ACKNOWLEDGMENT

■ Author appreciation goes to Yankee, Inc., Dublin, N.H., for permission to reprint the chapter, "Up on Apple Hill." This was published, in condensed form, in the September, 1975, issue of *Yankee*.

FOREWORD

With a sense of exaltation and of exultation, our nation has celebrated its 200th anniversary of independence. Pride in achievement and pleasure in benefits taken for granted all too frequently outweigh humility and gratitude in our appraisal of the gargantuan accomplishment that has brought America through a union of 13 colonies bordering the Atlantic Ocean to one of 50 states extending far into the Pacific.

Significantly, it was the effort of a son of the first state to join the original 13 that contributed much to the development of the 50th member of our Union today. A young Green Mountain farmer, turned missionary, Hiram Bingham, in the 1820s first reduced the Hawaiian language to written form, thus laying the cornerstone for the state. The essential ruggedness of body and of spirit, with which he toiled in the Sandwich Islands, had been acquired in his youthful labors among the rocks and trees of his father's pioneered acres, now the site of Bennington College.

From the New England frontier and the rest of the Atlantic seaboard, the American boundaries were laboriously extended, geographically, economically, and culturally, across the centuries, across continent and ocean.

Our National Department of Agriculture has said that it took "a great quantity of wood to build the United States." It likewise required a tremendous amount of hewing with resourceful and purposeful hands.

Hand-Hewn in Old Vermont tells a part of that story of building from the wood of the primeval forest and from the stone of the heretofore unopened quarry. The men, women, and children who did the hewing had been schooled by their own and their forebears' experience in the earlier settlements of Massachusetts, Connecticut, Rhode Island and New Hampshire. Unlike many today, who regard challenge as hardship, they accepted hardship as challenge.

FOREWORD

In order to appreciate our national heritage, we need an acute awareness of the way the early builders of our country wrought to accomplish their dream. Constant labor of both mind and muscle was the essence of that building. The love of home and family provided the basic impetus. With this love, there burned fiercely in the hearts of the pioneers a love of independence. Omnipresent within them also was Faith in their Maker and in His Purpose for them. Through stern discipline, they applied the essential thrift, self-reliance, courage, and endurance required to establish their homes, their industries, and their cultural institutions.

Recently, at a campfire gathering of members of the National Student Conservation Association, who annually come to the Merck Forest for land and forest research and operations, one of the youths from California made a poignant remark. "When we hear how the early settlers worked to build America, we seem like TWIGS compared with them as TREES. And it makes me want to get busy at doing something worthwhile with my life."

"A lot of others would, too," a boy from Ohio added, "if they could know what everyday life was really like in those early days."

It is hoped that *Hand-Hewn in Old Vermont* may tell at least some of today's young Americans "what everyday life was really like in those early days," as portrayed by a typical community in the northeastern part of the United States.

This is no political nor military history. It is an account of some of the daily customs and struggles in the lives of those who wrought together on the grassroots foundation of a Free America.

R.M.R.S.

Arlington, Vermont
August 29, 1978

Table of Contents

1

OUT OF THE WILDERNESS

High among the hills of Southwestern Vermont, a 2700-acre meadow-and-woodland preserve opens its well-marked trails to rich outdoor living and learning experiences for thousands of visitors each year. Near the entrance, which is barred to all vehicles except service trucks and jeeps, is the overseer's snug log cabin. A few rods beyond, the big weathered grey barn, "raised" in the 1850s, houses the chief administrator's office, a small wildlife museum, and some farm animals, including a team of workhorses. Rosie, the pet doe, occasionally seeks its shelter.

A woods road leads from the barn to the craft center a mile or so away. Within its spacious interior, heated by a big stone fireplace and lighted by great windows that face the vast panorama of mountains to the west, students convene for sundry creative activities.

Other structures on the preserve are a dozen or so camp lean-tos and a saphouse where four or five hundred gallons of high quality maple syrup are produced each spring.

This preserve is now known as the Merck Forest Foundation. It was established as The Vermont Forest and Farmland Foundation in 1950 by the late George W. Merck of the Merck Pharmaceuticals Industry. He donated the land, comprised of several abandoned farms, for a multiple land use program.

After his death, the Foundation was dedicated on October 3, 1959, as the George W. Merck Memorial Forest. His longtime friend, John P.

Marquand, the novelist, speaking on that occasion, noted: "He was always thinking of something constructive and useful, generally for others....Due to his vision....we are standing in a challenging and interesting area....It is fitting indeed that the Merck Forest should give help and inspiration to all who walk along its paths."

Within two centuries, these several hundred acres at the top of Rupert Mountain have come full circle. Until the late 1760s, a primeval forest of hard woods, birch, and evergreens covered the area.

More than three quarters of the 200 years since were marked by the characteristic pioneer struggle for establishing and maintaining homes in New England. Here the early settlers wrested from the wilderness a hillside community with more than a dozen productive and self-sustaining farms, a sawmill, a schoolhouse for 60 or more "scholars", a cheese factory, and a stagecoach line. All these were, in turn, merged into a half dozen or so comparatively prosperous dairy and/or sheep farms, from the mid-1800's to the early 1900s.

These subsequently abandoned upland fields and woodlands, crested by Harmon Hill and Mount Antone, now provide a valuable educational and recreational preserve. The 20-odd miles of hiking and cross country ski trails wind among lilac-marked cellar holes, tumbled stone walls, numerous streams, ponds, and meadows, a demonstration garden, a Christmas tree plantation, a sugarbush, a managed woodland, and a designated wilderness area.

The thousands of all ages, who constantly come from near and far to take advantage of the opportunities offered here, have shown great interest in the history of this mountain, so typical of Northeast American pioneer settlement.

According to legend, Reuben Harmon and Amos Curtis whoaed their floundering ox team to a halt at a rocky opening among the trees in the Big Woods here on the mountain one wind-whipped zero afternoon in mid-February, 1767.

"Whadya say we set camp here?" Harmon bellowed against the wind to Barnabas Barnum, Oliver Scott, and Isaac Blood, who followed close behind the ox-sled. Three coonskin caps nodded approval.

The year before, they had drawn their 50-acre allotments numerically from a hat at the Propriety Meeting in Bennington, according to the regulations for pioneer settlements established by the King of England and his representative, Governor Benning Wentworth of New Hampshire. They had purchased additional land from some who decided to sell their drawings for these Hampshire Grants.

The snowdrifted trail to this mountain had led these five of the first 64 Proprietors of Rupert township among tall trees that had been marked or "blazed" by Propriety Surveyors the preceding summer. From experience they knew that this was the best time of year to cut timbers for building. No sap was running in the trees so the logs would be partly seasoned before they went to the axe for hewing. For their homes, to be built in late spring, these young men would need logs that would lie straight and true. Therefore, they and their ox-team, Duke and Turk, had wallowed and lunged their way over the hills from Bennington to their new mountain holdings on these two blue-arched days in the "right time of the moon".

Hay and corn to supplement the woods browse for their oxen, corn meal, fat pork, and a keg of cider for themselves were their only provisions. But for the past several winters they had been accustomed to baking their cornmeal-and-water "journey cake" on a green slab of pine beside their woodlot campfires on the mountainsides of Bennington. Dipped in a noggin (wooden mug) of cider to soften and flavor the hard crust, and eaten with a thick chunk of salt pork, this johnnycake well comforted and fortified a man to swing an axe from the moment grey dawn outlined East Ridge until darkness blotted out the trees.

Twenty-four-year-old Barnabas Barnum, tall, broad-shouldered, and renowned for his Herculean strength, tossed the tow sacks of corn and bundles of hay from the ox-sled into a wall beside the flat rock that jutted up out of the snow. The cliff behind it somewhat eased the chill of the west wind. Here on the rock they would kindle their campfire, and nearby they would build their brush lean-to.

With only an axe apiece (no saws for use in the forest were available then), the other four deerskin-clad men soon gathered sufficient white birch twigs and branches to lay their fire. How glad they were to see the white birch, for it would burn when freshly cut, even in wet weather. The pile of ruddy coals which they had brought with them in an iron kettle, from their paternal hearth fires, soon set the bark ablaze. With the surrounding snow packed hard by moccasin and hoof and sled, the pile of glowing embers at the center of the walled-in circle gave ample heat for a night of renewing sleep. And for protection from any prowling panther, wolf, or bobcat that might come investigating this strange, penetrating, and ominous scent of ox and man.

Early the next morning, the mountain wilderness rang with the axe blows of the settlers.

One reservation of the British King, stated in the Rupert Grant issued by Benning Wentworth on August 30, 1761, as was likewise stated in most

English colonial grants, somewhat curbed the operations of these fron-tiersmen. In their "cut down", or chopping trees for their homes and for space to plant, as well as in all their subsequent timber slashing, they were commanded to spare every pine tree two or more feet in diameter, measured a foot from the ground.

"We found white pines on that mountain," one of the surveyors had reported earlier, "as much as 250 feet tall and six feet through the butt." Many that the settlers eventually cut there measured three or more feet in diameter "chest high" from the ground.

During the nearly two years since the first Rupert Proprietors' Meeting at the house of Captain John Fassett, Innholder, in Bennington on April 16, 1765, these young men who planned to come to Rupert had committed to memory the terms of the customary British Grant of that time:

"That every Grantee plant and cultivate five acres of land the term of five years for every fifty acres contained in his or their share—continue to improve and settle same—on Penalty of Forfeiture of his Grant—That all white and other pine trees fit for masting our Royal Navy be carefully preserved for that use, none to be cut and felled without our special License for so doing be first obtained—Yielding and paying therefore to us—for the space of ten years—the Rent of one ear of Indian corn only on the twenty-fifth day of December, annually—the first payment 1762—after the expiration of ten years December, 1772, one shilling Proclamation Money for every hundred acres, he so own, settles or possesses."

On each of their fifty-acre divisions that spring of 1767, Barnum and Curtis, Harmon, Blood, and Scott carefully avoided from day to day the "white and other pine trees fit for masting our Royal Navy" among those they felled. Those to be left standing had been marked with the customary "broad arrow" made by three hatchet strokes in the form somewhat resembling a crow's track, by Captain Jahiel Hawley, Thomas Burton, and Samuel Robinson, Jr., who were chosen by the Propriety to "lay out the first Division."

Subsequently, most of the pines so marked as "mast trees to the crown" actually were felled to meet pioneer need, without "special License" or penalty. However, as late as 1825, a few of the tall giants, two feet or more in diameter, bearing the "broad arrow" mark, could still be seen in remote sections of the summit woodland. Others by then had gone to mast the young United States Navy against the Crown.

Nevertheless, the five Grantees observed the terms of the Grant in those wintry days as their prodigious labor with ox-team and axe accumu-lated the piles of logs to season for the spring building. The ages-old humus of the forest floor had given to that first growth timber timeless strength and other factors for endurance. Its hardness daily tested the faculties of the axemen.

Those strong-fibered pioneers felt a kind of kinship with the primeval trees among which they worked. Their roots, too, would soon be going deep into the black earth, recently surveyed and recorded to them, and where their own footprints were now marking their individual boundaries. Muscle and mind exulted in this initial conquest of a new frontier. On this mountain they would find a fuller freedom, a greater independence. Here they would plow and plant. Here they would tend and harvest their crops. And here they would extend their acres, raise their families, and meet untold challenges of land and of life. Strength born of hope, aspiration, and faith in the Divine Guidance of their Creator surged high within them in the invigorating mountain air.

By late February, these five Proprietors judged that sufficient logs for their respective homes lay ready for their completed seasoning in the spring sunshine, wind, and rain, so they went back to their dwellings in Bennington.

In late May, they returned to their holdings, bringing with them their wives and children. Jonathan Eastman and a half dozen of the other Proprietors from the Flats to the East assembled also to help with the cabin building. Log homes for themselves they had just completed in the nearby valley of the Mettowee, allegedly meaning "good earth", and so named by the Mohawk Indians, some of whom had often roamed this area from their nearby settlements in eastern New York State.

The feathery green of new leaves canopied the mountain, sifting the sun's rays into shadowy patterns and elemental fragrance on the warming leaf mold. The carols of bluebirds and robins mingled with the beat of the partridge drumming for his mate. Warblers, vireos, and chickadees sang as they busied themselves with their nests. A fox and his vixen barked and gamboled on a lichened ledge. Beside the white water that gushed in sparkling cascades down the hillside streams, pink and yellow lady's-slippers spread their magic bloom. Everywhere, the woodland was burgeoning with its reawakening and its promise. As these first settlers here hewed at their new homes, they, too, felt the promise of the Power that rules the Universe. Throughout the summer, their confidence in the promise grew in fulfillment.

By fall, five log houses and a barn stood a half mile or so apart upon the Mountain Grants.

From the woodlot at each cabin door came maple for the plates, bowls and other greenware for table use; birch for household brush and broom; oak for bucket and tub, the green "popple" for the lugpole to hold the black iron kettles bubbling over the hearth fire, and ash, hickory, pine, and hemlock for many another frontier need.

More than building, however, occupied those Proprietors of Rupert during the summer days of 1767. Acres and acres of trees they felled or girdled by hacking off a foot wide band of bark and cambian layer a yard from the base to clear the land for planting. The rhythmic, muffled beat of the axe echoed continuously among the trees from earliest dawn through the twilight.

The method of cutting revealed daring ingenuity. A giant of the woods chosen as the kingpin tree was worked on by one man, usually Barnabas Barnum. Around it, within its falling range, the other men chopped partly through the trunks of other trees. Then, at a signal, the king tree was felled, crashing against the others, which in turn felled those partly cut ones against which they crashed. Caution and courage were the woodsmen's constant watchwords as they toiled among the trees.

This slashing of timber to clear the fields revealed an inspiring vista of mountains to the westward and northward, of well-watered valleys and wooded hills to the south and to the east. Dreams of crops-to-be, of neighbors gathering, and of clearing further ranges for future generations marked the labors in this wilderness.

The densely tangled crisscross trunks with their upreared branches lost much of their moisture to evaporation through their yellowing leaves here upon the ground throughout the summer. Then, one bright, dry day in early fall, Barnum, Scott, Harmon, Blood, and Curtis, each with a burning brand in turn fired their slashed acres at a point where the light breeze would carry the blaze away from their cabins. Red and orange flames leaped and crackled; grey smoke billowed and the mountain air was pungent with the scent of burning leaves and branches. As the fire died and cooled, leaving a blackened mass of stumps and trunks and larger limbs upon the woods-damp ground, the men set to work with their axes to prepare the mass for a second firing. They then hacked the great tree trunks into lengths that could be drawn by ox-team.

Then came the log rolling. Again the settlers from Mettowee Flats at the east end of the township joined the men on the summit for this "bee" of men and oxen. The faithful, powerful-bodied animals were yoked in pairs by a U-shaped ash bow placed under each neck and joined by a stout hickory bar across the top, so that the contrivance encircled the neck of each and held them a foot or so apart. The bar was pinned in place by whittled maple pegs. Hitched to a huge log by a heavy chain with a hand-forged hook at each end, the team was given the command. "Giddup"! Horny hooves gripped the earth and mighty shoulders bulged against the yoke. One after another, the semi-charred logs were snaked to the piling places, at each of which fifty or so of them were loosely stacked in windrows for future firing.

The following spring while the ground was still wet, consuming flames again roared through the pile of seasoned limbs and logs leaving a residue of fertilizing potash upon the woodland earth. Well did the men know the need for firing while the ground was damp so as not to impoverish the soil by overburning or heating too deep beneath the surface.

When broad acres had been thus cleared of timber, there still remained a dense growth of tough and craggy stumps. Again, with long days of "Giddup", "Gee", "Haw", and "Whoa", Barnabas and his neighbors urged their oxen to the tremendous task of yanking the toughest of those deep-rooted monsters out of the ground and to their field boundaries for fences of pasture and meadow. These were mainly the white pine stumps, for wheat and flax could be sown amidst the more widely spaced birch and beech, maple and basswood, elm, ash, and hemlock ones. Those would crumble within a dozen years or less anyway, even if left alone. The white oak and chestnut must be yanked out the following spring when there would be more time. If left to decay in the soil, they would last a quarter century or more. But the white pine crags would stand for a century or more if they were not removed. Besides, they would tear a wooden plow apart before the earth around them could be broken for planting.

By early July, 1767, Barnabas Barnum had seeded the first one-acre field he had wrested from the forest. A forked ash tree, hewn with the broad-axe, had given him his plow. For handles on this one-piece share and beam he had pegged a pair of slanting uprights cut from twin hickory saplings with a crook at the butt. This plow and its similarly fashioned successors, drawn by Buck and Bright, by Star and Brindle, and by succeeding ox-teams, mellowed the summit meadow soil for more than twoscore planting seasons. By 1820, the "Swallow Tail", a plow with iron point and mouldboard, was turning the furrows in the former woodland. Nevertheless, it was the earliest primitive wooden one, fashioned from summit trees, that first broke the wilderness floor for food-cropped acres. Fortunately, no weed seeds had found their way here to dispute the growth of grain the first year.

A two-bushel sowing of wheat on his holding the fall of 1768 yielded a fifty-bushel return to Barnabas the following summer. The next season, a bushel of rye brought a thirty-fold crop of flailed and winnowed grain. The fall of 1771 he harvested one hundred bushels of ruddy, full-kerneled ears of King Philip dent corn from the one-acre piece he had recently cleared. Reportedly, Reuben Harmon claimed a similar return, and the other Proprietors were "satisfied" with their harvests. With considerable gratification they paid their annual rent of "one ear of Indian corn only" that 25th day of December, for each 50-acre grant.

The flax grounds soon proved as productive as the other fields, insuring ample supplies of household linens, tow shirts, breeches, and dresses for the pioneer families. Grazing lands were also being developed to provide for the Jersey cows and Shropshire sheep, with their annual increase to flock and herd.

Though progress was constant, it was slow. It was also defined by long days of arduous labor to wrest a living and a margin from the hand-tilled, rock-and-stump-torn soil.

Worst challenge of all, the Tories disrupted the township in the 1770s. When Town Clerk Josiah Cass and his followers began burning log homes, barns, and stacks of grain among the neighbors, some of the First Proprietors packed up their families, with as much food and clothing as they could carry, and returned to their former homes in Bennington and Connecticut. There the women and children remained while the men served in the Revolution.

Reuben Harmon and Amos Curtis represented Rupert Township at the Grants Convention held at the home of Cephas Kent in Dorset on July 24th, 1776. Barnabas Barnum, who had returned to Bennington somewhat earlier, had been commissioned a First Lieutenant of the Green Mountain Boys at a meeting there the preceding year.

When the pioneers returned to Rupert, following the evacuation of the English from the New England area in the late 1770s, they were hugely relieved to find some cabins still standing and some household possessions still secure where they had been hidden. A fire shovel among the willows, a wedding ring at the bottom of a washtub full of water, bake kettles and iron tongs in a hollow oak, all were joyfully reclaimed and returned to service.

A few of the Rupert frontiersmen did not come back, however. Some remained in Connecticut or in other newly established homes, and some had given their lives in the cause of liberty. Barnabas Barnum was among the latter.

In December of 1780, the men of Rupert, in what had then become the State of Vermont, met at the home of "Jonathan Eastman, Innholder," "to establish their former votes and proceedings as some records had been carried off by Clerk Josiah Cass, a Tory."

A few years after their re-establishment of the township, those mountain settlers were pithily described by the Reverend Nathan Perkins of Hartford, Connecticut, who in 1789 made a "Missionary trip to Pollet, Rupert, and Dorset." His observations dealt particularly with the most remote section of hill country bordering Reuben Harmon's first grants: "Got lost in ye woods—heard ye horrible howling of ye wolves. Far absent in ye wilderness—among log huts. All people sadly parsimonious—many profane—yet cheerful and much more contented than in Hartford—and the women more contented than ye men—turned tawny by ye smoke of ye log huts—dress coarse and mean—Some very clever women and men—serious and sensible.

"Woods make people love one another and kind and obliging and good-natured.... They set much more by one another than in ye old settlements.

"Ye women quiet, serene,—peaceable, contented, loving their husbands—wanting never to return—nor any dressy clothes."

When John Graham, a lawyer from Rutland, visited a client in the same area a few years later, he wrote rather differently: "The inhabitants are good husbandmen and keep their farms, barns, and stalls in the best order and in a manner that proves Industry loves to reside among them. I do not know anything more creditable to a country than that neatness, which without doors as well as within, is a sure sign of cheerfulness, content, and plenty.

"The women of this State bear hardships in an incredible degree."

Fortunate it was that "Industry loves to reside among them." Securing fuel for the fireplace and brick oven, and later for kitchen range, for parlor chunk stove, and for even a 1930 furnace was annually an arduous operation in the mountain timber lot. Again, the moon exerted its influence. An almanac of the 1790s advised: "At this quarter (first week in January), cut fire wood to prevent it from snapping and throwing embers beyond the hearth."

Hard work though it was to procure the backlogs, fifteen to twenty inches in diameter and five feet long, as well as the somewhat smaller forelogs for those pioneer fireplaces, it was even harder work to acquire the stove wood of later years. Only an exceptionally "good man with an axe" could cut, split, and stack a cord of wood in a day. Approximately twenty cords, equal in fuel value to twenty tons of coal, were needed for each of those drafty mountain cabins during each year. Even a greater supply was required for each saltbox house or spacious Colonial that followed. The diary of one of Great-Grandfather's nephews gives some details of securing the family fuel one winter in the early 1800s.

"January 10: An uncomfortable day in the woods — heavy S. wind blew violently so the woods roared with it. A big basswood near me swayed terrifyingly. My dress was a woolen shirt with a neck handkerchief, coarse boots, old felt hat, long jacket, large overalls, a short strait bodied coat, and an old shortened great coat. In felling our third tree a big one, I was so unfortunate as to have it fall over a high ridge of rocks near which it stood, hoisting the end which was severed from the stump 15 feet in the air. I cut it off on the ridge which caused it to fall fast against the stump. Ira had now arrived with the team. Cutting the end of the log, contriving, prying, fastening the team to it and drawing stoutly finally removed it from the stump but she stuck fast to the rock. After tugging at it a long while, almost in despair, she was forced down the hill, but to our chagrin we saw it strike a beech tree. As the team attempted to draw it on, they broke the chain, which was the least ill we suffered. The end of the log was trimmed, but at the next pull, that and the sled slipped many feet down the hill, breaking the rod that passes from one beam to the next. We left it and came home.

"Jan. 11th: Severe cold this a.m. after stormy night. Roads frozen up edgewise. Good sledding on the hard crust—best this season. Drew down the big basswood and 5 loads wood altogether. Fastened a harrow on to hind end to hold back in descending the hill. Late in the day sledding bad going down, imminent danger of oversetting in several places. Oxen and horses together on the big sled, balling of the horses' feet made them slide to and fro. Off ox so unlucky as to tear off one of his dew claws (the small horny growth above and back of the ankle that touched the ground in going down a slope, thus helping the ox to brake the load by bracing his feet) so did not draw any more today. Would judge a good half cord, somewhat more than a ton on each load.

"March 8th: Snow thin as paper. The hill was heavy to rise. The friction was so great as almost to set fire to the runners. Brought down the last of what wood we calculated to get this season, making an aggregate of fifty loads or nearly thirty cords."

The same woodland supplied the timber for building the several commodious farmhouses and barns that succeeded the log structures in the mountain community. These woods also furnished the timber for a succession of two log schoolhouses, a crude frame one, and finally the District No. 8 red schoolhouse, where many a hill youth obtained his entire academic education. Built in 1851, it now is the vacation home of the Andrew Painter family from Darien, Connecticut .

A yellowed journal among Great Grandfather's family papers, dated 1858, gives an account of a certain rugged woodsman who had toiled on the mountain.

"In early days Joshua Moore of Shaftsbury came to work for Neighbor C at $7 per month, chopping logs all day in winter, eating coarse bread and milk for dinner out of a dish formed by making a hollow cavity in his leather shoe-making apron—laboring hard as long as daylight lasted— after which would return some distance to the house—sup on hasty pudding and milk or other very simple coarse fare and spend the remainder of the evening until 10 o'clock making shoes Go to bed and rise by 4 next morning & go through the same routine—So we presume he went on for years acquiring the habits of Herculean industry, rigid economy & all iron requisites for gaining wealth which resulted in establishing him among the most wealthy farmers in the county."

Joshua was one of a long line of lumbermen who have "logged it" on these hills. Sylvanus Wright and Abner Stone were two who worked here in the 1830s, earning $1 for cutting either 40 bass logs or 30 of the harder fibered ones and delivering them to the sawmill. For several days at a time, they camped out up on one of the highest slopes, their only shelter a rough log lean-to. With oxen, sleds, and provisions for man and beast, they chopped and sawed through days of wind and snow and cold. Each late afternoon they drew down a load of timber, one sled hitched behind the other to accommodate the longest logs, the double load drawn by the four-ox-team.

One January day, the teamsters reported an amazing "cut". This was an ancient ash, measuring four feet six inches in diameter several feet up the butt. It had required considerable strength and ingenuity to work up its four logs, each 12 feet long, and each totaling about 2300 board feet of trimmed timber. After delivering the logs to Noble's Mill in Kent Hollow, they returned to their camp by moonlight, there resuming their chopping at sunrise.

"Sylvanus," his partner reported on one such trip, "had the misfortune to get frostbitten in the toes of his right foot and in his right ear this morning." Regardless of such discomfort, Sylvanus returned to the timber lot that evening with Abner. The next four days the two men were weather-bound at their camp by a paralyzing blizzard.

When it cleared, Sylvanus' younger brother Bijah donned snowshoes and his warmest gear. Setting forth up the mountain, he hauled a flat sled loaded with corn, potatoes, ham, cheese, and cider through the white wilderness to the stranded men. "Saved our lives most likely". Sylvanus grinned in appreciation, as the three bearskin wrapped youths huddled around the campfire where slabs of ham were beginning to sizzle.

Another who chopped in those woods was not so fortunate. A few years later. when young Jonas Allen did not return from his woodlot for his evening meal at sunset nor even by late milking time, his wife ran the mile from her home to Great-Grandfather Joseph's house to ask him to go in search of her husband. Fearful of what he would find, Grandfather seized a blanket, a rope, and a bottle of brandy and urged his fastest horse up the cart track to Allen's woodlot, which bordered his own. The woods roared with an east gale. It tore and smothered his cries of "Jonas!"

At last, Grandfather came upon his friend—pinned beneath the oak that he had felled for fence rails. The white moonlight cast ghostly shadows upon the lifeless figure. Shuddering as with a fit of ague, Grandfather tried to force some of the brandy between the stiffened lips, but to no avail. The shock and horror of that tragic night haunted him all the rest of his days.

But Allen's widow stood in need of a fence around her meadow. Grimly, Great-Grandfather Joseph headed the "bee" that split and set the rails from the last oak that Jonas had felled. "He would have done as much for mine," Grandfather reflected in an agony of remembering their good years together, as he resolutely swung his axe to help fence the last field that Jonas had chopped, tree by tree, out of the wilderness.

In the late 1840s, a gang of other hardy loggers plied axes and crosscut saws in the Rupert Mountain Woodland. By then, Great-Grandfather and three of his sons owned most of the original grants on Windy Summit, Harmon Hill, and the adjacent area. Oliver Moore's and Jonathan Eastman's descendants held title to the neighboring ones. All these men had sold "on the stump" most of their oak timber to be cut for the railroad which was in the process of construction through the west side of the township. Again the runners of the heavily loaded sleighs creaked and sometimes nearly caught fire from friction. Nevertheless, down the hillside the indispensable logs for fast-developing American transportation were borne from woods to mill and thence to railroad site.

The Telephone Company, at the turn of the century, came stringing their revolutionary lines up among the hills. Again the Summit echoed to axe and saw as the timber lots yielded tall supports for the wires that wrought magic in communication. How the great peeled poles, equipped with glass insulators and wires, hummed on wintry nights, as though they, too, would speak to one another of the wonders of a changing world.

Between the 1920s and the 1940s the pulp mills of eastern New York State were a ready market for all available spruce and pine from these mountain acres. Thundering trucks then replaced the ox and sled for transportation. The chain saw bit through the tough-fibered trunks in a fraction of the time that was required for the old-time axe and hand-powered saw to do the job. But horses were still used here and there for skidding the four-foot logs down the steep descents.

Much besides the securing of fuel and timber marked the story of life in the mountain woodland. One summer in the early 1800s misfortune struck one summit. On July 13th, a newcomer, Freeborn Watson fired some pine stumps in a lot that he was clearing for a meadow. The past month had been hot and dry, so all the other settlers looked dourly upon this ill-timed procedure.

When flying sparks soon ignited the edge of the nearby woods, Great-Grandfather, his sons, and all the other men, as well as most of the women and children, hastened to stamp out the flames or smother them with shovels full of dirt. Some frantically chopped through tree roots where the fire was spreading underground, and dug trenches around their homes. Then, horrified, a few hours later, they saw two other sections of the woodland blaze up. A brief shower momentarily quenched the flames, but they flared up again as soon as a light breeze arose. With green branches wet in the brook and with more shovels full of dirt, the desperate men drove the fire up the mountain away from their homes. There it roared across the Height in a grim holocaust.

Helplessly, Great-Grandfather and his neighbors watched the sky darken with smoke. With religious fervor, they prayed for a drenching rain, but day after day passed, each seeming hotter, drier, more oppressive with smoke and despair than even its predecessors.

At last, on August 2, Great-Uncle Benjamin noted: "Thanks be to God—Our late three days of rain has put a final stop to the fire on the mountains around us. They raged dreadfully the last 8 days, 17 since the first one broke out. They have made a dismal appearance of the Trees that they singed. My loss is about $1,000."

In spite of its ruined appearance, Benjamin and his peers, as well as their descendants, found that the forest rapidly renewed itself after the Great Fire, and again after a devastating tornado, which ripped across it in 1855. That June day the shattering wind, accompanied by rain, hail, thunder, and lightning, uprooted, twisted, and broke off even the largest of the forest trees. Every tree in its path of a half mile width and several miles length across the mountain lay prostrate when the storm was spent.

Some of the neighborhood residents considered the tornado sweep more of a gain than a loss. They were the gum pickers, who found the fallen trees a convenient source of bounty in their work of supplying the Gum Man, Herbert W. Martin of Bennington. Martin reputedly shipped 12,000 pounds of spruce gum of "excellent quality" each year to Boston, New York, and other eastern cities. According to an article in a *Farmer's Almanac* of the late 1800s, much competition had developed in Canada, Maine, New Hampshire, and Vermont for supplying this commodity to flourishing markets from St. John, Canada, to San Francisco. All across the continent, "big consumers" were eager to buy as much as was available. Prepared in gin, it was prescribed by some physicians as a cough medicine. Mainly, though, it was used "just for chewing". The white or pale amber pitch oozed from seams or cracks in the spruce boughs and trunks during August and September. The lumps that hardened on the bark were right for gathering when they were a year and a half old. They were of better quality, however, when they were aged for three years. They did not deteriorate if they remained on the trees for ten years or so.

The relatives of First Proprietor Jonathan Eastman, John and Norman Jenks, who lived half way up the Rupert Mountain Road, made a business of gathering gum each year from early October to late June. Often they would spend three or four nights at a time in a rough shanty at the farthest side of the mountain woods. The best time to gather was when deep snow covered the underbrush and they could snowshoe close to some of the most productive trees. A fallen spruce likewise usually proved a bonanza.

Armed with a ten-foot pole with a chisel on one end and a pint cup attached directly beneath it to receive the chunks as they were pried from the tree, each gum gatherer daily hoped to fill a long tow sack which he carried on his back. A five-pound "picking" was their best days' record. All too often, from one to three pounds comprised a day's harvest.

At home their sister Mary cleaned the pale gold nuggets by removing all bark, moss, and needles. Two to five hundred pounds a year, sold at $1 a pound, maintained an excellent income for the "Jenks Boys" and their sister, on their small homestead, where, indeed, "Industry loved to reside among them."

Another bounty of the wilderness, where the trees had been felled, was the abundance of berries. Juicy red strawberries, some as big as the end of a man's finger; dusky blueberries sweet as ambrosia; tangy crimson raspberries oozing fragrant juice; and plump long blackberries, as big as a woman's thumb! Gathering those berries for pies, shortcakes, and cobblers, or for eating fresh with shaved loaf sugar and thick Jersey cream spelled refreshment for both body and soul.

The berry patches on the mountain teemed with brown calico sunbonnets, pink striped frocks, blue-checked shirts, shiny tin pails, wooden buckets, and birchbark baskets throughout the annual berry season from mid-June to early September. To protect themselves from gnats and mosquitoes, the berry pickers learned early to rub their exposed skin with the crushed leaves of the pungent herb pennyroyal that thrived in the clearings.

Great-Grandmother Vesta credited this "penneroil" with saving Great-Aunt Harriet's life one summer day in her infancy. Great-Grandmother had rubbed her baby well with the aromatic leaves and then laid her on the ground under a shady beech for little Harriet to sleep while the mother gathered blackberries. The profusion of ripe and juicy fruit lured young Vesta farther away than she at first realized .

Suddenly she heard an ominous snort! Terrified, she darted out of the thicket toward her little one. There a huge shaggy black bear was sniffing around the small pink bundle. Paralyzed with fear, Great-Grandmother momentarily froze in her tracks. She could not even scream at the bear. Then she went limp with relief and joy. The hairy intruder was shambling off, sniffing and shaking his head. Like the gnats and mosquitoes, he had an aversion for pennyroyal.

Honey from the trees where wild bees often hived was another especially prized woodland offering. This thick brown ambrosia was a popular sweetener in numerous foods and medications, as well as a favorite confection by itself. Securing the honey was considered a pleasurable outing as well as a provident achievement. One such expedition was vividly described by a nephew of Great-Grandfather's.

"One balmy Sabbath morning Hi Watters was walking home from church. He was dressed in the height of style, large trousers made of bed-ticking, a blue dress coat with brass buttons, a bright red waistcoat, and a stovepipe hat made of genuine beaver that added two feet to his stature. Near home, he met his cousin Shadrach Robinson, returning from Mount Antone where he had been to free a colt that had been caught in a thicket.

" 'Did you know that that big basswood up by the cave is a bee tree?' Robinson asked. Hi knew, for he had found it the day before but he was admitting nothing.

" 'When are ya goin' to get the honey?' he inquired, with an expression of guilelessness.

"'Tomorrow morning at daylight,' Shadrach answered, looking smug and well pleased. It was considered a great achievement to discover a bee tree but an even greater one to get the honey and divide it with the neighbors.

"As Shadrach disappeared around the bend in the road Hiram hurried cross lots to get his friend, Thankgod Harwood. Together, carrying their axes and two large milkpails, they set out toward Mount Antone.

"Arrived at the tree, they first stupefied the bees with smoke by stuffing the opening in the trunk with a chunk of smoldering woolen waste. They then chopped the big old cavern open and scooped out the dark amber sweet. So much dripped out that the pails were soon filled. Still quantities remained. Thankgod dexterously fashioned a basket from a large strip of birch bark lying near, laced it with strings of wild grapevine, and filled it, too, with the sticky delicious stuff. Hi filled his hat.

" 'Gol!' he exclaimed, 'there's gallons yet!' He hauled off his voluminous trousers, tied the bottoms with strands of grapevine, and poured them also full of the honey with its broken comb. Hanging them astraddle his shoulders and gripping his hat, pail and axe, he agreed with his broadly grinning partner that they 'Might's well go now.'

'The peace of this pious community was broken by the appearance of Hi Watters and Thankgod Harwood as they plodded along the road with their load of honey. Red flannel underwear never looked so red before or since.

"On Monday, everyone in the neighborhood ate some of the honey, that is everyone except the tything-man and Shadrach Robinson. It was the best flavor we ever tasted."

That bee tree was not the only sweets-yielding giant in the woods. The spring of 1891, Grandfather Seymour noted in his diary that a "Big Maple on the mountain has just been tapped—some 16 feet in circumference and about 130 years old. From 5 spouts and 3 buckets, it yielded twenty-one 12-quart pails full of sap in 36 hours. It has 99 half-inch auger holes in it." The leaf loam and wood ashes in which it had taken root in the 1760s must certainly have given the old giant a good start in life and then sustained it well.

Throughout the score of decades since surveyors entered Rupert Mountain Wilderness, the wildlife there has likewise played a part in the settlers' maintenance of life. The bear and raccoon provided the pioneers with meat, with clothing, and with extra bed and sleigh coverings in severest weather. So, too, did the deer throughout unlimited seasons. All gave fat for candles and for certain favorite home-concocted remedies as well.

One of these last was an ointment for sprains, swellings and rheumatism. Instructions for preparing it directed: "Simmer together for 15 minutes half a pound of soft bear grease or deer tallow, one gill of strong cider brandy, and half an ounce of cayenne. Apply hot to the part affected, after which wrap in flannel bandages."

Another curative derived from the wild animals was an application for cutaneous diseases. The "receit" instructed: "Take of the Seneca or sweet clover one handful and of lovage one handful. Bruise them together and simmer them in fresh bear's grease or skunk's oil for three hours or until the moisture is dried away, or the oil has absorbed the virtues of the herbs. Strain off and press the grains.

"This is an excellent softening and fragrant ointment for any eruption of the skin, such as salt-rheum, chaps, or cracked hands, or for scorbutic diseases generally."

Recently, Uncle Howard, who had grown up a few miles from Rupert Mountain Woodland, was badly mangled in a motor accident. A deep chest injury failed to heal during several weeks of treatment by skilled physicians in the county hospital. Finally, the patient's pleas to go home were granted. No one believed that he would ever heal, no one but Uncle Howard himself.

"Go 'way back in the woods up on the mountain and shoot me a bear," he begged his brother.

Uncle Roger brought in a fine black 250-pounder that very night. He and Aunt Dorothy extracted the chunks of fat from the still warm carcass, tried them out over a hot fire, and strained the oil into a crock. Daily, "for a while" thereafter, they filled the yawning raw cavity in Uncle Howard's chest with the soothing warm oil.

"You could just see the flesh heal," the recovered Uncle Howard reported with satisfaction a month later. "I learned about bear oil when I was a boy, and I never knew it to fail."

The menacing panther, bobcat, wolf, and lynx early retreated deeper into the Green Mountains. However, a hungry bear still ventures occasionally into the lumbermen's preserves.

A few summers ago, the longtime village doctor drove his sturdy old Ford up over a narrow, rough woods road bordering the Rupert Mountain Woodland to stitch up the head gashes two sawyers had suffered in felling a craggy elm. On his way home at twilight, he saw a dark figure, evidently one of the loggers, resting beside the bridge.

"Going to town for a Saturday night celebration," thought the doctor.

Halting his car, he called out genially, "Get in, and I'll give you a lift."

As he leaned over to open the door on the other side he had a momentary shock. A shaggy head loomed up, bloodshot eyes glared in through the window, and a startled lunge and snort unmistakably identified the pedestrian. Hastily snapping the door lock and stepping hard on the gas, the doctor shot down the trail.

"If I'd had my old-time horse, I'd never have gotten near the brute." Dr. Russell chuckled as he related the incident. "A horse can smell a bear half a mile away if the wind is right. And that scent drives a horse crazy."

Despite the innumerable hazards, eight generations of the Eastmans, Harwoods, and other Rupert Mountain men fueled and provisioned their homes from the former wilderness.

The crackling fires and embers, thus provided, cooked countless pans of beans and loaves of bread; pots of greens, hulled corn, and succotash; juicy pies and toothsome cakes; and all the other innumerable foods that produced sturdy builders of the township, state, and nation.

Simultaneously, those logs and limbs gave a heart to every home, where family life centered around the glowing hearth. Here, the Bible and other books were read, corn was popped, pippins roasted, love was told. Here, too, yarn was spun and woven, socks were knit, and cradles rocked. Amidst the flame shadows, the sheep dog drowsed and the kitten played. Children watched here for Santa Claus, emptied their stockings of his largesse at Christmas dawn, and later stuffed socks for their own children. Around these hearth fires, fed by the woodland, the daily activities and long discussions intangibly helped to shape the nation's policies.

After nearly two centuries of yielding physical and intellectual sustenance to the early Proprietors, "their heirs and assigns", these hundreds of former wilderness acres were sold to the one who here pioneered a new frontier.

Although this property is private land, berry pickers, picnickers, students, conservationists, and all other nature lovers are welcome to explore here, as long as they do so on foot.

Conservation education, as envisioned by Mr. Merck and established here by him, is still maintained as a year-round program, under the direction of an 11-member Foundation Board.

What thousands of young people, as well as many older ones, from all over the United States have benefited thereby. Scout troops and 4-H Clubs frequently hold study-Camporees at the Foundation. Classes from numerous public schools, from colleges and from churches, as well as study groups from libraries, are scheduled here regularly throughout the year, to acquaint students firsthand with the principles of ecology, with the ways of wild life in animal, bird, and plant, and with the fundamentals of forest management for long range benefits. A trained leader directs and instructs each group.

The Vachon, Washington-based, National Student Conservation Association each summer sends three groups of teen-age boys and girls from throughout the United States, with a staff of trained leaders, to a three weeks' program each, for work-study projects in land use, forest operations, and outdoor living, featuring wilderness survival, here on the Foundation. Mr. Merck's daughter, Judith Buechner, who lives in the area, is a longtime member of the Board of Directors of this Association, so this Forest offers an excellent permanent opportunity for student research and development.

Many of the boys and girls who have participated in this program have chosen some phase of conservation as a profession. Others, who have enjoyed field and/or camping trips here, have likewise chosen careers in ecology, horticulture, and other, related fields.

As I recently walked some of these Forest trails, I was filled with nostalgic memories of the years when we who grew up on Windy Summit roamed this woodland as a pasture land. How much we young ones wondered then, as visitors wonder here today, about the Curtises, Scotts, and Barnums, who opened the 1767 wilderness, established homes, wearied of tilling acres wedged between rock and mountain, sold to others, and pioneered westward.

How much we have wondered, too, about those others who further cleared the land and left us Convis Lot, Wade Lot, Gallup, Clark Hollow, Mylan Meadow, and Harmon Hill. What challenges they met! What struggle marked their achievement in hewing out their new frontier. What knowledge and skills emerged from their necessity.

In this first-tilled soil, human seed was planted and took root. From it came numerous generations of other hardy pioneers who went forth to help people in Wisconsin, Missouri, California, and many another state in the expanding American Republic. With them went the mountain-nurtured faith, ingenuity, and hardihood to support them and the torch of civilization which they carried.

In every age, people's resources meet their needs. Beneath the arching sky here today, nature and a staff of foresters, farmers, and educators work together to promote an extending frontier of knowledge and culture through the beauty, peace, and natural resources of what was once the Rupert Mountain Wilderness, now The George W. Merck Forest Foundation.

2

AT BARNABAS BARNUM'S LOG HOUSE

W e'll have the house built and the door hung before our little feller gets here." So Barnabas Barnum may have spoken, and his lean brown face may have smiled into Hepzibah's wide grey eyes beneath the matron's cap that half obscured her chestnut curls. His strong young arms swung her gently down from the bay mare's saddle, setting her feet on their new home ground.

It was a little more than a year since Parson Dewey of the Bennington Grants had recorded: "April 14th, 1766, Barnabas Barnum & Hepzibah Chelston was married & Declared Husband & Wife Before Me, Jedediah Dewey Clerk."

During that year, the 23-year-old husband and his somewhat younger wife had looked forward to establishing their home in the Rupert Grants. And to raising their family here.

The Bennington Records showed that "Samuel Robinson Gentleman" had deeded to "Barnabas Barnum Yeoman" for the "sum of One Hundred

Pounds York Currency 10 rights of Land in the Township of Rupert, on July 14, 1766, in the 6th yr. of His Majesty's Reign." Each right was identified by number and the name of the person who had drawn it out of a hat at a Proprietors' meeting earlier and had then decided to sell rather than settle the right. Seven of the 10 rights Barnabas sold two months later to Reuben Harmon, who would henceforth be his neighbor.

Now Barnabas and Hepzibah gazed with happy anticipation at their clearing here in the Rupert Mountain Wilderness. The logs for their house lay ready for building where Barnabas had felled them a few months before.

He had chosen this pinnacle for their home because the air would be drier here than in the valley and hence the risk of disease would be less. Too, his meadow would receive more hours of sunlight each day, would be subject to fewer frosts each year, and would therefore be more productive. Besides, his chosen site had a magnificent view.

The sunset cast a rosy glow upon the mountains to the west, and upon the nearby rock and trees and gurgling water. Chewinks and hermit thrushes poured their liquid notes through the gathering dusk. High above, Hesperus shone radiantly among the paler stars that seemed almost to touch the tops of the newly leafing elms and oaks and maples. The Big Dipper, with the North Star for its guide, was just swinging into sight above the whispering pines to the eastward. Tranquility and the fragrance of renewing life enveloped Barnabas and Hepzibah, as they tethered their mare and turned their oxen into the browse.

Joyfully, they thought of the new life that Hepzibah also carried, as they rolled themselves in their blankets, feet turned toward their campfire, and sank into the sleep that would restore them for the next day's labors.

As soon as dawn brightened the east and birdsong filled the woods, husband and wife arose, stirred up the embers, and breakfasted on the corncake that they had brought from Hepzibah's parents' home in Bennington.

When Oliver Scott's and Reuben Harmon's "Halloo" sounded along the woods trail to their holdings, axe and man were ready for "rolling up the house." Across the stump-studded clearing, the three men, soon joined by Amos Curtis, propelled the logs to the house site. Eighty tall straight pines, mainly 12 to 18 inches in diameter, with a few somewhat larger ones, Barnabas had cut and trimmed in February. He had chosen pine for his building because that wood was comparatively easy to work on, was lighter in weight and more resistant to decay, even when exposed to wet weather, than the other trees. Among the pine logs lay a dozen or so white ash ones of similar size, which he had split in halves to season for his new house floor. The ash had split well with axe and wedge, along its tough white grain, and Barnabas knew that the flat surfaces would rive to pleasing smoothness when he came to lay his puncheon floor. True, this would require some extra time and labor, but he was building this home to endure so he would build it well.

Twenty by thirty feet on the ground and twenty feet high, Barnabas and Hepzibah had decided should be the dimensions of their house. Accordingly, he and Harmon, working as one pair, laid two 34-foot logs, nearly two feet in diameter, in the most nearly level part of the clearing that May morning. At a point a foot or so from each end they notched these to one third the depth of the log from the top side. Curtis and Scott, working together, then brought in two 24-foot logs of the same diameter. These they cut in similar fashion from both the top side and the under, taking care that the depth, width and slope of the notch angle matched the notches of the first pair. The men then heaved the second pair of logs crosswise upon the first, dovetailing the notches to form a sturdy, tightly locked foundation, upon which to build. Across these at intervals they laid a dozen of the smaller logs to serve as the base for the ash floor to be added in "a slack season". Higher and higher the similarly notched logs were then rolled, lifted, and dovetailed into place during the next six days of sweating, back-bending toil. But guffaws of laughter, as well as the beat of the axe, rang among the trees, as the men dexterously vied with one another in their feats of muscle to erect the four walls of the house.

When the tiers of logs, notched and fitted transversely, reached the height of ten feet, another row of the more slender logs was laid similar to the one that provided the base for the ground floor. This latter formed the floor of the loft. Six more tiers of the 12-inch logs completed the walls. Smaller ones, secured to the top one by means of rootlets, provided the rafters. The ridge pole was notched into the top end logs, which had been "rived off" into the shape of a gable. Heavy sheets of bark stripped from the trees were laid lengthwise from the ridge to the top of the side walls, "with a jet sufficient to carry rain or melting snow."

When the outside was thus completed, a doorway and two, foot-square window openings were adzed out of the south side of the house. Later, the men collected a pile of flat, broad stones, a foot or so in length and somewhat less in width and thickness. These they walled up into a fireplace and chimney on the north side of the enclosure, placing the hearth directly opposite the doorway, to insure a good draft for the fire when "the weather should be damp or heavy." An opening was adzed out of the roof above the hearth to provide a place for the chimney smoke to escape. This would likewise admit some small amount of light and air. The men also hewed two more foot-square openings out of the north side of the house, one on each side of the chimney.

Almost as soon as the men had completed the window openings Hepzibah filled them in with bear-grease-coated tow cloth cut from worn garments, that she and her mother had prepared for this very need.

Day after day, as the men constructed the house, she gathered and chopped bucketfuls of coarse ferns and fine twigs from the nearby woods and clearing. These she mixed with wet clay, dug from the bank of the brook, and the resultant mass she plastered into the chinks of the logs, as high as she could reach, to harden under the rays of the sun. Sometimes, Harmon's young son helped her. Barnabas would finish chinking the topmost logs later.

During the week or so that the men worked at the building, Barnabas and Hepzibah's only shelter was a crude hut of evergreen boughs and birch bark. Their only hearth then and until the fireplace was finished late in the summer was a small arch or square box of stones nearby. Within it, the pioneer wife kindled and kept her cooking fire of the fallen dry limbs which she had gathered in the forest. Over the hot embers, she boiled with a chunk of fat salt pork the fiddleheads, or young ferns, as well as various other greens that she found in the woods. These brought pleasing variety to the pots of boiled succotash that she made from the dried corn and beans her mother had packed among their belongings in their ox-cart when she and Barnabas had set forth from Bennington. The sweet wild strawberries and whortleberries, the plump blackberries and the thorny gooseberries, which she gathered at the edge of the woods, likewise brought welcome change from the stewed dried apples and pumpkin from her mother's stores.

Occasionally, Barnabas shot a deer, and over the glowing coals of the outdoor fireplace, Hepzibah roasted the fresh wild meat to juicy brown goodness. On an oak slab beside the same red coals, she daily baked her crisp flat loaves of golden johnnycake. Inspite of frequent winds that blew he smoke into her eyes, and an occasional drenching rain that almost quenched her precious fire, she fed her husband and their helpers well.

By early June, the Barnum house was finished except for the hearth, the puncheon floor, and a door to swing on hinges. Those could be finished after the harvest time. Two other log houses, one for Curtis and one for

Scott, were similarly completed, though both were somewhat smaller and cruder than the Barnum one. Harmon's, which stood a mile away, had been erected somewhat earlier by another crew of Proprietors.

Hepzibah's trim litheness had become considerably plumper, but her movements were as nimble as ever, as she shook up her homespun bedtick, newly filled with dried pine needles gathered from a sheltered hollow, and smoothed her blue and buff woolen blankets of the previous winter's weaving upon her bed frame that Barnabas had built into one corner of their new house.

Upon the puncheon table that he had also fashioned, she set the maple burl bowl that would hold enough for a dozen hungry people, the poplar plates, and the hickory spoons, all of which he had carved for her the winter before their marriage. Beside the table, a half dozen pine chunks, nearly two feet in diameter and in height, served as chairs .

A ladder to the loft would be made in the fall. Then her second bedtick would be filled and laid on the floor up there for her mother's visit "when the baby comes."

All summer, after the homes were built, Barnabas spent odd hours from his land-clearing in peeling four- and five-foot strips of birch bark from the trees he had girdled, and from which the bark slipped easily at this season of the year. Layers of this bark he pegged to his roof covering, since he knew that these tough strips would insulate his house well against the heat of summer, the cold of winter, and the fury of every season's upland storms.

Several rainy days that summer and fall also gave Barnabas time to finish his fireplace and chimney, to lay his puncheon floor, and to hang the rived slab door upon its wooden hinges. Hepzibah later told her mother, "Oh, what a luxury it seemed to have a fireplace and a good hearth of my own and a nice white ash floor. And then, when the door was hung, I took down the blankets we had used for many weeks, and how nice it was when I could open the door and go out and shut it when I came in. I didn't have to worry so much about the bears getting in."

Most of the time that summer, however, Barnabas toiled at clearing his 50-acre home-lot, just as did the other Rupert Proprietors at clearing theirs. With his oxen, and his wooden plow, he broke a section of his grant to be used for seeding: a patch of corn, "scratched in" in June, and one of wheat that fall. More corn and rye and flax would seed his acres the following spring, when he would have cleared away more of the trees and stumps. The windrows of logs and limbs when burned would provide ashes rich in potash to fertilize the soil.

That same summer, Barnabas fashioned their "mill". This was essential for crushing the grain of his crops to come, as well as the several months' supply that he had brought from Bennington. This contrivance was really a huge mortar and pestle standing at the east end of his house, but it served as his grist mill for the next four years. Choosing a hickory stump, three feet high and two in diameter, he hollowed it out to a shell three inches thick, by means of a slow fire and his adze. The pestle or masher was a three-foot section of hickory sapling four inches or so in diameter. Until Oliver Scott's first grist mill of the township began operations five years later, every housewife on the summit drew her baking supplies from a similar contrivance at her own door.

During those three months and a little more that Barnabas was clearing his land and fashioning his mill, Hepzibah was providing for her household. Upon the two broad puncheon shelves that her husband had built beside the fireplace, she arranged the supplies that she had been accumulating even before her marriage. On the top shelf went a row of hollowed and dried pumpkin shells, filled with cornmeal, with shelled corn, and with dried beans. In the fall, she would fill others with beechnuts, hazelnuts, butternuts, and hickory nuts that she had discovered among the woodland trees. Throughout the summer, she filled other shells with dried berries, dried venison, and dried bear meat to meet their winter need.

Beside these pumpkin shells, she arranged her several dried gourds for dippers, cups and soapdish; a pair of snuffers, and a small stack of rush lights. These last she had made by stripping the bark from rushes that grew by the forest brook. The bare pith she then dipped in melted deer suet, after which she let these "candles for company" harden in a cool, dry place.

On her lower shelf, Hepzibah placed her winter blankets, the few extra garments for herself and her husband, and her twelve yards of fine linen for the summer baby clothes. The tiny garments of softest wool for the baby's first winter she had wrapped in a worn homespun sheet, as she and her mother had completed them, one by one, in the early spring. These she now laid beside the linen and next to the Family Bible. In this treasured volume, she had learned to read upon her father's knee, and in it she would find Divine Wisdom that would guide her all her days.

One of her happiest experiences that late summer was the hanging of her crane. On a chilly morning in early September, her big black iron dinner pot was suspended from the green lug pole set across her fireplace opening to be used as a crane. As the maple backlog burst into flame beneath it, her dreams were as bright as the flame. This fireplace would bring warmth, food, and comfort to her, Barnabas, and their young ones for years to come. She happily hummed a lullabye as she arranged her other two iron pots, her saltbox and bread trough, her iron tongs and wooden bellows beside the hearth. At the front, she set her covered iron bake kettle that had just arrived on Harmon's extra load from Bennington. Here she would bake better bread than she had been able to do outdoors. The bake kettle could easily be buried in hot coals and ashes upon this fine new hearth. No oak slab could equal a bake kettle in producing good corn bread.

Best of all, Hepzibah thought, the baby would be snug and warm here beside the purring logs, in the hooded cradle that Barnabas had made in the early spring. Only two months now and the wee one would be with them.

But the radiance of her brightest dream soon greyed to ashes. As she was gathering butternuts one fall day, she was startled by a sudden leap, a menacing snarl in the branches above her, and the hairy bulk of a bobcat crouched above her and ready to spring. Terror paralyzed her, body and mind, but for a second only. Seizing her gun, she aimed and fired. The bobcat fell with a thud at her feet, a young kitten beside her. A retching nausea gripped Hepzibah. The smell of blood and the sight of the lifeless bodies, mother and babe, drained the strength from her own. Clutching her gun, she crawled to her hearth.

When Barnabas found her that evening, she no longer carried the new life within her. And very little of her own remained.

There followed long days of rest in bed near her warm fireside and of tender care by Barnabas. Each day she found comfort in her Bible. Turning its pages, she read again and again: "Whom the Lord loveth, He chasteneth". Or, as frequently, "Blessed are they that mourn, for they shall be comforted".

Finally, Hepzibah regained sufficient strength to resume her household duties. A week long visit from her mother, who rode up the thirty miles from Bennington in an ox-cart with a neighbor, who came to look at some Rupert Grants for speculation, considerably aided the young wife's recovery. Joy in her hearth, in her fine new home, and in her husband also brought healing. They were young, they were strong, and the frontier held promise. Man and wife were soon dreaming of" another baby in a year or so".

For the next several months, as Barnabas busied himself outdoors with the surveying of a road through the wilderness and indoors with the making of ash axe helves to barter in the spring, Hepzibah set about making her husband a much-needed suit of clothes.

During the summer, she had saved the skins of the deer whose meat had helped supply her table. She had then moistened, packed, and sweat the hides until she could scrape off the hair. The stripped skins she had thoroughly rubbed with deer brains and tanned them in the smoke of her cooking fire. When these were sufficiently cured, she cut them into a loosely fitting jacket and pair of trousers, using a worn-out suit for a pattern. Proudly she surveyed the size of her cuttings. It was good to have such a big man as Barnabas for her husband. And such a kind and gentle one. With long rows of painstaking stitches, her deft fingers secured the seams and even added a fringe of the deerskin to the bottom of the coat and the sides of the breeches. From the left-over pieces, she fashioned moccasins for both her husband and herself. Barnabas' black eyes shone with pride and pleasure as he donned his handsome warm new suit. A wife like Hepzibah and a snug home like this gave a man good reason to clear the land, build a road, and open a new settlement in a wilderness frontier. Together, they planned for their flock and herd, for their grain crops, their flax field, and for their family.

Together, too, they worked for community growth and welfare. Their house was the one in which the first Proprietors' Meeting on Rupert Grants was held. The earliest Town Records contain the following:

"Application being made to me Clerk of Rupert Propriety by more than six Proprietors to warn a meeting for said Rupert pursuant to their request these are to give public Notice to the Proprietors of Rupert that they meet at the house of Barnabas Barnum in said Rupert on Wednesday the eighteenth of May next at nine o'clock in the forenoon, then & there to vote on the following articles

1st Choose a Moderator

2nd A Propriety Clerk

3rd See if the Propriety will lay out another division of lands

4th Choose a Committee for the purpose if necessary

5th See if they will raise money for arranging necessary changes in said Propriety & to vote anything else thought necessary, when met together. Bennington, April 12th, A.D. 1768

Proprietor Samuel Robinson Jr. Propriety Clerk

Notified in Bennington, Arlington & Shaftsbury fourteen days before said meeting.

Proprietor Samuel Robinson, Jr.
Rupert, May 18th, 1768

Then the Proprietors of Rupert met at time and place mentioned by Warrant & voted viz.

1st Chose Mr. Reuben Harmon Moderator

2nd Chose Josiah Cass, Clerk for the Propriety who was sworn to the faithful discharge of his office by Alexander King, Esq. (No one could foresee that May day how futile the oath would prove to be.)

3rd Voted to lay out a second Division of Lots to each Proprietor by pitches

4th Voted to draw a Lottery for the Rights or chances of pitching first & the Proprietor that draws No. 1 to lay out his lot first, No. 2 the second, & so on successively until the whole be finished, viz: to begin the seventh day of June next & lay two lots in a day which completed, always providing they shall be laid in good form, either adjoining one another or having at least fifty rods vacancy between lots; said lots shall contain 60 acres each & laid in undivided lands

5th Adjourned the meeting half an hour.

6th Met at the adjournment & voted further viz.

7th Chose Reuben Harmon, Jonathan Eastman, Barnabas Barnum, Oliver Scott, and Amos Curtis to lay out proper roads also to inspect 4th article.

8th Voted three Shillings on each Right for making roads and other changes

9th Chose Mr. Reuben Harmon to take care of the public Rights, Minister Lot, School Lots, &c.

10th Chose Mr. Jacob Fish to draw the Lottery for pitching being disinterested.

11th Chose Barnabas Barnum Collector for the Propriety

12th Chose Jonathan Eastman Treasurer

13th Adjourned the meeting to the 20th of this instant May at 3 o'clock in the afternoon to this place.

Attest Sam'l Robinson Clerk"

During the half hour of adjournment at mid-day, the men who had assembled on horseback or on foot that bright May morning withdrew to the clearing around the house to check their tethered horses, to lunch on their own "journey cake", and to ruminate upon the forenoon procedures. Hepzibah had gone to spend the day with Elizabeth Eastman, taking with her the socks that she was knitting for her husband.

Two days later, a dozen or so of the Proprietors reconvened at "three o'clock in the afternoon to this place" to vote a limitation of "sixty rods wide" on the lots or pitches in White Creek Meadow at the west end of the township. They also voted to meet again "the second Tuesday of September next" at "one o'clock P.M. at Barnabas Barnum's". Those pioneers really practised democracy.

During that summer of 1768, Hepzibah "scratched in" a patch of flax behind the house. Barnabas had removed the tree stumps, so the labor with her grubbing hoe and wooden rake was comparatively easy. Throughout the summer, she watchfully tended the plants and planned for a larger field the following year.

The surveying and laying of a road upon his holdings consumed much of her husband's time. So did his duties as Collector of the Propriety. Nevertheless, he found time to barter the axe helves, that he had shaved out during the winter, for a fine ewe and her lamb from a Bennington sheepfold. To the same owner, he gave his note for a cow and her calf. How happy he and Hepzibah were when they brought home this beginning of their own flock and herd. Pride surged within them as husband and wife penned the animals into their new quarters. And dreams of the future brightened each day.

By fall, Barnabas had fired his windrows of logs and branches, harrowed and seeded two acres of his land to wheat, another two to rye, and had harvested "a good krop of corn" from two more acres. The terms of his Grant had thus been fulfilled

The second Tuesday afternoon in September, the assembly of men at the Barnum home chose Reuben Harmon, Jonathan Eastman, and Amos Curtis to "settle all the disputed lines around the town." Disputes had become so bitter, and rebellion against rulings so rife that the assembly also voted "That in case our adjourned meeting shall die, our method for raising meetings for the future shall be by one eighth part of the Proprietors making application to the Clerk & his advertising it in Rupert and Bennington fourteen days before the meeting."

When the Proprietors next met in the Barnum house on the second Tuesday in November in 1768, their bitternesses were somewhat mollified by their having had good corn crops on even the poorest grants. "Finding nothing worthy of action," they voted to adjourn until the second Monday in May of 1769. Again, the meeting was scheduled "at Mr. Barnabas Barnum's". But it was not held there. Instead, the men met at the doorway only of the Barnum home, in hushed voices "adjourned the meeting six minutes", and reconvened at Simon Sears' house.

According to legend, Hepzibah had been ailing most of the winter. Although she had known that she was "in the family way", she had gone with Barnabas to Bennington when he paid his land "Rent of one ear of

Indian corn only on the twenty-fifth day of December." It had been a fatiguing ride for her on the pillion behind her husband's saddle. Their fleet-footed mare had made the journey in a single day each way, but during the 16-hour ride home, Hepzibah had become "chilled to the bone." Despite her daily draught of willow tea and of pine needle syrup, concocted from the woodland resources, she was tormented throughout the winter by a racking cough. A few days before the April meeting of the Proprietors, she suffered another miscarriage. Again, Barnabas tenderly cared for her and then summoned Elizabeth Eastman, who soon pronounced her "on the gain."

Again, Hepzibah turned to her Bible, repeating over and over, "If thou faint in the day of adversity, thy strength is small." And, "Weeping may endure for a night, but joy cometh in the morning."

Although his wife and the other women assured Barnabas that she was recovering well, he decided to curtail all further trips as Collector for the Propriety. Accordingly, at this April meeting, Simon Sears was appointed to the office of Collector "in the room of Barnabas Barnum, who has resigned."

Barnum did, however, continue his surveying and road building operations, giving all the time that he could spare from his crops and from his newly established flock and herd. In appreciation, the Rupert Proprietors, "at a meeting at Reuben Harmon's house the second Thursday in October, 1769, "1st Voted Mr. Barnabas Barnum shall have one acre in the undivided for his extraordinary labors in having the Highway through his land."

Hepzibah also engaged in "extraordinary labors" that summer. Having regained her usual rosy cheeks, lithe figure, and vigorous vitality, she had turned to her flax field for solace in her second disappointment in becoming a mother. However, she assured her husband that no doubt she would still bear him a robust family. One of her aunts had suffered two similar losses before bearing twin boys, followed by five other sturdy sons and daughters. Resolutely, Barnabas and Hepzibah applied themselves to the tasks at hand and trusted that Heaven would add to their numerous blessings.

Although in her father's flax field she had trod barefoot back and forth along the rows of tender plants to pull out the weeds, this was not necessary the first summer in her mountain sowing. No weed seeds had yet invaded the forest earth. How thankful she was for that. In Bennington, it had been tedious toil to tread each row, stepping always to face the wind, so that if any plants were accidentally trodden down, the wind would lift them back into a growing position. How beautiful her field was that July of 1769, when it bloomed into a blue lake behind her house.

Pulling the ripened plants in September and spreading them to dry a day or two in the sunshine was particularly hard work. Barnabas did most of that, but Hepzibah helped. She helped, too, with the rippling, or drawing the dried stalks through the teeth of the big wooden flax comb to remove the seed "bobs" or heads. These fell on a thin blanket laid beneath the comb to catch them. Flax seed was valuable for medicine, for re-seeding, and for barter, so none must be allowed to go to waste.

After the rippling in the field, the stalks were tied at the seed end into bundles and set up tentwise for further drying. When thoroughly dry, these stalks were piled solidly in the nearby brook, a frame of saplings anchoring them in place and chunks of wood weighting them down. After a week or so, Barnabas lifted these bundles, called beats or bates, from the water, and Hepzibah helped him remove the rotted leaves and spread the stripped stalks to dry again. They were then ready for the flax-brake or breaker.

That fall, the Flax-breaking was a festive occasion for the first settlers, just as it was for many other seasons, according to pioneer custom throughout New England and neighboring settlements. On a clear, sunny day in early November, when the flax could be kept as dry as tinder, as it must be, neighbors from miles around assembled at the Barnum home for the swingling-bee. Out came the cumbersome flax-brake, which Barnabas had hewn and pegged from seasoned logs. Three "knives", or split logs shaved thin on one edge, he had set between two wooden bars on legs. A pair of similar knives, hinged at one end to the lower ones, and with a heavy mallet attached at the opposite end, he had pegged into place so that the upper knives would work up and down between the lower ones.

The whole mechanism, five feet long and somewhat more than three feet high, was operated on swingling day by Jonathan Eastman, his son Enoch, Amos Curtis, Oliver Scott, and Barnabas, taking turns. The flax was laid on the lower knives and then pounded and worked by the upper blades to break or ret the hard center core and bark of the stalk. Hard work it was, but the men's arms were already hardened by work.

Israel Blood, Simon Sears, and Reuben Harmon then took turns at the swingling or scutching. This consisted of beating with a wooden knife the bundles of broken flax placed on an upright board set in a block. Hepzibah's eyes shone as she saw the bark and core fall in broken bits from the tawny bundles. Then, as the best of the plant, about one tenth of the whole straw separated from the waste, was hetcheled by drawing it a dozen times through a series of increasingly fine wooden teeth cut in a hewn timber, Elizabeth Eastman and the other women helped Hepzibah gather up the clean dry hoard of fiber for her spinning.

The swingling-bee was a social day as well as a day of labor. A dinner of roast venison and partridge, corn cake baked in the hot ashes on the hearth, boiled turnips, squash, pumkinsass, and cider was followed by a supper of similar fortifying foods. Then, by the light of the dancing flames of the hearthfire, the merry couples, young and middle-aged, swung blithely across the white ash floor to the strains of Oliver Moore's cherished fiddle.

Soon after midnight, the rattle of cart and thud of hoof died away in the distance. The only sign of life after this strenuous day and evening was the hearth smoke that drifted up from the solitary log house in the clearing on the brow of the hill. The moonlight whitened the flax-brake and hetchel standing lonesomely beside the chimney of logs and fieldstone and clay.

Early dawn brought renewed activity. As Hepzibah gazed upon her pile of tow, with the sunshine streaming across it on her puncheon floor, she thought, "Morning pours its honey on my good loaf of work."

With her fiber already prepared, the young wife was soon spending long days at her spinning. As she treadled the wheel with her foot, her fingers held the twisting flax which the turning wheel wound on a bobbin. This thread she then wound off on her reel. Forty strands made a knot, twenty knots a skein. Rarely could she spin two skeins a day now, though she had often done so before she was married Then she had sometimes earned as much as eight cents a day in spinning for the Robinsons of Bennington Grants.

Yard after yard of greyish tan linen later that winter came from her loom in the corner of her one-room house. Barnabas had worked early and late to hew and peg the big wooden contrivance for her. Often Reuben Harmon and Enoch Eastman had also lent a hand, with the understanding that Hepzibah would do a linen piece for each of their families. Day after day, the whir of the wheel and the thump of the loom were a busy accompaniment to the clink of the kettles on the hearth and crane.

There were occasional days when Hepzibah needed "woman talk" instead of her "loaf of work". At such times, she would tuck her knitting needles and yarn from her mother's spinning into her pocket and walk the mile or so to Elizabeth Eastman's "for a good visit". One February afternoon in 1771, she went to call on Patience Harmon instead. Her path that cut crosslots through the woods was marked by "blazed" trees.

As she and Patience exchanged bits of news and confidences, Hepzibah suddenly noticed that the sky was darkening. Five o'clock! Barnabas would be coming home from the woods for supper. Wrapping her great cloak around herself, she hurried toward home. She had gone only a short distance through the foot-deep snow when she discovered that she could not see the blazed trees in the storm-threatening twilight. She tried to retrace her steps over the logs and through the brush, but she still could not find the marked path. Nor her tracks from early afternoon. After walking blindly for what she knew must be an hour or more, she decided that she would have to sit down on a fallen log and wait till morning. She was so tired. And so cold. She might freeze! What COULD she do?

Stiff with chill and fatigue, she clung to a tree trunk, letting her almost numb body sag against the rough bark. Just then the moon shone out—surely she could now find her way.

Brief hope! Almost immediately the light was obscured by clouds. Panic seized her. She now realized that in spite of her knowing the woods well, she was lost. After what seemed hours of mental and physical struggle in the wilderness, she became calm. She had her Heavenly Father. She looked up at the sky—there was the North Star! She would take that for her guide.

With a new surge of energy, keeping her eye on the Star, she plodded on. An almost overwhelming joy filled her as she finally came into a clearing. A log house with a dim light showing loomed up in the shadows. Struggling through the snow to the door, she fell against it. In answer to her cry, a strange man flung the door wide open. Although he and his wife and son urged her to spend the night, she insisted upon going on after only a short rest at the friendly fireside. Already Barnabas must be frantic.

Taking a pine knot torch, the two men each gave her an arm and practically carried the nearly exhausted but prayerfully grateful Hepzibah to the path among the trees and then along it the mile or so to her home.

Barnabas was not in their house. The numerous footprints around the doorstep and leading along the path toward Eastman's told her that he and some of the neighbors had gone to search for her, for it was now past nine o'clock. Taking from the shelf the ox horn that was notched so it would produce a shrill blast when one blew violently into it, she trumpeted a powerful signal out through the forest. It was answered by a similar blast.

Up to the door Barnabas, the Eastmans, Scotts, and Harmons all came running. At the Harmons', they had learned that Hepzibah had left there hours before. Following the path, they had found where her tracks had left it a quarter mile from the Harmons'. She had headed directly toward the Deer Lick, a place where the settlers left salt to attract deer so they could be shot for food. There, also, wolves were frequently heard howling after they had killed a deer or bear at the Lick.

"We expected every minute to find your mangled carcass torn by the wolves," Amos told Hepzibah. Barnabas, still shaken from his fright, wordlessly helped her untie her hood and pull off her moccasins.

After the others had headed toward their respective homes, the Barnums prepared a poultice of wood soot and deer tallow. This they applied to Hepzibah's frostbitten feet, and by morning she declared that they felt "as good as new". Thanks to the North Star, the wood soot and tallow, her husband, and their good Samaritan neighbors!

But Hepzibah herself was not so "good as new". Slowly, but insidiously, a fever burned inside her throughout all the cold damp spring and even more distressingly, all the following summer. She could no longer tend her flax field, spinning-wheel, and loom. Both she and Barnabas fought their distress and despair with all the hope and faith that they could muster, but Hepzibah became weaker day by day.

Just before the autumn gales and cold struck the mountain, man and wife quenched their hearth fire, barred their door, and stowed their personal possessions into their ox-cart. Barnabas had already left his cattle and sheep with his neighbors, to be kept for the winter. Both he and Hepzibah reassured each other that they would return in the spring, ready to begin anew, as she mounted their bay mare and he turned the oxen toward Bennington. As they descended the mountain, neither could bear to look back at their log house, standing abandoned in the clearing.

By spring, Hepzibah's life had ebbed away, and Barnabas had no heart to re-settle in the home that he had built with such high hope on the mountain.

Heartsick, he sold his Rupert holdings to Jonathan Eastman's son, Enoch. There, the 24-year-old and his bride soon established a flourishing family, the fulfillment of a dream that had been denied to the builder of that log house and cultivator of the surrounding acres.

Young Barnum went into land speculation in various areas of the Grants and was reputed to be doing well. Then, according to legend, he did return to his log house in late July of 1775. He had attended the "Meeting of the Committees of the Several Townships on the New Hampshire Grants, West of the Range of the Green Mountains, convened at the house of Mr. Cephas Kent in the Township of Dorset, July 27th, 1775." There he was chosen one of the seven First Lieutenants of the Green Mountain Boys to serve in the Revolution.

After the meeting, he succumbed to the desire to see the house which he had built on the nearby mountain, that had been a wilderness a little more than eight years before. What his feelings were as he visited briefly with Enoch Eastman and his wife, tending their two small children near the hearth that he had laid, no one ever knew. They knew only that he rested a big hand tenderly for a moment on a shelf that he had fashioned for Hepzibah, and on which she had kept her dried pumpkin shells of winter stores, her rush candles, and her baby's clothes.

Most of the next five years, the log house stood empty. Bitter strife between the Tories and the Revolutionaries of the township caused most homes to be abandoned.

In 1780, when its owners returned to help rebuild the town, the log walls reflected news of their builder. He had served heroically and successfully at the taking of Ticonderoga by Ethan Allen and again at the Battle of Bennington.

Shortly thereafter, he had married Abigail Harwood, a girl "a lot like Hepzibah", whose home was near Bennington. A few months later, he had been summoned as second in command of a troop of Green Mountain Boys, to Shelburne, 115 miles or so to the North. A blockhouse there was being menaced by Tories and Indians. With meager rations of food and clothing, the dedicated and resolute men marched through the trackless wilderness. Half starved, nearly frozen, and almost exhausted, they finally arrived at Shelburne. There they barricaded themselves in the blockhouse and awaited attack. It came the night of March 12th, 1778.

Led by Colonel Thomas Sawyer of Clarendon, the brave boys in green finally routed the enemy. But their gallant Lieutenant Barnabas Barnum lay dead when the battle was over.

"He never knew that he had a son," Enoch Eastman sadly observed.

That son, born the summer of 1778, however, felt that he knew his father. His mother and his stepfather, Colonel Ezra Whipple, who had held Barnabas Barnum in high regard, often told young Jehiel about his own father's patriotism and bravery. "We named you for your grandfather, because your father did so want a son to carry his father's name," Abigail explained to the boy.

One of the most treasured family possessions was a ballad about the Shelburne Attack, written by its survivors. This was frequently sung in the Whipple home:

"On the twelfth day of March in the year seventy-eight,

The Britons and Indians invaded our state.
'Twas in Shelburne brave Sawyer these wretches did meet
And fully determined not to retreat.

'The first in command was Sawyer by name,
The next unto him were the elements of fame—
'Twas young Barnum the hero, he fought like a man,
Saying, 'Fight on, brave boys', but quickly was slain.

"Our men numbered twelve and the enemy fifty-seven;
But with this vast odds, when aided by Heaven,
We drove them, we beat them and caused them to fly,
While others lay wounded and left there to die.

'There are three of our men lying dead on the ground,
The rest have returned and are yet safe and sound;
The enemy lost twelve, and the rest they soon fled—
Some went on their feet, others drawn on a sled.

"May the name of the hero be never forgot,
Who determined to beat or to die on the spot;
Let the youths of our land his example pursue.
Give the glory to God AND to whom it is due."

The summer that Jehiel was eighteen, his Uncle Zechariah bought a piece of what had been the Rupert Mountain Wilderness. When he went to claim his deed from Reuben Harmon's son Nehemiah, he reportedly took Jehiel with him to see his father's log house.

The Eastmans, having built a fine new clapboard home, were then using the log structure for storage. As Jehiel stood at its hearth and gazed out across the productive surrounding fields, he recalled the words of the ballad, "May the name of the hero be never forgot."

Closing the door firmly behind him, he observed to his uncle, "I only hope that I can be as great a man as my father was."

3

A LOOK AT THE POTASH KETTLES

Here and there throughout the Northeastern States, an ancient potash kettle may still be seen. One of the several-barrel-sized, half-eggshell-shaped iron relics is sometimes slung up to log supports by heavy iron chains in front of a "maple sugar house", reminding the passerby of the early method of boiling sap. Another, filled with petunias, geraniums, or other bright blossoms, graces a lawn. Still others provide drinking-places for farmyard stock.

One that has long been especially well known as a wayside watering place "for man and beast" inspired the name for its neighbor, The Iron Kettle Restaurant on U.S. Route 7, a few miles north of Bennington, Vermont. Here many a local citizen has lined up in times of drought to fill pails, bottles, jugs, and other receptacles with the clear, cold water that pours into this huge black kettle from a never-failing hillside spring. The date "1796", cast into its corroding side, signifies its ancient origin.

"Ye might say our country was born in the potash kittles," an octogenarian generally known as Uncle Will, used to comment. "When I lived up in Dorset Hollow about 1900, some of us boys used to ride our horses up to the end of the road to look at a pair of 'em. They'd prob'ly weigh 500 or 600 pounds apiece and would mebbe hold four barrels each. A yard or so across they were, and about as deep. They looked just like the Shaftsbury Iron Kittle, only they didn't have any date on 'em. We used to poke around 'em to find the but'nuts and hick'rynuts that dropped from the trees nearby. We'd sit there and crack and eat nuts and talk about what our grandfathers had told us about those kittles when our ancestors were clearing the farms all over Northeastern America. They chopped off the trees to make meadows and pastures and then turned the wood into potash to sell. Most all the money they had around here from the 1760s to 1812 came from potash. After the War, they had two or three spells of making potash again, but it didn't last."

Uncle Will grinned as he added, "Some of our forefathers made their fortune in the Embargo Days around 1810. The young fellers around here called 'em 'O Grab Me' Days from embargo spelled backwards. They made a regular game of smuggling their potash loads into Canada, after Jefferson ended their sending it out from New York and Boston. Pretty near ruined the trade of those old six-master sailboats that had been carrying it to England. But our Boys got it out through Montreal, and none of our ancestors around here was ever caught, as I know of."

Various 18th and 19th century newspapers and personal journals in the Bennington Museum piece together a typical tale of the earliest commercial industry in Vermont, and the one from which most of the Northeastern states profited.

One who was active in the industry was Reuben Harmon. Some time before he settled on his Rupert Grant the spring of 1767, he had read about the "black gold" that could be obtained from burning the trees from the heavily wooded hills. A pamphlet sent him by a relative in Boston reported that in 1751 the British Parliament had passed an "Act for encouraging the making of Pott Ashes and Pearl Ashes in the British Plantations in America." Unlimited quantities of this pott ash or lye salts, Harmon had learned, were needed for making the soap indispensable to processing the wool, for bleaching the linen, and for manufacturing the glass of the Mother Country industries.

The pamphlet stated further: "The Process is easy; the Expence small; the Profit certain." The price quoted for 1765 was "£35 Sterling per Tun."

As soon as he had gathered his first grain crops, therefore, Reuben set to work to obtain his black gold. Between autumn harvest and spring plowing, whenever the snow was not too deep, he chopped tree after tree upon his second division lot. With ringing strokes of his axe, his powerful arms brought down one after another of the tall monarchs that had been growing for a century or longer. Hacking the trunks into lengths that his oxen could draw, he then rolled up numerous piles of logs, brush, and branches to burn for their potential wealth.

As soon as the fires were dead, his wooden shovel scooped the ashes into the hollowed log sections that he had adzed and placed conveniently near. Into the bottom of each, he had packed a thick network of branches and had elevated this stump barrel on a hollowed out split log laid horizontally on the ground. With small stones, he wedged this base log firmly in place. Over the ashes in the barrels he then poured wooden bucketfuls of water from the nearby brook. The water seeped down through the ashes and leached out the valuable lye. This liquid dripped on down through the brush network, out through a hole carved in the base of the barrel, and into the half-log trough beneath.

Meanwhile, Reuben had prepared his boiling place. This consisted of a 10-foot log, six inches or so in diameter, set in the crotches of two trees, about eight feet apart, so the horizontal log was approximately six feet from the ground. In this rectangular framework, with the help of a neighbor, he suspended by means of heavy chains his 600-pound iron kettle, shaped like a half eggshell, with sides an inch thick, and with a handhold projecting from each of two opposite arcs of the rim. Beneath the kettle, he laid dry sticks to be ignited when his leach was ready.

As soon as he could tell by his eye that the liquor in the trough was of sufficient strength for evaporation, Reuben carefully baled it with his wooden bucket out of the trough and into the kettle. Well he knew the need for caution throughout this entire operation. The caustic lye would eat away any skin or clothing with which it came in contact.

When the cauldron was three quarters full, Reuben lighted a fire beneath it by means of a brand from his hearth fire. Confident that his pott ash kettle, which he had brought from Bennington, had a particularly thick bottom, cast especially for withstanding the strain of evaporating lye to a solid mass, the Rupert pioneer watchfully tended his fire. During the next several hours, his yard-and-a-half long heavy iron rod, flattened at one end, frequently stirred the boiling solution to loosen the alkali salt deposit from the inside surface of the kettle.

Finally, all the water was evaporated, and on the bottom of the cauldron appeared the desired great hard cake of black salts.

To hasten the process of cooling this, he raked the embers and live coals into a heap on damp ground a little way from the kettle. His iron rake, with close set teeth, separated these ashes, which would in turn go into the leaching barrel, from any bits of unburnt wood.

As soon as the salt had cooled, Reuben set to work with his broad iron chisel and wooden mallet to break up this mass and pry it from the kettle. Blow after blow resounded through the mountain notch as the concrete mass was broken into chunks. These he then scooped into his deerskin sack to be carried on horseback to the export merchant in Albany 60 miles away. Exultation peered out from his black-browed, sweat-streaked face, as he thought of the wedges and hammers, the gunpowder and shot; the salt, molasses, pins, needles, and even a book now and then, which he would bring home in exchange for his pott ash. And also the silver coins! The words of the inspiring pamphlet from England lurked in his mind: "The Process is easy, the Expense small; the Profit certain."

By the end of his third year on the mountain, Reuben had cut, cleared, and burned the wood from several acres of his holding. A little more than five tons of pott ash he had by then sent by his neighbors or carried himself over the rough trail to Albany. Over a thousand cords of wood had gone into it. Almost 3,000 bushels of ashes! Hard work it had been, but the pott ash had yielded him his only cash income, about £250 sterling for those three good years. Pott ash prices were rising, and much of the route to Albany was now a road instead of just a trail. The years ahead seemed full of promise.

Reflecting upon his success, Harmon ruefully recalled one especially bitter experience. Having learned from working with a veteran woodsman, Timothy Fields, some years before in Bennington, that elm, black ash, maple, hickory, beech, and basswood were the trees richest in "black gold", he had felled these mainly from his thick stand of timber. The evergreens he had left for building, for tanning bark, and for the "masts for our Royal Navy."

Then, one morning early in the summer of 1770, he had come upon a gigantic water elm. Five tons he estimated the weight of its several cords of wood. Timothy had once told him of a Bennington man who had gotten two hundred pounds of pott ash from such a tree as this, though the usual yield would have been only about forty pounds. So rich were the ashes that they had fused into big chunks of salt before they were ever leached and evaporated. Two hundred pounds! At the current price of 34 shillings per hundredweight, this one tree would be worth $12 or more. As much as a man could earn in a month at chopping. Reuben's long hard body tingled with excitement at the thought of such riches.

With high hope, he felled the elm and fired it where it lay, as soon as it was dry enough to ignite. He whistled as merrily as he had when a boy, before care had sobered his days, as he watched his prize leap into flame, glow to embers, grey to ashes. Tenderly he crumbled a cooling pile with his rod. Sure enough, the ashes were fusing.

Then came the storm. Black clouds poured down a drenching rain flooding the ashes, leaching away every vestige of hope as well as of pott ash. Drearily, Reuben turned again to his chopping. Only twice besides had he lost his lye in a shower, and both of those times his burning had been small. Yes, he had had good years mainly.

Four more profitable years followed, with the pott ash trade in varying extent becoming the main source of cash for practically every land-owner in all the Green Mountain townships, as well as in the neighboring colonies.

Then came the Revolution. Forced by the Tories, including Josiah Cass, the traitorous Clerk of the Propriety, to leave or to defend their Grants, Reuben and his neighbors enlisted with the Green Mountain Boys or returned to their former homes in Connecticut and Massachusetts.

After the War, the British Government placed a tariff on its "American alkali" imports. Begrudging the payment of any money to the young United States, and preferring to import from her own colony, England turned to Canada's inexhaustible forests for her pott ash.

As the Rupert Proprietors gradually returned to their lands, they also gradually discovered that their woodlands and pott ash kettles were still a rich source of revenue. A pack horse could be loaded with the crude black stuff here in the Vermont township on a Monday morning and be un-loaded at the Canadian border by friendly merchants there on a Saturday night. No one in England could distinguish between the Republic of Vermont and the Province of Quebec product. Most of the European countries were requiring greater quantities of the black salts for their manufacturing. The American mills, which were increasingly coming into production were likewise in need of the alkali.

An article in *The Farmer's Almanac*, published about that time, urged New Englanders to utilize their woodland resources. It gave a detailed account of the process which involved the use of lye salts for scouring wool, as convincing evidence of an assured market.

"In the west of England where the finest cloth is made, Spanish wool is bought by the manufacturer ready sorted. When the bags are brought to the mill for use, they are cut open, and the bagging carefully taken off. A woman is employed to pick off the straws, lint &c. The wool is then taken to the scouring house where a ley (lye) had been prepared, composed of one part stale urine and a small quantity of American pot ash: the last is more commonly used from the idea that the pot ash neutralizes the urinary acids. When the ley is heated to such a degree that the hand if immersed in it, can be retained in it for but a short time, a small quantity of wool is taken from the heap, thrown into the ley and well worked until the yolk (natural filth from the sheep) and grease are removed; it is then thrown on a railing set across the furnace (of heated solution) and resting on the curb so as to be kept warm by the steam. A second portion is then thrown into the furnace and worked as before; by the time this is done, the first lot will be sufficiently drained for washing; it is then taken to the swilling (washing) basket, small quantities washed at a time and the instant it is immersed, the workman moves it backwards and forwards to open the wool and that the stream may pass through it to carry off the yolk and grease. When well washed, the wool is thrown into baskets with handles, and left to drain till next day; it is then carried to the next pasture field, and spread on pieces of sail cloth, previously laid down for the purpose and then left until sufficiently dry: should the day be fair, the wool is taken in before it is quite dry; should it be cloudy, it cannot be made too dry.

"In the United States, when wool is purchased in the fleece, it is necessary to have it well sorted: bagging the wool is attended with considerable loss; the bags by being tumbled about on the wharves, streets, ware-houses, and mill-seats, gather a large quantity of dust, which packing through the bagging, soils the wool and adds considerably to the weight; the lint from the bagging mixes with the wool, to separate them after finishing costs two pence sterling per yard, & if not separated will show white upon the surface.

"In scouring, the greasy matter attached to the wool chemically combines with the alkali of the ley, forming a soponaceous compound which mixes with the water in washing, and thereby becomes detached. The natural oil, exuded from the sheep, would be preferable to artificial oil could the yolk be separated; leaving the yolk in the oil makes the wool work hard and leaves so much filth in the cards of the machines as to fill them up and prevent them from working; the separating the one without the other appears impracticable; therefore scouring must be considered absolutely necessary.

"Urine to be used should be stale, that it may have decomposed, for when fresh it abounds with acid; that which is voided by persons living high and drinking much is not so good as that of those who live low; for this reason one bucket full, collected from a prison or poorhouse, is worth two from families living well.

"A ley, when made, may be used for 14 or 15 days, by adding a sufficiency of the mixture to keep up the original quantity; when new it does not scour so well; it is well to let the old liquor settle, to skim off the filth, and throw one third of it into a cask to mix with fresh making.

"Wool of the same quality loses in scouring from one to three pounds in twenty:

"Wool when scoured should be used as soon as possible. A lot made up at once is worth from 10 to 15 per cent more than one made up three months afterwards. Always be sure to use enough potash in the liquor but not too much.

"Before carding, 3 pounds of hog's fat should be worked into each 10 pounds of wool."

Reuben Harmon, returning to his Grant the spring of 1781, was among the many who resumed the felling of trees to clear more land and to produce more pott ash. His iron cauldron, though somewhat rusted, his stump barrels, and his leaching trough were exactly where he had left them, sheltered by a high rock in a clearing at the foot of Harmon Hill.

Reuben Jr. by now was clearing his own land in the nearby Mettowee Valley, so father and son took turns at transporting their black salts to the Canadian border. Often two or three of the other townsmen took loads at the same time for themselves and their neighbors.

Returning through Burlington, they would usually tarry there for a day to do their marketing. Often their purchases had been carefully planned in family consultation, each one listed by a piece of charcoal on a sheet of birch bark: 1 axe head, 5 lbs. salt, 2 King's Rose tea cups and saucers, 6 pewter spoons, 1 copy of *Robinson Crusoe*. Satisfaction with their homes and families, freedom to sow and harvest their crops and to carry on their profitable pott ash industry, as well as their ambition to "lay up" as much as possible of their "pounds sterling", left them with no desire to carouse, so the trade-trips to Montreal were profitable.

In 1785, the Vermont Legislature granted the younger Harmon the right to coin copper money within the State for two years, so his father carried on the pott ash business near Harmon Hill by himself for a while.

According to legend, when Silas Harwood began clearing his Rupert farm in 1791, he set up his potash kettle and barrels near Harmon's and learned much of the trade from that First Proprietor. Soon he heard of a new process in producing potash and pearlash from a Samuel Hopkins of Pittsford, some miles further north. For this advanced method, Hopkins had been granted, on July 31, 1790, the first patent ever issued by the then three-months-old States Patent and Trademark Office.

When Silas' brothers, Oliver and Joseph, came to Rupert a few years later, the three men developed an increasing interest in potash. They noticed that the farmers of the county were becoming engrossed with their flocks, herds, and grain fields. Only a few lumber wagons, which had replaced the pack horses, were taking loads to the potash merchants who were by then legally operating at Albany, New York, and Boston, even though the product was in demand.

About the same time, the Harwood men saw the newly published *Natural and Civil History of Vermont*, which further fired their interest.

"The manufacture of pot and pearl ashes," the pages stated, "is extensive and useful. The immense quantity of wood, with which the country is everywhere covered may supply any quantity of ashes for this purpose. And the greatest economy takes place in collecting the ashes, made either by culinary fires or those which are designed to burn up the wood, where the inhabitants are clearing the land. In almost every new settlement, one of the first attempts is to erect works for the pot and pearl ash manufacture. It is reported that there is now one in every town. The business is everywhere well understood; and there is no better pot or pearl ashes made in any part of America than that which is produced in Vermont. It has hitherto taken 450 to 480 bushels (or more) ashes to make 1 ton of pot ash. Attempts are now made to extract more salts from ashes....thrown aside as useless".

The statistics quoted showed that in 1791 Vermont had produced 1,000 tons of pot and pearl ashes and that in succeeding years, the production had rapidly increased. The page stated further: "As the mountains will not fail to supply wood for this manufacture for centuries to come, it seems that Vermont will be one of the states in which this manufacture will be attended with greatest perfection and profit."

Having duly considered the many currently favorable factors, the Harwood Brothers decided to set up an Ashery. On the hillside, slightly back from the road, they laid flat rocks for a 20-by-30-foot fireproof foundation. Upon this, they constructed a stout log shed with a door and a window facing the lane that led to the road. The logs for the back of the Ashery were pressed tight against the high perpendicular bank that rose directly behind it to a narrow plateau on the hillside. In the log roof, the men inserted a sliding door for unloading ashes from vehicles on the plateau into the row of leaching barrels set directly beneath the opening. These barrels, formed of 3-foot oak stumps, hollowed by adze and slow fire kindled within them, closely resembled the ones that Harmon had set up in his woodlot more than a quarter century before. The 1806 ones, however, were lined at the bottom with wheat straw instead of tree branches. They were set on grooved stones, instead of a split log, that permitted the lye to drip into iron containers below. These in turn could be emptied directly into the 126-gallon caldrons, set three in a row, each on its separate stone arch.

In one corner of the shanty was a stone oven somewhat less than a yard square and of similar height, to be used for making pearlash.

A 10-gallon iron kettle on another arch, with a sassafras stirring-stick beside it, provided for the making of soap, as well as potash and pearlash, here in the new Ashery.

Beside each of the cauldrons were set up the tools similar to Harmon's in 1768: a heavy iron rod, somewhat more than a yard long and flattened at one end, similar to a gigantic chisel; an iron scoop instead of a wooden one; and an iron rake with close-set teeth.

The day that the Ashery window was glazed and its wide door hung, a new announcement appeared on the respective doors of the village store, the meetinghouse, and Moore's Inn. It stated: "The subscribers will purchase good house Ashes delivered at their Potash Works on Rupert Mountain at 10d. (10 cents) per bushel, and field Ashes at 6d. or 8d. per bushel. Those who cross the Turnpike with Ashes for us will be paid 10d. extra in cash for every load of 12 bushels or upwards.

Rupert, November 1, 1806   Silas Harwood & Brothers

The tollgate on the Turnpike had been completed only a short time before. Remembering that the notice posted there required: "For each cart or other carriage of burden drawn by two beasts, 10 cents," the advertisers had providently facilitated delivery of their essential supplies by guaranteeing to pay the toll.

The Harwood Brothers estimated that 500 bushels of ashes at 10 cents a bushel would produce a ton of potash, worth $120 or more at the current market. That allowed for a good margin of waste and still should return a high profit.

Soon business was thriving at the Ashery. Many a townsman scraped up a few bushels of ashes o deliver, just to satisfy his curiosity about the new enterprise. Daily, the horse or ox-drawn carts or sleds loaded with ashes made their way up the steep lane to the plateau at the top of the bank behind the shanty. Daily numerous bushels were dumped from the dust-greyed vehicles through the sliding door in the Ashery roof to the barrels below.

Besides the loads of "good house ashes" from fireplaces and baking ovens throughout the township, there came also tons of ashes from the woodlands. These latter commanded a lower price with good reason, since the dirt, twigs, and other foreign matter mixed with them considerably decreased their potash content. Also, many of these were already partially leached by dew and ground dampness. Nevertheless, when the Harwood freight wagon or sleigh made its twice-a-month trip to Albany the next two years, potash comprised the main part of its market-bound load.

Pearlash was soon a part of the Ashery output. For this, pure potash was dissolved in clear spring water and the solution filtered through clean wheat straw into an iron bake kettle. This was then placed in the stone oven which had previously been heated to a high temperature. Silas and Oliver could determine when the kiln was hot enough by thrusting a hand into its cavity to test it. By intuition, too, they knew at what stage of the baking the evaporation was completed.

This bluish white mass, fused out of crude potash from which the carbon had been burned by the intense heat, was then broken and pulverized into the product commercially known as pearlash. This commodity was increasingly in demand by those who had formerly used only potash. Housewives were also finding it a valuable asset in their cooking.

In Great Grandmother's cookbook appears "A Receipt for Baking Powder: Pearl Ash-6 ounces; cream of tartar-8 ounces; dry on separate papers in a cool oven; then mix and keep dry in a bottle; a heaping teaspoonful to a quart of flour is about right for this kind of powder."

When the "Receipt to Cure Fresh Wounds & Old Sores" appeared in *Beer's Calendar* or *Vermont Almanack* about this time, many of the townsmen, as well as Dr. Graves from the village, began coming to the Ashery for Pearl Ash for medicinal purposes. The "Receipt" advised: "When you are troubled with diseases of this kind, only apply this simple though cordial medicine, viz—Dissolve a little Pearl Ash in some good smart Vinegar, and by applying soft lint to the wound, use the liquor frequently as a wash."

Another "Curative Receipt", published in the *Albany Almanack*, not long thereafter, likewise increased the demand for the Ashery wares. This "rule" directed: "Let a person bitten by a dog or other animal, known or suspected to be mad, have as soon as possible the wound washed with hot water having as much pearl ash or potash as possible dissolved in it. This done change the water for another of the same kind, and let the bitten part be kept long in pot ash water (or strong ashes ley). Let this be repeated as frequently as the patient can bear, or as conveniently as can be done. There will then be no danger. The patient may be considered cured on the third day."

Dr. Graves widely recommended this remedy. He also began calling at the Ashery for another medical aid when he learned from Joseph that a skin irritation on his face had been relieved after an accidental splashing with lye solution. A favorite prescription for the King's Evil, also called tetter in the face, thereafter was to wash the face with a "not too strong" lye solution, let it dry briefly, and then neutralize the alkali by washing the area with "good vinegar."

For whooping-cough, Dr. Graves frequently recommended a nightly foot-bath of warm lye-water. "Botheration" though the Brothers often felt that it was to put up these supplies for local medical use, they never refused. Good will was still a business asset, and good neighborliness was a universal practice.

So profitable was the production of pearlash at the Harwood Ashery that the owners began offering the few local farmers who were still making potash a "good price" for their black salts to be processed at the Ashery into the purer commodity. The Brothers likewise raised the price of the ashes that they themselves would collect from the homes to 14 and 15 cents per bushel. Householders who had no dairy often exchanged a bushel of their "good house ASHES" for a pound of the "best BUTTER" churned from the cream of Joseph's Jersey herd.

In 1807, the fulling-mill owners at Pawlet made the Harwoods an excellent offer for a weekly supply of another product soon available at the Ashery. This was soap for conditioning the woolens processed at the mill. Barrel after barrel of soft soap was soon being conveyed to the Pawlet fuller.

Then one day a young boy who was helping at the Ashery "spoiled" an entire batch of the soft soap. Thinking that sour cream was as good grease as any, he poured a bucketful of the thick lobber into the grease barrel. When the soft soap made from this mixture was cooling, it hardened so it could barely be removed from the barrel. This apparent misfortune soon proved beneficial. The hard soap became so popular that the Ashery undertook manufacturing a regular stock of the cakes.

After several experiments, the men were able to produce a fairly standard product for the trade. Their rule for soft soap was modified only by substituting "properly soured cream in the proper amount" and proved "reasonably successful." The rule directed: "Take 15 pounds clear grease, 12 pounds potash, 3 pails rain water in the potash, and when dissolved for the lye to bear up a potato so as to show a piece of it as large as a York shilling it is the right strength to mix with the grease. Have both potash and grease boiling hot when put together. Add a pailful of sour cream or in the proper proportion. Stir frequently, a sassafras stick is best. Let it stand 24 hours. Add 3 pails of water to the residue of the potash and pour it in, a pailful at a time, at intervals of 6 hours. Then fill up the barrel with cold water added the same way."

A simpler rule for making hard soap appeared somewhat later in the family cookbook: "Take 3 pails good soft soap, 1 pound rosin, 1 pound borax, 2 1/2 quarts salt. Put in kettle and let it just boil, then set in a cool place over night. It will rise like tallow and can be cut in pieces. The longer it is dried the better it is."

From 1797 to 1807, potash was selling at $200 to $300 per ton. Then, as the conflict between France and England worsened, making the export business increasingly hazardous, the price more than doubled. Fireplaces and woodlots were scraped bare of ashes. The Harwood Brothers hired two additional men so the Ashery could be operated night and day. They planned an extension to the log shanty, bought two more wagons, one for collecting ashes, the other for delivering their increased output, and their plans for the future loomed bright.

"They motion to money, and it rolls their way," one of the less ambitious neighbors once observed, according to an old diary.

To this, Oliver Harwood was said to have retorted, "If you've got enough gumption to wad a gun, you can feed where you scratch. But if you don't the one, you don't the other."

By New Year's Day, 1808, the potash business in Rupert, as in the rest of New England, had reached a previously unimagined peak. Then came word of President Jefferson's Embargo passed in late 1807 as a reprisal for the search of American ships by France and England. United States ships were henceforth forbidden to sail to foreign ports, and foreign vessels were prohibited from taking cargoes from American ports. No longer could Vermont potash be shipped from Boston and New York. The Act, however, did not take effect on "Goods and Merchandise shipped in sleighs only", so overland trade into Canada was still legal. The Harwood freight sleighs, loaded with potash and pearlash, almost immediately were making weekly trips to Montreal.

On March 12th, 1808, Congress passed the infuriating "Land Embargo." Embittered by what seemed to them a highly unjust Act that spelled ruin for their commerce, the ashery owners in the Green Mountain State defiantly set about exporting their product in spite of the enactment.

"O Grab Me" (Embargo spelled backward) became both a derisive joke and a working slogan up and down the State.

Military and civil authorities had been ordered to enforce the law on all "insurgents", but the militia were in sympathy with their fellow Vermonters and would not fire on them. They declared that it was impossible to prevent smuggling over the network of roads, paths, and trails that crisscrossed the New York and Vermont sections of the Canadian-United States frontier.

By moonlight and even in broad daylight, the smuggling sleighs and wagons made their way northward to Montreal. Many drivers boasted that they snapped their whips at the Vermont Militia and that those boys in uniform discreetly turned their backs.

The Harwood Brothers felt that they were in no position to do that. A friend of theirs, Israel Smith, was Governor of the State. He had been directed by President Jefferson to enforce the Embargo Act by "all means in his power."

Silas, Oliver and Joseph were torn between their resentment of the Embargo and their loyalty to their longtime friend and former townsman. As a practising lawyer in Rupert from 1783 to 1791, Israel Smith had successfully defended two of the Harwood land claims against the challenge of some shrewd impostors. Attorney Smith's only fee for his legal services to Silas had been a request for "a vote of confidence" from him and his friends when Smith ran for office as town representative to the State Legislature in 1790. This had led to his becoming the Vermont Congressman for four terms, the Chief Judge of the State Supreme Court, the United States Senator from Vermont, and now Governor. In all these campaigns, the Harwood Brothers had given their full support. They could not now undermine their longtime friendship, in spite of their neighbors' urging them to join the profitable caravan to Canada.

The fall of 1808, taxes were soaring. Money was hard to obtain. The potash barrels accumulating at the Ashery were a frozen fortune. More and more the Harwood Brothers' minds were in turmoil.

About this time, the Harwoods' nephew John, who was living just north of the Canadian border, came to visit. Born on Rupert Mountain just before his father's death 21 years before, he was now establishing himself in what had become a thriving business for many in his adopted country. According to legend, he and some of his friends had excavated a cavern beneath a barn on the north side of the Vermont line. From this, they opened a passageway into another cavern on the south side of the line, north of Smugglers' Notch. Since all imported goods, legally or otherwise exported from another country, were required by Canadian law to be recorded at the customs house at St. John, the enterprising young men had arranged for an inspection officer to visit their entry-barn and record his manifest there.

Silas' sons, John and Philo, aged 16 and 14, excitedly listened to their cousin's account of the cache transfers through the tunnel. Begging permission to have a part in it themselves, they argued that there was no law against what they would be doing in transporting potash, and any other commodities that they might include, to another point within the state.

About this time also there was a change in governorship. The Brothers felt no great allegiance to Israel Smith's successor, Isaac Tichenor, so their potash freight wagons resumed operations.

For a considerable time the business flourished. Then, in 1813, the War closed the British market to all Americans, and prices slumped to an all time low of $45 per ton.

The Harwood Ashery did continue to supply potash, pearlash, and soap to some of the woolen mills, the linen mills, and the general stores that were springing up throughout New England, as well as the rest of America. Prices slowly rose to $120 per ton but the demand was limited.

The production of potash was also limited, due to a scarcity of ashes. In 1816, often termed "Eighteen Hundred and Froze to Death", however, ashes and salts of ashes provided the only source of cash income, and sometimes a medium of barter, for numerous New Englanders.

According to an old family diary, eight to ten inches of snow covered the Bennington County fields that June 6th to 9th, with more falling later in the month. Cattle and horses, unable to find grass, turned to the brush and tree branches for their browse. Apples and plums hung hard, green, and undeveloped in the orchards throughout the summer. Most of the young corn shriveled and died. The little that survived was cut for the starving animals after a severe freeze in August covered ponds and pools with ice a half inch thick. Although some poor quality wheat, barley, and rye, reaped that September, gave limited rations for bread, the meager supply of grain left from the 1815 harvest was rigidly hoarded for the next spring's sowing need. The price of corn soared to $5 per bushel and was hard to obtain even at that price.

One of the Harwood nephews, whose family had had no bread for weeks, backpacked "as much potash as he could carry" to a friend in Connecticut that fall, "paid $2 to boot" for a "bushel of maize" (almost a sixth of a month's wages for his chopping in the woods the preceding winter) and back-packed it the two hundred miles home again on foot.

Desperately, the men throughout many of the states turned to their woodlands. The Harwood men and boys reportedly chopped in the woods that summer of 1816, frequently wearing a "great coat, fur cap, and woolen mittens." The blows of axes felling trees to burn for ashes resounded louder and louder, day by day, throughout the northern woodlands during the summer, the fall, and the winter.

That year, as in all the years from 1812 to 1830, Rupert potash went primarily to local markets. By the latter year, only a few men were "chopping for salts" between fall harvest and spring plowing, so ashes were scarce. Oliver Harwood had died, leaving no sons to help at the Ashery. Joseph and his sons had become more interested in their tilling of the land, and in their flocks and herds than they were in the Ashery. They and even Silas had also become convinced that both the European and the American manufacturers would henceforth buy most of their alkali from Alsatian and German salt mines instead of from New England woodlands.

With ambivalent memories of their more than a quarter century in the potash business, the Harwoods decided to raze their Ashery in 1832. They gave the best of the equipment to one of the nephews. Possibly, though it is not provable, the two potash kettles that stood in the woods of Dorset Hollow were the ones that had long been used in the Rupert Mountain Ashery.

Silas gave the potash residue to his neighbors, who put it to widely varied uses. The local doctor made up a supply of liniment from a rule that he had recently found in his medical book. It directed: "For Rheumatism— To one pint of alcohol, add one tablespoon pulverized potash and a lump of gum camphor the size of a walnut. Apply daily to the diseased part."

Silas' son-in-law used some in his orchard, following instructions in his agricultural magazine. "To renovate pear trees, when fruit is stunted in growth, the bark thick and partially dead: Scrape the outer bark well; take off the moss and dead bark in to the green or living bark and wash the trunk with potash dissolved in water, united with soft soap in equal quantities.

"Spade up the soil around the tree and mix in a scattering of hen manure each spring. Add some potash, and mix it well into the soil."

Most of those who received the "salts of lees" (lye) from the discontinued Ashery used it to revitalize their land. Many of them had been using their wood ashes for that purpose for some time, hence the frequent shortage of supplies at the same Ashery. The practice had been promoted by the general discovery of the value of the alkali among the farmers throughout Northeastern America.

One, who was also a lawyer in Rutland, wrote to a friend in England: "These pot ashes amply pay them (the early settlers) for the clearing of the land. The method they adopt in order to prepare it for a crop is to cut down their timber about two feet from the ground, then chop it in pieces, and place it in heaps at a proper season when they set fire to them—after this they collect the ashes, make them into salts of lees & pot & pearl ashes: these ashes amply pay them for the clearing of the land, which they then harrow over, sow their wheat or plant their Indian corn, without any further cultivation, and the produce of wheat is usually from 30 to 40 bus. per A. Thus the landowner gets his grounds cleared without any expense and with little trouble (Amazing statement to us in the 20th century!) and his first harvest seldom fails of yielding him double the original cost of the whole land so cultivated."

Some astonishing tales were told about one of those who received the Ashery largesse, Darius Clark, regarding the immense specimens that he produced from his potash-fertilized land. He reported that many of his Early Rose potatoes at digging time weighed from three quarters to one and a quarter pounds each. He observed also, "I never plant in the new of the moon. If you don't want all tops and vine, plant when the moon is old." One of his most gigantic potatoes weighing four pounds and six ounces, had grown from a hill where "one small cupful of air slacked lime, one half cup of pulverized potash, and one barn shovel of old manure" had been applied to the soil. No doubt the seed had also been planted in "the old of the moon."

From similarly enriched soil in the same garden had come "a cabbage weighing 30 pounds and measuring three feet ten inches in circumference."

Most astounding of all was Clark's winter squash. This giant, according to witnessed records, weighed 94 pounds and measured 69 inches in circumference. The vines of the two roots reportedly extended 610 feet or more than a ninth of a mile. None of the others who fertilized with potash ever quite equaled Darius Clark's production, but all reported excellent results.

A *Farmer's Almanac* about this time recommended a quart of wood ashes to be used in place of pulverized potash, stating that its benefits were equal and much more easily obtainable. It likewise advocated the application of a mixture of paris green and wood ashes to prevent squash and cucumber pests. All in all, the potash and ashes from the razed Ashery served the community well. Even today, many gardeners use their wood ashes to improve the quality and quantity of their berries, squash, and cucumbers.

Soon after the Civil War, Joseph Harwood's son Oliver was living in Dorset Hollow when his neighbor, Sam B___ persuaded him to help build two stone arches near the road on his farm at "the head of the Hollow." Upon each of these, the men set an old potash kettle, both of which Sam had bought at a neighborhood auction. He had been inspired to try making potash by having read an advertisement in the local newspaper for March 2nd, 1866. The notice stated: "Ashes—At Boston pots have been in fair demand, with sales of 8 1/2 to 9 1/4¢ per lb. cash. Pearls have been selling at 11 1/4 to 12¢ per lb. cash, and are scarce and firm."

Sam had learned from his own father and grandfather the art of making "pots and pearls," so the prospect of selling such a product at $175 to $240 per ton as a side operation on his farm was full of appeal. As Oliver helped to set the kettles in place, he felt certain that they had come from his father's former Ashery. He hoped that they had and that they would continue their tradition by fulfilling Sam's expectations.

Although ashes from brick ovens, open hearths, brush piles and wind-falls throughout the county were soon being transformed into potash at the Hollow kettles for the Boston market, the venture was short lived. Good ashes were difficult to obtain, transportation was expensive, the work was arduous, and farming was much more lucrative than potash making.

Nevertheless, whenever a supply of his own ashes accumulated in his barrels, Sam would "run off" a kettle of potash to meet local need, mainly for making soap or a washing fluid.

The family manuscript cookbook contains the directions for "Grandmother's Washing Fluid—Take 1 ounce muriate of ammonia, 1 ounce salts of tartar, 1 pound of potash. Dissolve each one separately, putting the potash in some large earthen dish, pouring boiling water over it. When all are dissolved, put the three together into 1 gallon of rain water and set away in a jug or something that can be tightly closed. Pour 3 large pails of rain water and two thirds of a cup of the liquid into a copper boiler on the stove. Soak the white clothes over night, rub soap on the soiled places, put them back in the boiler, cover, boil twenty or thirty minutes. Take out, suds well, rub out all the dirt and rinse thoroughly. The colored clothes may be soaked in the boiler with the water not too hot." (Do "the good old days" include the "wash days" too?)

Beneath these Washing Fluid instructions there is a "Receipt for Home-made Soap: Clarify 6 lb. bacon or other grease by frying a large, sliced, raw potato in it until the potato is brown. Strain and cool the grease. Combine a can of lye with 5 cups warm water that has 2 tablespoons granulated sugar dissolved in it. Add 1/4 Cup borax, and let the mixture cool, while stirring constantly. When cold, pour into the fat, which should be luke-warm, stirring all the while. Add 1/2 Cup each of ammonia and kerosene, and continue to stir until the mixture is as thick as maple syrup. Pour into dripping pans, each lined with a cold, damp cloth. Let set for 24 hours, and then cut into bars. Set it away to harden for 24 hours more. Cover and store in a cool dry place. Take care that not even a speck of lye touches the skin, hair, or clothing, as it is highly corrosive and can cause severe burning. Especially beware of any contact with the eyes."

This homemade soap was frequently used for purposes other than cleansing. When some of the men were preparing to plow their fields for spring planting, they relied on this household staple to ease their labor. By smearing a "pinch" of the early soft soap, or by rubbing a dampened piece of the later bar variety, on the soles of their feet before pulling on their socks, they provided a fortifying emollient for their plodding the tedious miles of furrows behind their horses or oxen. Today, numerous people prepare for long runs or walks by rubbing the bare soles of their feet with a moist cake of the hard soap.

Men, women, and children similarly applied the soap to faces, necks, ears, hands, arms, and even legs, whenever they set forth to pick berries, pull weeds, or otherwise face the attacks of gnats, mosquitoes, or other pesky insects. Currently, this soap is recognized as a most effective relief for mosquito bites.

During the early 1900s, the potash kettles in Dorset Hollow were taken over by one of the local farmers for use in his dairy yard.

No one seems to know the individual history of the oldtime potash kettles now performing other roles here and there throughout the North-eastern United States. Nevertheless, several of the indestructible relics of early days still render valuable service. Two hundred or more years after they served as "borning kettles" for our country, they are dispensing spring water, floral beauty, and rudiments of Americana to refresh the obser-vant passerby.

4

FROM EBENEZER SMITH'S PENT ROAD

A leisurely-winding, woods-bordered lane forks off the Rupert-Dorset Highway on Windy Summit. A stout brown ribbon of hard-packed earth, it ties together two centuries of a Vermont "backwoods" way of life. Although it has been the unbarred entrance to the Merck Forest Foundation since 1950, it had been a pentway for over a century and a half, having been established in 1781 as Ebenezer Smith's Pent Road.

In Rupert Township, as in most New England townships, the early settlers laid their first trails, which were to become roads, along the edges of their fields as fast as these were cleared. Where a side road passed through the land of one owner to that of another, a gate or set of bars was often placed in the line fence by the owner of the land to be entered. This would prevent animals straying from their own fields. The traveler along the road was expected to close each barrier behind him, therefore each of these highways was called a "pent" or closed-in road.

Although highways were built by order of the town to accommodate the settlers' needs in going to market, mill, meeting, or their neighbors, many a landowner felt that a "back" road was an encroachment upon his private property and would sometimes nail his neighbor's gate shut. This naturally led to considerable inconvenience and discord.

The Rupert Town Records give an interesting account of the origin of Ebenezer's Pent Road. Near the end of the Revolution, Peletiah Dewey wished to build a frame house to replace the log cabin on his farm which was well situated on the main highway. The War, however, had considerably impoverished him, so he lacked funds for building. Ebenezer Smith, the landowner who had recently moved from Bennington to his holdings back of Dewey's, on the other hand, possessed some ready cash but no access to the town highway. Although it was rumored that both men were "as tight as the bark on a white oak tree," they finally worked out the following mutually beneficial agreement.

RECORD OF EBENEZER SMITH'S BOND FROM PELETIAH DEWEY

"Know all men by these presents that I, Peletiah Dewey of Rupert in the county of Bennington and State of Vermont, am holden and Stand firmly Bound and obliged unto Ebenezer Smith of Rupert in the County aforesaid in the Sum of one hundred pounds lawful money to be paid unto the Said Ebenezer Smith his Heirs, Executors or administrators or assigns to the which payment well and truly to be made I bind myself and my Heirs, Executors and administrators firmly by these presents.

Sealed with my Seal   Dated the 13 Day of August 1781

'The Above Instrument is such that if the Said Peletiah Dewey Does let the said Ebenezer Smith quietly and peacably have Liberty himself and his Heirs and Assigns to have a pent Road with gates or bars and free passage on the South Side of the lot he now lives on Said Ebenezer Smith is to maintain the one half of the fence between Samuel Gookins and Said Dewey then the above Instrument is void and of none Effect Otherwise to remain in full force and virtue according to law.

Nehemiah Harmon   Peletiah Dewey
Selah Harmon

August the 13 Anoque Domini 1781, being the 5th year of independence, the above named Peletiah Dewey appeared and acknowledged the above written Instrument to be his voluntary act and Deed before me.

Nehemiah Harmon, Justice of Peace"

By this "written Instrument", Peletiah Dewey and Ebenezer Smith thus insured Justice and Security for both parties, as well as for their "Heirs and Assigns."

In June of 1781, Ebenezer and his family had moved their first household equipment to their new home on an ox-drawn stoneboat—a stout, flat wooden dray without wheels, generally used for hauling stone. Their load consisted of two brass and three iron kettles, sundry hearth-irons, a few blankets and linens, some pewter ware, and a large mirror wrapped in worn pieces of red flannel and packed between two feather beds. The mirror was an heirloom that Mrs. Ebenezer's grandmother had brought to Connecticut from England when she was a bride. Rosebush and lilac bush roots in a dirt-filled stump keg topped the load. Puncheon tables and chairs, as well as a plank bed frame, already equipped the rough small clapboard house which had been built on the holding just before the War and into which the Smiths were now moving.

At intervals along the mile stretch between the main highway and the backwoods cabin, they had to halt long enough for Ebenezer and the three sons aged nine, ten, and eleven, to chop down the obtruding trees so their equipage could be drawn through. Both this stoneboat and the ox-carts that jounced over the right-of-way later that summer could be heard banging over the boulders for miles away.

As soon as Peletiah's bond was recorded, work was begun on the Pent Road. From rock and tall timber, from rank undergrowth and steep hillside, Ebenezer, his sons, and their neighbors hewed and dug their "free passage" from their remote farm to the main road.

During the more than a century and a half that followed, they and their successors intermittently toiled with shovel and wheelbarrow, pick and crowbar, ox, horse, and aching joints to maintain their indispensable route. A mile long and a cart track wide, it was pent off at the neighboring landowner's line fences of stones and rails by three sets of bars, later gates. Near each of these latter was a crude set of steps, called a stile, for pedestrian convenience. Cattle, sheep, and occasionally hogs grazed in summer and exercised in winter in the two pastures and the meadow across which the narrow lane wound.

At first, Dewey's grazing hogs posed a problem as they sometimes rooted their way under the gates. Ebenezer was dismayed one morning to find a mother hog and her nine pigs, less than a week old, grunting beside his doorstep. The "coarse hobs" and deep ruts made it a too hazardous operation to convey the young Swine Family back to their owner's lot in a wagon. But Ebenezer favored peaceful relations with Peletiah. Therefore, he directed his oldest son Peter to help him pack the nine young squealers into a flat bushel basket, in which he lugged them on his shoulder back to their home yard. "Miss Sow", Peter reported later, "made a great commotion as Brother Micah and I guided her along behind Father and her pigs by a rope attached to one of her hind legs."

Fortunately, Peletiah Dewey shortly thereafter gave up his pig-raising, much to his neighbors' relief. However, as the animal population on the

Summit increased during the ensuing years, cattle and sheep sometimes broke through or jumped over the fences that crossed the pent road. Careless travelers there also sometimes failed to secure the bars or gates. About 1800, Great-Grandfather and his brothers, having bought the land on the main highway, were pasturing their flocks and herds where Peletiah Dewey's had formerly grazed. To prevent disputes, each of these men registered their animals' "Ear Marks" with the Town Clerk, who likewise kept a record of identifying marks for numerous other farmers of the township.

Upon the yellowed pages may still be read: "May 16th, 1802: Oliver Harwood's mark a half penny cut on the underside of the left ear and a Swallow's fork on the end of the same.

"Joseph Harwood's Mark: two half penny cuts the underside of the right ear and a slit in the end of the same."

Ebenezer and his son registered no marks, the lack of cuts in their animals' ears being sufficient proof of ownership by contrast. Whenever strays mingled in the pent-road pastures, their owners amicably sorted out and reclaimed their property. The terms of the Peletiah Dewey to Ebenezer Smith Bond for "Quietly and peacably to have Liberty himself and His Heirs and Assigns to have a pent Road with gates or bars and free passage" were still working well.

While the men were laboring at their dugway that first year of 1781, Jane Smith busied herself with meeting the demands of her household. From the sugar, or rock, maples that they felled, she selected some "with the grain sound to the heart" for the treenware (dishes made from trees) to fill her table needs. She then persuaded her husband to hollow out a huge abnormal growth or burl on one, by adz and knife, to make a bowl eighteen inches in diameter. For more than a half century, this great bowl, placed in the center of the table, daily held the family stew of meat and vegetables, the breakfast hash, the hulled corn, the hasty pudding, and many another fortifying dish.

From the same tree, sacrificed to the pentway, came the smaller bowls for serving individual portions from the burl one; the eating-plates with edges slightly raised to form a rim; the noggin or mug with a handle, from which to drink; and the innumerable dippers and ladles, spoons and tankards, tubs and kegs required for preparing and storing butter and cheese, herbs, berries, and other staples for the family larder.

The hulled corn, which was the primary essential in that pioneer family's bill of fare, depended in part upon the same maples that were cut to clear the pent road and that supplied the dishes. A century-old cookbook gives the "receipt": "Boil maple ashes in a kettle of water till it will hold up an egg. Put a quantity of shelled corn into this lye and boil till the shells will come off with a little rubbing. Wash free of lye—This will require several waters. Boil again till soft." This hulled corn required many hours of preparation in the two-gallon iron kettle hung on the crane over the glowing coals, but it was an economical and nourishing dish.

When it was soft, Jane Smith, as well as many of her neighbors and descendants, ladled this kind of mush out of the kettle into a big burl bowl. Over it she shaved sugar from the "loaves of maple" stored in the cellar, poured on rich Jersey milk from the piggin or wooden pail with one stave projecting for a handle, and supper was on the table. Enough hulled corn was often left over in the kettle to provide breakfast. This, sliced cold and fried crisply brown in butter from the dash churn, was eaten clear or accompanied by maple syrup.

One lean year, when food was scarce in the 1780s, the Smiths found that the red and the white oaks that grew near the maples were also a source of valuable food. Having learned from the Indians, who sometimes pitched their wigwams along a nearby river, that the acorns from the oaks could be made into bread, they gathered a supply of the ripe nuts. These they shelled, pulverized with a mortar and pestle, and thoroughly boiled to a thick paste. This dough they then baked in a flat cake and found it a nourishing and palatable food. And grateful they were for the knowledge.

The Smiths, as well as all others who have lived near the pent road, found the butternut and beech, the hickory and chestnut trees that grew on the adjacent hillsides likewise a source of bounty for many decades. In my own childhood, it was an annual delight to go nutting in those pastures every harvest season. How the squirrels and chipmunks scampered and scolded among the drifts of red and gold leaves as they watched us loot their largesse. And how sweet were the chestnuts roasted on an open hearth. What a never-to-be-found-elsewhere flavor were in all those nuts, too, as we cracked them by the dishpanful on our back doorstone for our mother to use in cakes and frostings, ice-cream, cookies, and fudge. Like the Smith family, however, we ate most of them just as salted meats.

Some of those same trees that gave nuts often supplied another household need. Each October for many years, the Smiths annually filled large homespun sacks with dry leaves from the beeches, and on these they slept soundly.

Remembering the stories of this use, when his oat field occasionally yielded a less than abundant crop, Grandfather Seymour would drive his lumber wagon along the pent road to gather filler for the stout towcloth casings used as mattresses under Grandmother's plump goose feather beds. There the beech trees were shedding their leaves. From their sun-bright rustling crop he would fill his three yawning limp ticks, button their corpulent bellies, and trundle them home on his hay rack. But that was nearly a century after the Smiths first settled there.

For several decades, the yellow birches along the pent road, as well as the maples and nut trees, provided for the backwoods family need. Shortly after their arrival on the mountain, it became ten-year-old Micah's daily chore to sweep the kitchen and "other room" floors. Peter's duty it was to procure the broom. For this, he chose a straight-trunked yellow birch, five inches in diameter. After chopping a five-to-six foot length, he set to work with his jackknife. Fourteen inches from the butt-end, he marked a two-inch-wide ring in the bark. Below this ring, he removed the bark and split the wood into tiny flat slivers lengthwise up to the bark ring. He then removed the bark from the trunk above the ring and likewise slivered this wood down to the two-inch circlet, leaving a somewhat more than four-foot length, an inch or so in diameter, to serve as the broom handle. The latter lot of slivers he pulled down smoothly over the first lot and bound all tightly in place with swingling tow. This sheaf of slivers he then trimmed off evenly, smoothed the handle, and added a tow loop at the top by which to hang it. For more than a decade, the birch broom or Indian broom, so-called because its use had been taught by the Indians, was in service at Ebenezer Smith's.

During the late 1700s and early 1800s, the Smiths and others who lived near the pent road plied a profitable trade in their birch broom industry. A good one, requiring three evenings to finish, would sell for as much as six cents, all earned in spare time. The brooms that went to market along the pentway were always good ones.

Ebenezer himself helped to produce these. In addition to the logs that blazed in the fireplace, he sometimes required a pine knot impaled on an iron spike above the hearth stone to give him light. A supply of the knots gathered along the pent road he always kept on hand. These he secured by cutting from a white pine "the right kind" of limb, a little below the point at which it joined a larger limb or the trunk of the tree. The slender part would serve as the handle. The knot at the joint, filled with pitch, provided a font of lighting fluid. When thoroughly dried, these would provide fragrant lights, that could be carried around the house or barn or spiked in a convenient place, usually to the mantel. Although Jane sometimes complained of the "mess of pitch" that "the stick dripped", she did not discourage the home industry in broomcraft.

As Ebenezer whittled away at his brooms or flails or sap spiles or snowshoes or parts for Jane's spinning-wheels and loom, he was inspired to become his children's teacher, as well as a craftsman. Although by 1786 there was a log schoolhouse here and there in the township, the nearest one was a mile and a half away. The pent road, choked with snowdrifts in winter, was often impassable. And in other seasons the young ones were needed to help with the work of farm and household.

Remembering his own first lessons in reading and ciphering back in Massachusetts more than a quarter century before, he began to teach Eben and Alma, aged four and five, their letters from the Bible. Their numbers he taught from rows of beans, pumpkin seeds, and barley corns, estimating what number of each would equal an inch. The inch was first defined as the length of "three barley corns round and dry" when laid together. For the older boys there were more perplexing problems.

"How many barley corns will reach round the globe?" became a favorite. "The distance is 360 degrees and 69 1/2 miles equals 1 degree."

Seated on the extra backlogs which Ebenezer providently kept, one on each side of the fireplace, the children figured their sums on a block of wood with a piece of charcoal or pored over revealing pages. Each evening in winter brought their lesson hour, lighted by the hearth flames. Snowflakes and rain on nights of storm beat upon the roof and hissed upon the embers. But beside their unquenchable fire, the family pursued their learning. Amidst the howl of wolves and the roar of wind in the treetops, they read their Psalms and Proverbs and built their strength in the security of knowledge and of unity here at their own fireside.

Strangers occasionally traveled Ebenezer's pent road and sought shelter at the Smith house. According to legend, one bearskin muffled traveler appeared at their door on a stormy evening in early 1787. Tarrying only an hour or so to drink a cup of hot toddy and consume a slab of johnnycake, following his query as to the way "over the mountain to Sandgate", he disappeared into the darkness. No urging on Ebenezer's part could persuade him to spend the night in the snug comfort of the Smith home.

Most intriguing to Peter, Micah, and Matthew was the gun that the stranger carried. To their wondering questions, Ebenezer replied that this was known as a "Long Tom" and had been made in England before the Revolution and about the time the first settlers came into Vermont. He explained further that King George had had 500 such guns issued to the American colonists for barter with the Mohicans who were then roaming the Bennington area and hunting beaver. The Indians were eager to have the "long guns", and the English were equally eager to have the beaver fur.

The terms of trade required that beaver skins of the first quality be piled flat and tight until they reached to the top of the 6 1/2-foot-long gun barrel when it was set upright. A six-and-one-half-foot stack of beaver pelts of top quality gave the British a tremendous advantage in the barter, but the Indians had seemed satisfied with their part of the trade.

"Anyone could want such a gun," the boys agreed. But who was the stranger that was toting it toward Sandgate? And how did he come by it?

They never discovered how he came by it, but they did learn somewhat later the identity of the stranger. He was one Daniel Shays of Massachusetts who was fleeing from prosecution following his recent tax rebellion violence in his home state. In seeking refuge in Sandgate with his fellow-officers of the Revolutionary War, he had chosen the pent road and crosslots path through the woods as the least traveled route. Reportedly, he had taken particular care to leave most of his tracks in the rut water so as to outwit his man-and-bloodhound pursuers.

When the Smith boys learned of the subsequent death of Shays in a town far from Sandgate, they wistfully wondered what had become of his "Long Tom".

Another who traveled the pent road about that time had to contend with more than gates and rut water. Jane Smith's aged uncle from "over in Middletown" had decided to visit the family. Driving the more than forty miles in his two-wheeled chaise drawn by his faithful old mare Fan, he encountered a "terrible thunderstorm and powerful rain" accompanied by heavy wind just as he reached Windy Summit. Darkness had fallen, but he had been here before, so he pressed on. As he whoaed his rig and stepped out to open the second gate on the pent road, he found himself completely entangled in the top of a giant oak that had been uprooted by the wind. His thrashing around among the limbs merely entangled him further. Old Fan whinnied and patiently waited. Resigned to his lot, Uncle Jason curled himself up amidst the bushy branches. Next morning when he had finally extricated himself and driven Fan on to Ebenezer's, he reported, "I laid my hand over my ear to keep out the rain and slept soundly there till daybreak."

About 1811, Great-Grandfather Joseph extended his land titles to include those of Ebenezer Smith's. That family had decided to move off the mountain. Ebenezer and Jane felt that they were too old to carry on the place without their sons, who had "gone West", so they gladly deeded their premises and pent road to their neighbor.

For a while, one of Great-Grandfather's hired men lodged in Ebenezer's "old house". To his employer's offer of a horse to ride to and from the main farm, the eccentric Norman replied, "I never did like horses. I'd ruther walk." And walk he did. Each morning the summer of 1812 his cheery whistle mingled with calls of the robin and the bobolink, each twilight with the thrush and whip-poor-will, along the grassy-centered pent road.

According to a neighbor's journal, one July day the forty-year-old Norman "walked two miles from his lodging to the upper hay field. There he mowed (with a scythe) three and a half acres of meadow and then returned to his lodging after supper. There was upwards of two and a half tons of hay on each acre, much of which was lodged or flattened by the recent storm. Norm mowed the meadow clean and close and never touched a drop of spirituous liquor all day. Did you ever?"

When Great-Grandfather's oldest son, Joseph B., was married to Eunice Farrar in March, 1832, the father set off 300 acres or so of what had been the Rupert Mountain Wilderness, including Ebenezer Smith's land, to the bride and groom. There, in the "old house" at the end of the pent road, the young couple set up housekeeping.

Eunice, who had grown up near the village, was lonely in her isolated new surroundings. Besides, almost immediately, she became pregnant. In those early 1830s, no woman of modesty made a habit of appearing in public when her "in the family way" was apparent. Nor was the pent road conducive to her riding out over it, since the jolts and jounces might "upset her delicate condition".

Therefore, the summer of 1832 was marked by a series of tea parties "over the hill at Eunice's". Once a week or so, six or eight of her or her husband's relatives and other friends would wend their way along the pent road to the "old house". From two o'clock until four in the afternoon, the ladies, dressed in their best malines and summer silks, would hem ruffles and handkerchiefs or set tiny stiches in fine muslin baby clothes. And all the while, their tongues brought the sweet music of news of church doings, of courtships and marriages, of "bees" and personal confidences to the ears of young Eunice.

At four o'clock, the ladies would gather around the tea table, which Eunice had set by the front window facing the glorious view of the mountains to the west. Upon it was her finest linen cloth, woven by her grandmother in 1806. The scent of lavender always clung to its creamy folds, edged with knitted lace in a rose-leaf pattern. In front of Eunice was the Paul Revere silver service, also from her grandmother, and at each place one of her dowry teaspoons of coin silver, known as the 1810 pattern.

What sumptuous teas they were, for usually the guests would bring tidbits from their morning baking. White bread and brown, feathery golden-crusted raised biscuits; rich red apple butter and Damson plum preserves; amber honey, pear and cucumber pickles; firm-textured cheese from the home dairy; dried beef in thin rosy slices; rich dark fruit cake; and molasses cookies, doughnuts and tea.

Eunice was among the first in the community to abandon the custom of boiling the tea until it was black and bitter. The amber stream from her silver teapot, hot and fragrant, and "with a firm but gentle touch" upon the palate, brought delight to her guests.

Another delight was the variety of cups and saucers. Since Eunice as yet had a limited supply of china, she followed her grandmother's custom in earlier days of having each guest bring her own. Her mother-in-law, Great-Grandmother Vesta, usually took her pink King's Rose, a gift from her Aunt Pamela in 1795. Vesta's daughter Harriet often carried her favorite green sprigged Chelsea. Each guest took her most prized and her best, all of which were frequently discussed and admired.

At half-past five o'clock, shortly before Joseph would be driving the cows up the lane from the pasture to the barn for their milking, the ladies would start homeward, just in time to prepare their families' suppers. Never would Eunice and her guests forget those summer teas in 1832.

A score of years later, Joseph and his sons were driving their cows up to a big new barn. As the men of the community finished raising it, they agreed that this was about the biggest and sturdiest set of framed timbers that they had ever raised.

Sturdy it has proved to be. Its weathered grey bulk still stands against the winds that have whipped it for a century and a quarter. Long used as a cow barn, it today houses farm animals and machinery, a small museum of natural history, and the administrative office for the George W. Merck Forest Foundation.

Eleven children blessed Eunice and Joseph during that score of years from 1832 to 1852, though three died in infancy. Another, Heman, would have died, the family believed, had it not been for his grandfather. Great-Grandfather had been studying the use of botanical medicine in *The Thomsonian System of Medical Practice*, which he had purchased from a traveling representative of Dr. Samuel Thomson in 1840.

Late one raw night in October, 1842, frail little four-year-old Heman was "sinking fast". Great-Grandfather was summoned, and in desperation he administered a powerful concoction of dogbane which he had gathered near the pent road the preceding summer.

The "receipt" in his book of botanical remedies may still be read. "The powder of the newly dried dogbane root acts as a sternutatory when taken as snuff, and as an emetic, in doses from half to a teaspoonful or more. The root should be dug in the fall, the bark bruised off and carefully dried, after which it should be pulverized. . . It may be used in small quantities for the dropsy, as it is a powerful hydragogue, cathartic, emetic, and diuretic. It is also a sudorific, as it causes opious perspiration.

"Take of the pulverized bark of the root one ounce, three fourths of an ounce of witch-hazel leaves, and one fourth of an ounce of bayberry, all made very fine. Mix, and they make a powerful snuff for catarrh and other difficulties of the head. This snuff is frequently used in the last stages of acute diseases with small children. If there is vital energy sufficient left for the child to sneeze, we conclude there is yet hope for the little patient. This is the best way to test the immediate vital action, in these extreme cases, that has yet been discovered by us. No injury can arise from a trial of this means."

Little Heman that night must have sneezed. At least he lived. Twenty-three years later, having survived the forced marches and other rigors of the Civil War, he tramped home along the pent road. Beside the last stile there still grew a great clump of dogbane.

By then, this plant, as well as much of the other vegetation along the pentway, was increasingly popular in the farm homes. In those days of no refrigeration but nature's own, and of transportation only by horse and ox, these hill dwellers had from earliest times drawn their "restoratives" from the pent roadside. Along this leaf-dappled way, several generations filled their homespun sacks with dock leaves, hemlock twigs, bunches of lobelia and pennyroyal, and a hoard of other herbs, roots, barks, and berries for various healing decoctions and tonic teas.

Heman's sister, Aunt Delia, as she was fondly called by relatives and non-relatives alike, had early learned much from her ancestors and from her grandfather's *Botanical Physician's Book*. Even as a sixteen-year-old, she began dispensing herbal aids for various ailments. Although she moved out onto the main highway after her marriage to Uncle Elon when she was nineteen in 1861, she frequently returned to her home pent road to gather from its banks her essential ingredients. Goldthread root for sore mouth in babies; the scarlet bobs (berries) of the staghorn sumac for dysentery; witch-hazel leaves for sore eyes and canker; squaw-weed or starflower root for a general stimulant; goldenseal root for a "morbid state of the liver"; aspen bark to "restore the gall"; dogwood for female weaknesses; skunk cabbage root for an emetic; bittersweet berries for nervous disorders; and the seeds, herb and root of the princess pine for rheumatism.

Dressed in her long black cape and grey fascinator (a half-hood covering the top of her head and her ears), Aunt Delia might be seen any hour of day or night between 1861 and 1915 jolting over the main highway or the pent road on the high seat of the buckboard driven by her husband. Uncle Elon's urgent "Git-up-git-up-git-up-I-tell-ya" to his heavy-footed white nag, Jerry, brought her again and again to her neighbors' doors to assist at birth, death, or the revival of sundry ailing.

Heman and Delia's brother, Charles, likewise developed an absorbing interest in the healing potential of the wild growth along the pent road. As soon as he could be released from working on the home farm, he went away to study medicine, for a few months, at a "school" for botanical physicians. Becoming a successful general practitioner, he, with his wife Miriam's assistance, concocted in his own kitchen many of the remedies that he used. For these, he employed numerous ingredients about which he had learned as a boy and which he was now gathering from the pent road banks. One of his favorites was "an excellent drink for bad humors": "Take one pound of pipsissewa (princess pine), one fourth of a pound of fine ginger, one pound of green osier bark, a fourth of a pound of burdock seeds, and a fourth of a pound of lovage seeds. Pulverize the whole quantity, and put it into three gallons of soft spring water, and boil for an hour. Then strain off and press out the juice and sweeten it with molasses. When about milk warm, add half a pint of yeast, and in from twelve to eighteen hours it is fit for use. This is a valuable beverage."

Dr. Charles and Miriam likewise frequently prepared an ointment from their pent road resources. The instructions directed: "For an ointment, take of lovage seed, burdock seed, and prickly ash bark, each one ounce; bark of green osier, the flowers of yarrow and pipsissewa each two ounces. Pulverize and simmer all the articles well together in two pounds of fresh butter or lard for two or three hours over a slow fire; or it may be kept in a brass kettle, where it will simmer very slowly for a day or two, in order that all the strength of the articles may be extracted. Then strain and press out all the liquor. This is a very valuable article for the piles (which if neglected may become cancerous) and every species of old sores. Before using it let the sore be washed with clarified lime water. This is also an excellent ointment for stiff joints and rheumatic pains. Let it when applied be always dried in by the fire or by holding near some heated substance." Long after Dr. Charles and his wife were gone, their ointment was in use.

The green growth along the pent road provided another essential also. From it came the dyes for the coverlets and blankets, clothing and yarn, that Jane Smith, Aunt Eunice, and her daughters spun and wove from the flax and wool that the families produced on their wilderness-cleared acres. Shades of yellow came from the bark of the wild cherry, the cones of the spruce and the leaves of the willow. Browns, buffs, and tans, varying with the season, came from the bark of the butternut, maple, and birch, the oak and the alder. From the fruit of the sumac and from the young shoots of cedar came purple. The pent road women found joy in experimenting with those barks, roots, leaves, and berries for coloring their bed quilt linings, coverlets, and rugs, as well as an occasional dress or other garment.

Those same women and girls likewise enjoyed their gathering of the Bouncing Bet or Soapweed which grew beside the pent road. From its lush drifts of white, pink, and deeper rose bloom, they picked armfuls of the European-born weed during July, August and September. The girls used the soapy juice, that its stems exuded, for washing their hair, especially when a favorite beau was expected or when a kitchen dance, quilting frolic, or husking-bee was in the offing.

In the early 1850s, Joseph B. began operations to replace the old house with a handsome big new one. Daily, the ox-drawn loads of logs from the woods on Harmon Hill, the Stone Lot, and "up on Gallup" headed along the pent road to the East Rupert sawmill. Back came siding, planks, beams, and clapboards. Soon the two-and-a-half story house, thirty-three by forty feet on the ground, was raised against the mountain backdrop. Its nine bedrooms, back and front parlors, sitting-room, kitchen, pantry, and dairy gave the growing family ample space to work and to entertain. This latter was considered an essential, for the girls would soon "be sparking". Proudly, Eunice confided to her mother-in-law that she would no longer be tending fireplaces—the rooms in the new house were well equipped with "even-heating chunk stoves".

The dairy, too, was an asset. Its stove and vats, its big marble sink with piped-in spring water, its hand-cranked cream separator, and its big wooden barrel churn all promoted the production of cheese and butter for which the pent road farm was famous. Cheese-making ceased there at the end of the century, when the home dairy could no longer compete with the cheese factories of the town. However, until the 1920s, customers came from near and far to buy the firm, golden butter balls for which Aunt Eunice, and later Aunt Martha, her son John's wife, were famous.

Since the big dark cellar was not quite cool enough to keep the cream for churning "just right" in hot weather, ice annually had to be hauled over the pent road to the ice house built deep inside the poplar grove near the second set of bars.

HAND-HEWN IN OLD VERMONT

Each February, when the pond in a neighbor's meadow had frozen solidly to a foot and a half depth, the summer supply of ice was harvested. The men sawed two-foot squares, or a trifle smaller, in rows by hand. These they dug out, hauled ashore by ropes, and heaved aboard sleds which the oxen then dragged to the log shanty in the grove. There the blocks of ice were packed with layers of sawdust and shavings left from the sawing of firewood and the sharpening of fence-posts. Blocks extricated from this ice-house provided the treats of ice-cream made in the two-gallon freezer, cranked by hand, as well as sweet cream and butter throughout the hottest days of summer.

One of those who frequently drove his buckskin colored mare, hitched to a shining black four-wheeled buggy, along the pent road to procure butter for his household was John Lillie of Dorset. Beginning as a carpenter and builder in the late 1800s, he often drove the mountain roads of the county for the erection of houses, barns, and other buildings. Gazing down the valley from the dugway, he was deeply impressed by the vast panorama of mountains, forests, and meadows, of the animals and the farm operations the saphouse in the sugar season, the loads of apples going to the cider mill, and of other wagons drawn by plodding teams along the narrow road. All these scenes he was inspired to capture in paintings, so he was soon setting up his equipment at the roadside. Consisting at first of odd paint cans, brushes, and scraps of board from his carpentry work, it later became a chest of finest art materials. Between 1915 and 1942, the work of this self-taught artist was selling throughout America and some foreign countries. Some of his paintings still hang in the Metropolitan Art Gallery.

Many, who had first known John Lillie as a carpenter, often paused to watch him paint his pictures as they drove homeward from delivering their loads of maple sugar, cheese, and butter, of wool, potatoes, and their other produce to the Dorset, Manchester, or Salem markets five to twelve miles away. By then, the loads of hemlock bark were no longer in demand for the tanneries as they had been in Ebenezer Smith's time.

The road was still traveled, however, by "scholars" going to district school. From the 1780s on, education was held in high regard by those who were linked to the outside world only by Ebenezer's Pent Road. Their interest was aptly stated in one family diary of 1810: "I pushed forward to the main road searching for our stray colt, all the time saying over my rules of Syntax to myself and learning a small addition, having my grammar with me."

"I tucked up my time-book and spectacles and came whistling, musing, and fluting along home through the handsome white woods," the young man reported on a frosty evening soon afterward. He was then returning home after escorting a neighbor girl to "singing-school".

From the first family to occupy the rough cabin at the end of the pent road through the last residents in the big white frame house that replaced it, resourcefulness, self-reliance, and the application of learning marked the accomplishments of all who there worked out their way of life. The road was never actually pent to any who possessed the strength and will to surmount its barriers.

Over frozen hubs, through knee-deep snow and heavy mud, children from 1796 till the late 1920s daily during the school year trudged this mile-and-a-half route to the one-room red schoolhouse at "the center of the district".

From white-tailed bunny, from nuthatch and bluebird, from fossil in the roadside rock, from waterfall, curling frond, and arching elm along the way, they acquired firsthand knowledge of the natural laws of land and of life.

One of those "scholars" was stricken with excruciating pain one autumn afternoon in the early 1900s, as he strolled home from school. At the foot of the hill, he had found a reddening vine loaded with the pungent sweetness of frostbitten wild grapes. Filling his tin lunch pail with these, he enjoyed the juicy fruit until distress in his middle terminated the pleasure.

Uncle John and Aunt Martha, who with their three sons and two daughters, then occupied the farmhouse "over back of the hill", were likewise distressed. Fred showed no signs of improvement even after numerous draughts of warm sage tea, catnip tea, and peppermint tea.

At midnight, the telephone-on-the-wall rang a toll call to Salem. Four receivers clicked off the hooks of the neighbors on the party line. As soon as the summons for emergency had reached Dr. McGuire in Salem, Aunt Delia and two of Uncle John's cousins spoke across the wires to offer assistance. An hour or so later, their lighted lanterns were bobbing along the pent road.

Long before daybreak, Dr. McGuire's roadcart rolled along the same lane, his black gelding breaking into a brisk trot on the level stretch beyond the last steep pitch.

Aunt Martha had a big pan of water boiling on the dairy stove, but as was her custom, when she saw the expected vehicle reach the broad-branching oak out on the flat a quarter mile from the house, she stirred up the wood fire in the kitchen range and set the teakettle on to boil. A cup of good tea always brought a body comfort.

By the light of six kerosene lamps, each held by a parent or other relative, young Fred was laid out on the kitchen table, chloroform was administered, and a troublesome appendix was removed. Before dawn, all were sound asleep in the nine bedrooms. All but Aunt Delia, who "took the watch" with Fred. Even the doctor had some rest before heading back the twelve miles to Salem. He knew that his patient would be safe with Aunt Delia.

In early September of 1911, Fred's older sister, Caroline, was married to the young doctor who had been her classmate at a boarding-school in Poultney, Troy Conference Academy. Hers was the first wedding that my brothers, sister and I had ever attended, and what a never-to-be-forgotten day it was in our simple way of life.

Shortly before two o'clock in the afternoon of that sun-blessed day, about fifty of the relatives assembled, standing along the walls, in the "double parlors". The elaborately carved white archway between the two rooms was framed with branches of red and gold maple leaves mingled with pots of goldenrod and golden-glow. Other bouquets of the same banked the deep windowsills and the mantels in those rooms and the dining-room, or sitting-room.

As the clock on the stair landing chimed the hour, the beloved young pastor of the village church, the Reverend J. Duke King, came through the front parlor entrance from the dining-room, just as Will and Caroline and their attendants, Fred and Laura, entered at the rear. Having grouped themselves in the archway, they proceeded with the marriage ceremony, which was completed in such a few minutes that we young ones hardly knew that it had happened. We felt almost tearful as we pressed close to kiss the bride who had been our first teacher at the district school.

Then came the merry babble of voices, the gales of laughter over sundry tales and reminiscences, the singing of the tea kettle on the stove, and the clatter of silver and china. The fragrance of brewing coffee filled the rooms. Soon we were all balancing on our laps our plates of pressed chicken and wee sandwiches of Aunt Martha's freshly baked bread and freshly churned butter, green olives, and later, a slice of each of the cakes gold cake, silver cake, and fruit cake. My five-year-old sister and I curled up at the bottom of the stairway to enjoy the goodies. All but the olives! To us, who had never seen any before, they were obnoxious, but we had been taught to eat what was served. To hide our shameful conduct, therefore, we tucked the offending hard lumps under the edge of the stair carpet. For years thereafter, we were haunted by a sense of guilt and wondering what Aunt Martha must have thought when she cleaned and found the olives. *And Knew That We Had Put Them There*, for Aunt Martha was a meticulous housekeeper.

As we stood with our cousins, Spencer and Jessie, Julia and Austin, Fred and Harold, and watched wide-eyed the bride and groom being driven away in the first automobile that had ever come over the pent road, we could hardly bear the thought that The Wedding was now an event of the past. No longer could we count the days, the hours, until——. The mile home seemed longer to our feet at sunset than it had when we had tripped happily to Uncle John's earlier that afternoon, carrying the silver forks and spoons and the white Wedgewood cups that Aunt Martha had asked to borrow from Mother for the occasion.

The spring of 1944, fire consumed the nearly a century-old farmhouse, then owned by Spencer and Jessie. Chemical engines rumbled and rushed along the dugway from every neighboring town. Men swarmed to the hillside brook and did their utmost to quench the roaring crimson wall of flame. But to no avail!

When hopelessness and the agony of loss were somewhat healed by the passing months, the cellar hole was filled in and leveled off. The family settled in a village home, but the men continued to till the land, coming each day to seed and tend and crop the acres there for five more years.

Then, in 1949, the land once opened to Ebenezer Smith by his bond from Peletiah Dewey was sold to George W. Merck of New Jersey, who already owned the adjacent farms. Bars and gates were removed along the entrance road.

Since then, truck, tractor, jeep, and touring-car have plied this unpent-way for Merck Forest operations. Foundation representatives and various educational groups, now utilizing the area for studies in ecology, conservation, forestry, wild life, and scientific land development, circulate along the former pent road.

The voices of numerous nature lovers seeking recreation likewise mingle with the sounds of foresters and students in the mountain echo. Sheep, ox, and cow no longer here sniff the pedestrian's hand for salt along the roadway, but doe and fawn often stand in prick-eared, soft-eyed wonder to watch these passersby.

Surrey and lumber wagon, buggy, pung, and sleigh have all gone the way of the buckboard. So, too, have the horsedrawn power-saw and threshing-machine that once crawled along the lane on their annual rounds of the neighborhood. Smoothly purring motors have replaced the slower traffic line.

Nevertheless, research and labor for helping to build a better nation still prevail where Ebenezer Smith, his "Heirs and Assigns" once wearily shoveled, foot by foot, to make their way to mill and market, church and school.

The Pent Road ribbon, stamped with the imprint of almost 200 years of a small segment of an expanding America, continues to bind together the ever-extending aspirations and achievements of those who search for progressive ways of living off the land.

5

AT MOORE'S INN

A well-kept, and somewhat modernized, rambling old white farmhouse tranquilly reposes in sunshine and shadow, gale, and storm at the foot of Rupert Mountain. If its weathered walls could speak, however, they would tell of much besides tranquility.

From 1786 to the 1850s, this stout pine plank and beam structure, known as Moore's Inn, was a center of community activity representative of an emerging America. A Historic Site Marker identifies it today.

March 4th, 1791, marked its most noted event. That was the date upon which Vermont celebrated its becoming the first state to join the original thirteen.

Almost as soon as day broke over the hills to the east, up to the tip of the newly set tall pole beside the front door went the glorious red, white and blue Stars and Stripes. Above the opposite side of the entrance floated the Vermont State flag bearing the official seal of a pine tree and a cow in a wheat field on its indigo background.

The rippling folds of both banners had barely caught the breeze when excited citizens from all over the township came thronging into the Inn yard. Men in tricornes and great coats or in coonskin caps and leather breeches, women in fine woolen cloaks and velvet bonnets or in homespun coats and "pumpkin hoods", with children dressed like their elders, streamed from sleighs, pungs, and horseback into and around the Publick House. A hubbub of voices filled yard, Inn, and even the road.

Ten o'clock had been set for "The Reading". As soon as the sundial marked the hour, the Reverend Increase Graves from the "West Society" (Congregational parish) appeared on the front steps of the Inn. As he raised The Parchment and began to read, all strained their ears to hear the stirring words. Ever since they had elected a delegate here to attend the January 6th Convention at Bennington for ratifying the Constitution and for applying for Vermont's admission to the Union, they had eagerly awaited this day.

"Act for the Admission of the State of Vermont into this Union", read Parson Graves. His clarion voice continued: "The State of Vermont having petitioned the Congress to be admitted a member of the United States

"Be it enacted by the Senate and House of Representatives of the United States of America, in Congress assembled, and it is hereby enacted and declared, That on the fourth day of March one thousand seven hundred and ninety-one, the said State, by the name and style of the State of Vermont, shall be received and admitted into this Union, as a new and entire member of the United States of America.

Frederick Augustus Muhlenberg
Speaker for the House of Representatives
John Adams
Vice President of the United States and President of
the Senate
Approved February 18, 1791
George Washington
President of the United States

As Parson Graves completed the reading, there was a moment's silence. Then a volley of gunfire burst forth in a salute to this event of Union. As its reverberations subsided, shouts, laughter, drum notes, and the strains of numerous fifes rose against the hills and re-echoed in the revelry. All day the merrymaking continued.

Hostler Moore "stood treat" with apples, gingerbread, and cider for all who surged in and out of the open doorways. Those who wished could purchase additional refreshments: pumpkin or mince pie, baked in a long pan and cut in squares; roast venison or turkey with bread stuffing; crusty corn bread; stewed beans; milk, apple jack, rum, or tea.

Soon after dark, about eighty of the young people continued their celebrating at a ball in the ell chamber. Diaries kept by some of those who attended the Inn balls of the period gave some of their writers' observations: "We had a ballroom celebration that night. Everyone came from far and near, and the Inn yard was full of horses." "Some of the boys collected some of the girls with sleighs and wagons. In the chamber, I was requested to bring in my flute which I did but could assist the musician only in the sounding which I followed up so vigorously as to rob myself of almost all my breathing timber. Gazing at the performers I discovered much multiformity in the motion of the legs and feet of the gentlemen performers—but they beat the time regularly enough so it all went well. I had but little conversation with the ladies who I dare say regretted it as little." "They danced 'Speed the Plough', 'Yankee Doodle', 'Soldier, Soldier, Will You Marry Me?', 'My Days Have Been So Wondrous Free', and 'Song of Vermonters', intermingled with a march which would have appeared very graceful had it been accurately performed but everyone was feeling too gay to pay attention."

"When the apples were brought forward in large pans, some were used for 'toss and catch', some were eaten in hand, and some were stuffed into the girls' bosoms, not always without protest. The company conducted not so bad when the raisins and eggnog were distributed." "Ball closed between 1 and 2 A.M. Going out, we fired one last salute of guns. Great day for all!"

Nearly five years before that "Great day for all", there had been another great day at the Inn site.

"Heave! O Heave!" echoed against the adjacent hills shortly after sunrise one June morning in 1786. This was the day for raising James Moore's new house which would replace his log dwelling and later become a hostelry.

At the close of the Revolution, the forty-five-year-old farmer had come to Rupert from near Suffield, Connecticut. With him came his wife Mary, his two teenage daughters Aranie and Lois, and his six sons: James, Grove, Jabesh, Zophar, Seth, and Oliver, ranging in age from twenty-one years to six months.

For six years, the Moores were busy acquiring and tending the various lots of land that finally made up their 365-acre farmstead. By June of 1786, James Moore was ready to erect his two-and-a-half-story frame house,. similar to the many other New England and New York farmhouses that were fast replacing the early primitive homes.

The previous winter he had brought home the lumber that he had sawed at Noble's Mill from trees cut the year before. These had been quarter-sawed so the grain ran at right angles with the width of the board to prevent warping. Much of the lumber had been split and hewn by hand with broadaxe and adze, however, to save the time, expense, and work of hauling logs to, and lumber from the mill, seven miles away over a rough and mountainous road. These hewn and sawed boards had been soaked for two weeks in the nearby brook and then set up where the sun and wind could thoroughly dry them to prevent warping and rotting. Even in these 1970s, those "first growth" pine boards of the 1786 doors, an inch thick and two feet wide, which were thus weathered and cured, are still unwarped by time and use.

All spring, James Moore, his sons, and his neighbors, Enoch Eastman and Stephen Harmon, who helped him whenever their own work permitted, had been preparing for the "Raising of the Big House". Mainly, this had progressed well, although there had been a few setbacks. As the 12-year-old Zophar had straddled a log to cut the deep notches along its surface preparatory to hacking off the bark and squaring the timber one morning, he drove the blade of the broadaxe into his own leg. Such occurrences were not rare, but Zophar's gash was unusually deep, so work was halted long enough for Grove and Jabesh to apply a tourniquet and then help him hobble to their log house.

In spite of minor accidents, one after another of the 20-foot posts, the main beams, and the cross supports were hewn, split, and formed into the four frames for the ends and sides of the building. The men then split and whittled great oak pins for fastening the timbers where the pod-augurs bored. These square pegs they then forced with a heavy elm mallet into the round holes in the beams when these were hot and dry. The pegs would swell from the slightest moisture and be anchored fast forever. When the four huge frames lay completed on the broad meadow near the road, Moore set June third for "Raising Day".

One of the hardest jobs that spring had been the riving of the shingles from the pine blocks. Kenaz Kinne one day set a record by splitting five hundred of those yard-long, eight-inch wide slices from the resounding chunks of wood. In steady rhythm, hour after hour, his sinewy arms swung his weighty maul upon his froe (or frow), a narrow iron blade set at right angles to its handle, driving it through the block to cleave from it half-inch-thick slices radiating from center to circumference. Each of these sections he later clamped into a "shaving horse", or vice-equipped bench, where he shaved it to an eighth inch thickness at the thin edge, which would be overlapped by the thick edge of another in the shingling of the roof. These shingles, split with the grain of the pine, did not water soak easily, dried out quickly, and provided a dry shelter for nearly three quarters of a century, after which they were replaced by slate. By the designated June third, the required hundreds of shingles for main part and ell were stacked in bundles of two hundred each.

Near the assembled mass of building materials yawned the cellar hole, forty feet long, twenty-five wide, and seven deep. As this was to be a "sun line house", the site had been chalk-lined squarely east, west, south, and north, and the excavation performed accordingly. Laboriously, shovelful by shovelful, James Moore and his sons, James, Grove, and Jabesh, had dug out the earth by hand the preceding summer and fall. Then, with the aid of ox-teams, they had hauled numerous loads of stones from the meadow. These they had packed tightly into the soft dirt, walling up the excavation so that the stones fitted and locked into place without the use of any binder. They had laid three huge flat stones in the center of the cellar dirt floor to provide the foundation for the central chimney of the eight-foot fireplaces which would be laid later.

At sunrise on the appointed June morning the boss carpenter, Hiland Cooper, arrived at Moore's log dwelling just in time to help roll out the three barrels of hard cider which would serve to reinforce the men's strength for this day's labors. Within an hour, fifty men and women streamed on foot, on horseback, and in ox carts into James Moore's home meadow. With them they brought their axes and crowbars, their pike poles and handspikes, their children and an occasional dog.

"All ready?" Cooper as master builder demanded of the score of men crowding around the timbers and wiping their cider-flecked chins with the backs of their hands.

"Ready!" they chorused, bending over one big side frame, to the upper outside corners of which long pike poles, called "follerin' poles" were chained.

"Heave 'er up!" shouted Cooper. Feet braced, bent backs straightened, muscles strained, and the bulky timbers rose as high as arms could reach.

"Up with follerin' poles," Cooper urged. The men gripped pike poles and hand spikes and heaved again, till the tenons sank into place in the mortices of the foundation beside the cellar hole, and one 20-by-40-foot side stood perpendicularly in place. Asa Kinne, Titus Grove, Daniel Harmon, and Amasa Yale, as the most experienced of the men, had been assigned to tend the foot posts to guide tenon into mortice, and they performed their task skillfully. When this side was braced with temporary stays, the men turned to the second one which they similarly erected and braced.

Wearily then, they stretched out under the trees for a brief rest. The young boys who had been lugging spare tools, as well as wrestling and racing with one another, came running with pails of cider and of cold water to refresh the sweat-streaked men. Dogs scampered at their heels and tumbled over one another, yelping with the excitement of Raising Day.

Again Cooper's "Heave! Oh Heave!" echoed against the hill. By the time the sun stood directly overhead, both ends were likewise up and braced. The men gazed with satisfaction at the box-shaped frame which they had set in perfect precision upon its stone foundation.

Long tables of planks on wooden blocks, laden with tempting victuals, had been prepared at the edge of the meadow by the women who now called the men to dinner. A feast it proved to be, composed of the favorite dishes of the community housewives. Mary Moore had prepared a five gallon kettleful of boiled dinner, drawing on the thick slabs of corned beef, the potatoes, beets, carrots, and turnips that had wintered well in the pit excavated from a hillside behind her log house. Minerva Kinne's contribution was another five gallon mess of mustard greens cooked with salt pork. Corn bread, cheese, pickled young butternuts, cider applesauce spicy and sweet, a trout stew, a partridge pie, baked pork and beans, and loaves of molasses cakes were among the other offerings.

After eating abundantly and enjoying an hour of talk, the men returned to the building. Enough of them possessed knowledge, judgment, and experience in fitting the parts so that all went well, except for what proved to be a minor accident.

One of the helpers, young Tim Prescott, was placing the tenon of a girt between the beams of the garret when it slipped and fell to the second floor. Tim was on the stick so was carried down with it, barely missing several of the other men directly under it. They jumped out of the way just in time to avoid the crash. Tim jumped up and was about to return to the place from which he had fallen but found that he was too dizzy. A doctor in the group "let his blood", and Tim was laid out on a blanket under a tree. It was decided that he "was only badly bruised and would recover", so all hands except Tim returned to the building.

The two oldest Moore boys, James and Grove, won the race between themselves and two Eastman boys in pinning the ribs, to which the shingles would be fastened, so they had the honor of setting the ridgepole in place.

The Raising was finished with three loud cheers that echoed against the hills about sunset.

For the next several months, three carpenters and a joiner labored with skillful hand and eye to finish the house. Two others laid up the tall chimney with its five mammoth fireplaces opening into the kitchen, the owner's bedroom, the common room, and the parlor downstairs, and into one of the four bedrooms on the second floor.

The window frames, sashes, and doors were built by hand as needed, and 6-by-8-inch panes of handblown greenish grey glass were then placed, 12 over 12, in each of the window frames and in a single row around the front door frame.

Floors of 32-inch pine planks planed smooth, then tongue-and-grooved by hand, were tightly laid in each room. Doors and wainscoting were paneled, as was each wide Georgian mantel throughout the house, and the walls above were smoothly plastered. A double coat of whitewash lightened the interior of the rooms, seven and a half feet in height, and gave a pleasing contrast to the oiled pine sheathing and carved black walnut balustrade, handrail, and newel post of the staircase in the wide front hall.

Even the garret on the third floor was tightly sided over to be used for storing seed corn, frozen sheep pelts, and cow hides. This would also be used for extra sleeping space when all the bedrooms were filled by the ten Moores and the travelers who might come to their door.

Slabs of marble from the Dorset Quarry were laid for doorstones six years later, but blocks of fieldstone from the meadow served as steps at first. From the Dorset Quarry, recently opened, came the stones for the fireplaces and another slab which was chiseled into a 3-by-6-foot sink for the kitchen. Its drain pipe was a bored pine log, 4 inches in diameter. Several years later, James Moore's house received a coat of red paint, and later yet, a coat of white. At first however, only the weather colored the clapboards.

By fall of 1786, the story-and-a-half ell, sixty feet long and twenty wide, had likewise been raised, sided, and shingled. Here were the cheese room or summer kitchen, the woodshed, workshop, and wagon house. Over the first two of these extended a 20-by-35-foot lathed and plastered chamber, 4 feet high at the eaves and 7 at the peak. This "hall" was reached by a steep, unpainted stairway built against the woodshed wall but entered through the workshop. Like the rest of the house, this chamber was floored with pine boards 32 inches wide and 1 1/2 inches thick. Already this room had been designated as Rupert Town Hall, since Moore's house was located at the exact center of the township, and the chamber had been built large enough to accommodate all of the Rupert men of voting age.

Near the angle where main part and ell joined, Moore and his sons dug a well ten feet deep and walled it up three feet above ground with stone. Twelve feet east of the well curb a crotched tree trunk, eight inches in diameter, was set in the ground to support the well sweep. This was a twenty-foot poplar pole, four inches in diameter, set into the crotch to operate like a seesaw. A heavy rock was firmly bound with rope to the end of the pole that was away from the well. At the other end of the sweep was fastened perpendicularly a long slender oak sapling, at the lower end of which was secured an iron-hooped maple bucket. This was lowered into the well by pulling down, hand over hand, the sapling on which it was suspended. When the 10-quart bucket was filled with water, the sapling was released and the bucket was raised by the rock weight on the other end of the sweep.

This never-failing well of sparkling, ice-cold water and the four rain barrels placed at corners of the main part and ell provided the Moore residence with an ample supply of water until the mid-1800s, when a more convenient supply was piped from a nearby hillside spring into the kitchen sink.

When James Moore with justifiable pride paid the last of the total cost of $675 and moved his family into his commodious new house with greatly extended furnishings in December of 1786, he was reputedly "possessed of a comfortable estate and moral virtue." He was therefore eligible to keep an inn where the traveler could get a meal, a bed, and if so desired, provender for his horse. Because there was little profit from the business of inn-keeping, the town customarily granted a tax concession to one who would maintain an acceptable "Publick House". James Moore was a genial and ambitious farmer; his wife was an excellent cook and house-keeper; and their six sons and two daughters were willing and capable helpers. Therefore, when he petitioned the Town Board of Civil Authority for an appointment as an inn keeper, his petition was promptly granted.

In spite of all the essential services he had been rendering for more than a year, James Moore learned the fall of 1788 that he faced the loss of his appointment as inn keeper. His annual nomination the following March was to be indisputably challenged. The tything-men, who frequently came to the Inn to inspect it for suspicious characters or to collect funds for the meeting-house, had become incensed by Moore's refusal to support his town's newly erected Congregational Church. In retaliation, they pro-tested to the Town Authority that here was a person "not fit and suitable to keep a house of Publick Entertainment" since he was not a communicant of any church whatsoever.

Reluctantly, the Selectmen promised that they would recognize this fundamental qualification when making their appointments the spring of 1789.

James Moore and his family were well established in, and happily adjusted to, their hosteling. Cancellation of the appointment would mean a loss of some bed-and-table revenue; of the exhilaration of providing a social center for the town; of the special regard of the townsmen; and of the beneficial tax concession. Consequently James Moore moved to insure his re-appointment. In January, he presented to the Town Authority the following credential.

"Dorset, January 26, 1789: These may certify that James Moore is a professor of the Episcopal Church and has put himself under my Pastoral Care.

Bethuel Chittenden

Rector of the Episcopal Church in Tinmouth"

With considerable relief, the First Selectman handed the certificate to the Town Clerk who promptly glued it inside the front cover of his Town Records Book, where it has remained ever since.

Throughout the next sixty years, James Moore, his widow, his son Seth, and his grandson Calvin in turn continued to operate their Inn "at the foot of Rupert Mountain, on the west side."

During those years, also, heavy leather boots and sheepskin moccasins tramped up the stairs of Moore's ell chamber to perform much town business above the cheese room and woodshed.

The first meeting held there was scheduled by a Warrant, posted on the doors of the village store and of the church, as well as on various tree trunks along Rupert Highway. The document stated: "Whereas application hath been made to me the Subscriber by more than one Sixteenth Part of the Proprietors of the Township of Rupert in the State of Vermont to warn Said Proprietors to meet at the house of Mr. James Moor in sd. Rupert on the second Wednesday of March next at ten o'clock in the forenoon then and there to act on the following Articles Viz. 1st to Choose a Moderator & other necessary officers

2dly To see if the Proprietors will proceed to lay out a Sixth Division. Rupert December 20th, 1787   David Sheldon Just Peace"

The record of that meeting reported that the meeting was held "as mentioned by Warrant." David Sheldon was chosen Moderator; Amasa Yale as Clerk, to whom the former Clerk, M. Harmon, was directed to "Deliver the Proprietors' Records; and Daniel Reed, David Sheldon, Saml

Kent, Enoch Eastman, Moses Sheldon and Phineas Sheldon "a Committee one of which are to attend at the Surveying the Sixth Division Lots" they to be "Drawn for as the Law Directs", each to consist of fifty Acres.

A 6-foot trestle table stood in the center of the shed chamber for that Proprietors' meeting. At one end sat the moderator and clerk, and on plank benches around it were gathered the Rupert voters.

The next year, the first Town Meeting, replacing the Proprietors' Meeting, was likewise held at James Moore's hall, on the second Monday in March, beginning at nine o'clock in the morning. At this meeting, David Sheldon was again chosen Moderator, and fifty-three other town officers were elected. These included James Moore as Town Treasurer; his son Grove as Constable; his son Jabesh and his friend Oliver Eastman as Hog Howards (or wardens) to check the free range of hogs in the town; three Tything-men; two Leather Sealers (to check and stamp the quality of tanned skins to meet standards for leather), and other officials to meet the township needs.

The assemblage also "Voted to raise a tax of one penny on a pound to be paid in wheat at 4-6 (4 shillings, 6 pence) per bushel, rye 3-6, and corn 3. To be paid in the fall next coming to defray the town charges."

At the annual Town Meeting throughout the next seventy years, the voters who assembled in this same hall considered, and provided for, a variety of changing needs.

During the first decade of meetings there, drastic changes were voted concerning the free range of township animals: "Horses, Mules and Swine shall be prohibited from running on the Common." "Sheep shall not be suffered to run at large." "Any Ram found running at large within the term fixed by law (August 15 to November 10) shall be corded or castrated at the risk of the owner." "The Town shall be divided into two pound districts: the first in the West Society (section), the second in the East Society." Perez Harwood was elected pound keeper in the West District to "take up" and impound in his barnyard any of the prohibited stray animals until the owner should "pay costs for the same".

In 1796, it was voted to establish eight or more school districts to provide education for "scholars between the ages of four and eighteen years." It was further voted "that Damon Porter of Pawlett and Major Martindale of Dorset shall be called to confer with the elected committee in arranging the school Districts."

On March 2, 1804, it was "Voted that the poor masters should have a right to provide a work house (with such other advice as the law directs) for the purpose of employing poor & idle persons who are wasting their time & endangering the town into expense." This was to be located on a farm where the residents would perform the labors of raising crops of produce to sell, as well as to maintain themselves.

That same year, another meeting of the "votable inhabitants of Rupert" was held "to examine into the propriety of admitting the small pox by inoculation." It was subsequently voted to do so "under the direction of the Select Men."

For seventy years, too, each September and/or November that county, state and national officers were to be elected, the Freemen's Meetings were held in that ell chamber. "After the sun was down, the poll was closed, the ballots sorted and counted, and were stated in the certificate of the presiding officer."

The last meeting of the Rupert voters was held in Moore's Public Hall on March 1, 1859. The 24th item of business that day was: "On motion the town voted by 28 majority that it is expedient to remove the place for holding town and freemen's meetings from Calvin Moore's (grandson of James) to some other more central and convenient place." By then, the township population was centered in Rupert and West Rupert villages, so subsequent meetings were held there.

During most of those seventy years, the main house served as a hostelry for travelers, and, with its spacious yard, as a community meeting place.

Shortly after noon one grey day in December of the early 1800s, the Inn yard was the center of considerable agitation. There, on the top of a high pile of wood, stood one Lorenzo Dow from Connecticut, out on a "preaching perambulation". The district schoolhouse was closed at this season to save fuel, the church and parsonage were three miles from the center of the township, and so Preacher Dow, tramping the hill road on his mission of exhortation of the Gospel, had begged permission to speak from Seth Moore's woodpile. (Young Seth had become proprietor of the farm and inn upon the death of his father in 1800.)

A crowd of the "curious as well as the sanctified" soon gathered, pressing close to hear this haggard, harsh-voiced, wildly gesturing "prophet of the Lord" expound his interpretation of the Scriptures. A peculiar figure he was in his homespun grey woolen greatcoat, his wide-brimmed hat, and his long, dusty, red beard. Only beggars were then wearing beards, and this man seemed to speak the language of the beggar and the vulgar, yet he knew his Bible, too. His labored speech shouted warning to the sinner from a throat raw with a cold that he had contracted while struggling through hip-deep snowdrifts in the woods along his pilgrim's way. His flaying arms, his entertaining allegories, and his strange knowledge held his audience agape for an hour until an icy gust of wind roared through the Inn yard and swept it clear of both the pious and the scoffing.

In compassion, Mary Moore and Seth's wife, Rhoda, persuaded Dow to drink a mugful of hot tansy tea beside their kitchen fire before he resumed his perambulation. Hunger stared out from the deep sockets in his thin face as he eyed the fat festoons of apple and pumpkin chunks drying around the chimney, and sniffed the rich aroma of ham and beans simmering in the brick oven. The broad seat of the inglenook invited his chilled and weary body, but he was a man of determination and dedicated to his belief. Hastily into his voluminous coat pocket, beside his *Testament*, he stuffed Hostler Moore's offering of corncake and a birchbark container of soft soap with which to soothe his frostbitten hands. Then once more he resolutely set forth upon his journey of religious devotion.

From the first, Moore's Inn was a popular center for learning the news of the day. From 1790 until the early 1800s, when the stage took over the function, a post rider on his regular circuit from Bennington delivered a weekly newspaper at Moore's residence. In the evening of the day of its arrival, numerous townsmen came to the Inn for the reading of the news sheet. Both James and Seth were "good readers", so they were usually elected to perform by the light of the betty-lamp and the hearthfire in the common room.

One of the first items read there that early winter of 1787 was an awe-inspiring Advertisement in *The Vermont Gazette*: "just published in Litchfield and now selling at the Printing Office in Bennington, price a pence, *A Voyage to the Moon* by Count D'Artois & his Friend in an Air Balloon. Giving the most pleasing account of the objects they had a View of in their Passage; and likewise the Circumstances of their Landing in that Planet; as also of its being Inhabited by a Noble order of Beings,—their Language Manners, Religion &c.—The whole highly entertaining and worthy of the Reader's Attention."

Previously, Rupert people had heard of the Balloon Ascension at Versailles in September, 1783, when a sheep, a rooster, and a duck had been carried aloft in a balloon filled with hot air. They had marveled then, but even more somewhat later when two men in France had similarly ascended into the high atmosphere. Well, who could tell? Perhaps men on earth *might* some day visit the Man in the Moon. The men at the Inn chuckled over the preposterous thought.

Two other advertisements appearing in the *Green Mountain Farmer* somewhat later likewise seemed awesome but at least credible: "Notice is hereby given that I have obtained from the President of the United States in the month of June, 1809, the patent right for the following highly important discoveries which will be disposed of on moderate terms.

"No. 1. Patent for a Telegraph,—which will show a whole word at one view as written in the book, at eight miles distance—The great utility of this is so well known that it requires no comment.

"No. 2. A Patent Pump, to work perpendicularly; which will deliver double the quantity of water with little or no friction, and one man can do as much work as two otherwise with ease to himself.

"Enquire at the office of the *Baltimore Whig*.   William Schultz"

Similar pumps were soon in use in Rupert dooryards, including Moore's, but it was nearly a half century before any telegraph instrument arrived in town, and then it was a different kind from the one advertised at the *Baltimore Whig*.

Another advertisement, read at the Inn a year or so later, created much excitement, both in the hope of winning a reward and in the fear of losing property in similar fashion.

"Forty Dollars Reward"

"Stolen from the subscriber on Wednesday night, the 23d inst. a large Black MARE, four years old past—natural trotter, strait limbed, handsome carriage, with large mane and tail; was quite fat when taken away, shod all around, had no artificial mark, nor any white spots, but perhaps a few white hairs may be found upon her.

"Whoever will take up said Mare and the Thief, and return them to the Subscriber, shall receive the reward, or Twenty Dollars for the Mare without the Thief.

Canaan, County of Columbia
State of New York, August 24, 1811   Daniel Hawkins"

By some strange editorial quirk, on the same page appeared: "To color a bay horse black: Take 4 ozs. quicklime mixed with 4 ozs. litharge; boil in fresh water & use the scum."

So far as was reported, none of the audience at Moore's ever won an award for "taking up" a stolen mare. However, one who often joined the reading group, Eli Smith, did tell of catching a thief in the act of coloring a "bay horse black." "That Dan White, just moved into the shack in Frog Hollow, was out back of his barn, when I came along looking for my bay colt that got out of my barnyard in the night," Smith told the Inn assemblage a month or so later. "I saw him scurry into the barn with a bucket when he saw me coming. I went right in after him, and there was my bay colt half blacked over by that damned son of a gun. I almost kicked him out of the barn. 'Here, Nell,' sez I to the colt, and she came right along with me. That old crook slunk off toward the house. If he hadn't looked so sick himself, I'd have turned him in."

Another advertisement, read from *The Gazette* in the 1820s, likewise stirred much comment: "Whereas Rachel my wife being lawfully married to me, but she being previously infected with the venereal disease unbeknown to me, and thus greatly injured my health and reputation, and has deceived me in such manner that I am determined not to live with her any longer—this is therefore to forbid all persons trusting or harboring her on my account, for I will pay no debts of her contracting after this date. Manchester, Jan. 10th, 1827   William Edy"

Since such advertisements protected inn-keepers, store proprietors, and citizens in general, many of them were read at the inns, where by then mail was brought by stage. One of these so-called "postings" rated a reply from the wife and created considerable amusement among the Moore's Inn assemblage about 1840.

"Notice is hereby given that my wife Annie E. Baird has left my bed and board without sufficient cause and provocation, and that all persons are hereby cautioned against trusting her, as I will pay no debts of her contracting from and after this date. Signed Stephen D. Baird".

To this, Mrs. Annie E. Baird replied:—"Notice: No bed or board as yet I've had of Stephen D. or Stephen's dad, but since the time that we were wed have furnished HIM with board and bed; and for just cause and provocation have sent him home to his relation.   Annie E. Baird." (Was "Women's Lib" beginning to bud?)

The main events of the day, as well as the advertisements, were also conned at Moore's Inn. The trial of Aaron Burr in 1807, the imposing of embargo on American trade previous to the War of 1812, political campaigns, elections, slavery, the Gold Rush, and innumerable other news topics were read, discussed, and ruminated upon in the common room.

A report on the state of the national treasury was heartily approved in December, 1810, when Albert Gallatin, Secretary of that Department, declared that "the actual receipts into the Treasury have exceeded the current expenses of government, including the interest on the debt, by a sum of five hundred thousand dollars."

That approval was turned to gall in December, 1827, however, when Secretary Rush announced that the National Debt then stood at 60 million dollars.

"Sleigh runners groan when there's no snow,' Perez Harwood sagely observed, as he knocked out his pipe on the common room hearth .

One of the last items of news to be read at Moore's Inn concerned a lighter issue. *The Vermont State Banner* for July 26, 1851, carried the announcement. "It is said that the young ladies sent out by Governor Slade of Vermont as teachers to Oregon, although put under $500 bonds not to get married within a year of their arrival, are in danger of going off with a will. The Oregon Land Bill makes every lady worth 320 acres if taken before December next, so that the inducements to get married more than counterbalance the fine imposed."

Celebrations, Town Meetings, Freemen's Meetings, stage arrivals, and news discussions were not the only occasions for the males of the town to convene at Moore's Inn. For many years, they likewise met there for Training Days in the nearby meadow.

The same year that Moore's house was raised, a Vermont State Militia Law was passed. It provided that "Every citizen so enrolled and notified (as being a member of the 'guard') shall within nine months thereafter provide himself at his own expense with a good musket or firelock, with a priming wire and brush, a sufficient bayonet and belt, with a cartouch-box, with three pounds of lead bullets, suitable to the bore of his musket or firelock, a good horn containing one pound of good powder, & four spare flints (stones for striking sparks) and shall appear so armed, accoutred, and provided, when called out to exercise for duty if thereto required."

Most of the Rupert men between the ages of eighteen and forty were members of this militia.

In 1797, the State Legislature further requested that "Every captain or commanding officer of a company shall call his company together on the first Tuesday of October annually at 9 o'clock in the forenoon for company discipline; and once on the first Tuesday of June annually for the express purpose of examining and taking an exact account of every man's arms and equipment."

Therefore, on the designated days, the men of Rupert Township tied their horses behind Moore's barn and proceeded to the orders of the Day. The high notes of the fifes mingled with the thunderous throbs of the drums, as the officers prepared to call the roll. One of the drummer boys, Perez Harwood, Jr., who often came to the Moores, was so inspired by his beating out of "Yankee Doodle" at the edge of the Inn Meadow that he resolved to make the Militia his career. This he did, rising from the position of drummer boy to that of Major General, with command of the Vermont Troops. One of his cousins, Silas, who trained with him sometimes used to comment, "At Moore's, he could beat even me at eating doughnuts and drinking flip.' This flip was a favorite drink served at Moore's Inn. It was a concoction of hard cider, sugar, stick cinnamon, cloves, and beaten eggs. A fire-poker, heated red hot, and plunged into the mixture rendered it especially appealing.

Another cousin recalled that recruiting for the War of 1812 occurred at Moore's Inn, as it did in many another inn. "Much grog was served," he reminisced, "to stir up patriotism and animation. When men are drunk, they are ready to fight or enlist for fighting. The fifer and drummer played martial pieces all afternoon. Money and goods were hard to get back then in 1813. Everybody felt a kind of hopelessness, so a good many of the young fellows enlisted for action. They left from the Inn in farm wagons for Manchester at sunrise on June 13th. By then the grog had worn off, and some of them looked pretty sober."

Silas was not among those who enlisted, but he did continue to attend Training Day each June and October. He noted that through the years, Mary Moore, her daughter-in-law Rhoda, and HER daughter-in-law Ruby, each in turn served warm gingerbread free to every man at "The Muster" as it was also called. "The pans were set on the drums, and we helped ourselves—they were empty in no time."

He also recalled one special day in June, 1821. Each officer had been notified of the new requirements for uniforms, which must meet certain specifications: "Blue coat reaching to bend of the knee and collar up to the chin, single breasted with 10 buttons, cuffs not less than 3 1/2 inches. The skirts faced with blue. Vest and pantaloons white, blue pantaloons may be worn in the winter. Boots to the calf of the leg. Black stock, leather or silk. Black cockade of leather or silk, 4 1/2 inches in diameter. A white feather to rise not less than 8 inches. White leather waist belts not less than 2 inches wide. The uniforms similar to those of the United States.

"John Farrar and Hiram A. Harwood were in charge of the militia that day, T. S. Beebe and A. C. Beebe were Captains of the Artillery. They had exercised themselves to get their uniforms ready for the State Brigade Major who came to inspect that day. They all looked smart when we began drilling at 9:00 A. M., but they had wilted some by sunset. Wash Kinne and John Perkins kept us all laughing at our noon-out. Nobody else could boast quite like those boys. The townspeople that were watching us perform were having a good time, too. The Moore women didn't expect to sell so much that day, so they had all they could do to keep us supplied with gingerbread, cider, maple sugar, and buns. They most always filled in the gaps in October with apples and nuts, but that day they finally brought on popcorn, and that kept everybody eating."

From the opening of Moore's Inn in 1787 until its closing in the early 1850s, its main role as a Publick House was to provide food and lodging for those who came to its door seeking such accommodation. "Keeping everybody eating" and lodged well therefore absorbed the Moore women's days.

During the 1790s, while her own family kept her busy at the kitchen hearth and bake oven, Mary Moore seldom had vast crowds to feed, except on Vermont Union Day and on Town Meeting Days. For those occasions, she had laid in ample supplies—baked beans and corn bread being the mainstay on the days when voters climbed the ell stairs to the "Publik Hall."

Then, the summer of 1800, her husband was killed by a tree that unexpectedly slipped from where it had lodged when he was felling it. Their son James already had settled in another part of town, so twenty-two-year-old Seth almost immediately assumed the proprietorship of the Inn, bringing his bride Rhoda to help with its management. From the first, the two women worked well together.

Rhoda's dowry of wooden plates and bowls, of pewter spoons, mugs, and porringers, and her steel knives greatly added to the household equipment. So did her creamy white handwoven linen tablecloths and towels in her favorite M-and-O pattern; her woolen blankets, her buff and blue coverlet of Rising Sun design, all from her loom, and her thirteen bedquilts, twelve pieced, and one appliqued. The blues and reds, the greens and browns and pinks, pieced from dress scraps into the Nine Patch, the Double X, the Dusty Miller, Hovering Hawk, and other gay designs, brought a delight of color to the whitewashed walls, the pine-planked floors, and the maple four-posters of the upstairs bedrooms and the one behind the parlor.

Her appliqued quilt, "The Harvest Rose", done in shades of red, pink, and green, colored with barks and berries on linen of her own weaving, was her "bride's quilt." Rhoda spread this one for luck on her and Seth's plump feather bed atop a freshly filled straw tick in the bedroom behind the kitchen. This was known also as the "borning room", and here Rhoda hoped to give Seth as fine a family as Mary had given James, back in her Connecticut home so many years before.

Rhoda brought color to the dooryard, too. Seth set her flower slips, roots, and bulbs in the sunniest places around the now maple-and-oak shaded yard. Lilacs were soon flowering at the corners of the house; lilies banked the western wall; clove pinks, foxglove, rose geraniums, moss roses and numerous herbs filled the space between the grape arbor and the Red

Astrachan and Pound Sweet apple trees. The green sweep of grass in the broad dooryard was protected from hoof and wheel by a new picket fence the spring of 1802. The sleigh and wagon approach to ell and "ordinary" was henceforth confined to a crescent-shaped drive from the road to the wagon house door and back to the road. From this drive, a marble flagged path led to the front hall door and to the kitchen steps. Mary shared Seth and Rhoda's pride in this "Handsomest Inn of Rupert Township." And a handsome home as well!

Abel Dodge, the driver of the stagecoach which began its run over Rupert Mountain from Manchester, Vermont, to Salem, New York, twice a week, about this time, was more interested in the food and beds at Moore's Inn than in its beauty, however. Having heard good reports of this hostelry, he stopped here with his first load of passengers, all men. Thereafter, he made this his regular "halfway" stop. Soon, more travelers were flocking in. All joined the townsmen who smoked their pipes and drank their flip in front of the blazing logs or "summer embers" in the common room's 8-foot fireplace. And all joined in ruminating over the topics of the day.

In bed by nine o'clock that March night in 1802, the first coach travelers to stop here slept soundly beneath the homespun blankets until they were called to breakfast and to resume their journey. The night stars, according to the almanac, indicated the hour as three o'clock when Seth Moore's summons sounded through the bedchamber. Yawning their steaming breath into the chill atmosphere, heated only by coals in an iron kettle with a perforated lid, the four men jumped from the "big bed" and the "spare" and snatched their greatcoats from the wall-hooks provided for hanging extra clothing. Since boots were forbidden in bed, each man claimed his own that had been yanked off with the aid of a boot jack when he retired, from the pile in the corner.

After paying thirty cents apiece for the night's lodging, late supper of cold ham, fried eggs, warmed-over beans from the oven, corncake, apple pie, tea, and cider, and breakfast of the same, the men crowded into the stage and rumbled away up the dark road.

Mary Moore energetically rolled up the buffalo skins on which two pedestrians, rather the worse from overindulgence in their cups before their arrival the night before, had been required by Seth to sleep in the summer kitchen. She likewise put away her sewing-box, having stitched up a rip and sewed on a button for Driver Dodge. Then she went to shake up her feather beds.

Much to her surprise, she discovered a fat wallet under the blankets in the "spare bed". Fortunately, it contained the owner's identification so it could be returned by way of Driver Dodge on his next run. Widow Moore that very morning posted a notice on the wall of her upper hallway. Burned into a sheet of birchbark by a hot poker, it advised: "Put your wallet or other valuables into one of your boots when you retire, and keep your boot beside your bed. Then you won't leave them unless you go barefoot."

No wallet was ever again found in a bed at the Inn, but the "Notice" remained on the wall for many years.

Another precaution taken against calamity by the Moores was a lantern hung on a peg beside the common room door. This punctured sheet tin appliance with a peaked top always contained a "good length" of tallow candle, and a "tight hook" was attached to its door. More than one inn keeper had lost his barn because a careless driver or rider had gone to see to his horse with a "naked candle" for a light. The Moores always insisted upon the use of the lantern.

They were likewise provident in laying in an abundance of supplies for their table. This was a tradition begun by James Moore himself. The fall of 1787, when he was appointed as "A Keeper of a Publick House", he had established an impressive reputation by having put into his cellar: 23 bushels of butternuts, uncounted barrels of apples, vinegar, cider, salt pork, corned beef, hams, maple sugar, molasses, and flour of various kinds. There, too, were huge bins of potatoes, shelled corn, dried beans, pumpkins, squash, cabbage, and other "garden sass". Frozen milk, cider applesauce, spruce beer, and parsnips in sand filled several stump barrels directly outside the back door of the kitchen. On hand, too, through the years, were bountiful stores of dried apples, pumpkin chunks, blackberries, strawberries, gooseberries, plums, and prickly ash bark to be ground and used as pepper. A pile of corn cobs was also kept on hand to be burned, pulverized, and mixed with pearlash for use as leavening, later replaced by baking soda. Jars of pickled elder buds, pickled walnuts, salted shadfish and trout, and jugs of raspberry cordial occupied one special shelf in the cellar. With good reason, the Moores were famous for the meals they served on the trestle table in their common room.

In her later years, a granddaughter of James and Mary Moore recalled stories of some of the cavalcade that had taken meals "baited" (fed their beasts), and/or "lain over" at the Inn.

Early in his hosteling days, James Moore had a harrowing experience. Two sorry-looking men, identifying themselves as Mac and Eli, and rather uncertain on their feet, stopped for the night. At the Inn bar, they added to their uncertainty of foot and befuddlement of head, finally letting rage overcome discretion. When Mac accidentally or otherwise dropped a hot poker on Eli's foot, the enraged victim lunged at Mac and bit off the end of his nose. In the pandemonium that broke loose, Mary Moore's treasured Windsor chair from her wedding dowry was smashed to kindling wood. What occurred in James and Mary's private quarters that night was never revealed, but thereafter, a rigid rule was practised at Moore's. Inside the Inn, no grog was permitted to anyone who had already had as much as he could "sensibly hold."

On one occasion, nearly a quarter century later, "sensibly" was ill-defined. A cattle drover from "Up North" and a tin peddler from Connecticut arrived one fall evening when all the Inn beds except one were filled. As the evening advanced, the two late arrivals partook of so much "cheer" that they became far from cheerful in their rivalry for the attention of one of the pretty young Moore girls. Although that young lady discreetly withdrew from the scene, Mike the drover glared belligerently with his snapping black eyes at the handsome curly auburn locks of Abe the peddler, as they climbed the stairs to bed.

The next morning before dawn, Mike left with his lowing herd of cattle. Abe, whose slumbers were deep and prolonged from his previous evening's indulgence, descended to breakfast only after the sun was an hour high. As he caught a glimpse of himself in the hall mirror, he let out a bellow that reverberated clear across the road to the barn. His handsome chestnut hair had been grotesquely riddled. The fastidious dandy had been transformed by a pair of shears over night into a clownish lout. Either that shearing or the currently developing temperance movement permanently closed the bar at Moore's Inn.

Numerous hoboes regularly stopped at the hostelry. If corn needed to be hoed, wood sawed, potatoes dug, or some other job attended to, the Moore men offered a "good, square meal" for two hours of labor before-hand. Their doctrine was against alms in general, but they would gladly offer (often manufacture) employment and pay well in goods and/or services. If the traveler worked diligently, he would leave directly after dinner, his pockets bulging with the Moore women's extra donation of apples, doughnuts, cheese and buns.

If a hobo declined the offer of work, he was urged along his way, fortified by a slice of bread-and-apple-butter only.

One of the salesmen who annually stopped at the Inn was Tom Williams. His stock-in-trade was mandrake pills, known as "Simpler's Joy."

These were a favorite family remedy at Moores', one that was freely dispensed to guests, as well. A year's supply rated supper, a bed for the night (usually shared with one or two others) and breakfast.

An entry in an old diary well described a family who once spent a night at the Inn. "A man on foot with his wife and four children, seven months to seven years, took up lodging here this night. Said they had lost all they had in a fire. They were walking (about 250 miles) to the homes of their fathers. They asked for and paid for 'a light supper', not wishing to be beggary—We fed them well. They marched off with a light pace and cheerful countenances."

Another, who had met with greater misfortune, spent one night in the hostler's bench. This was the long, backless bench with a seat hinged to lift, that stood at the back of the common room. Beneath the hinged cover, the box was fitted with a straw tick, topped by a thin feather tick and a blanket. This "spare bed" could accommodate a child or a small adult. It gave sanctuary, and relief from wind-driven sleet and biting cold, one March night to a cringing young woman who frantically pounded on the front door.

As Rhoda opened it, the small figure huddled against it nearly fell at her feet. Regaining her balance, the girl begged to spend the night though she admitted that she had no money and refused to tell her name. Touched by the sight of such misery, Rhoda guided her to the hearth and brought her a cup of hot catnip tea. At the same time she noticed that the stranger kept a tight grip on the bundle that she clutched to her breast beneath a handsome Paisley shawl. In reply to Rhoda's questions, the girl would say only, "I must leave early," and she clung ever more anxiously to her bundle. As Rhoda looked back from the doorway, she saw the hollow-eyed, white-faced waif sink wearily into the feather bed and pull the blanket up over her shawl and bundle.

Just before daylight, another disturbing knock thudded upon the front door. When Seth peered out, a fur-coated young man agitatedly inquired, "Is my wife here?" A wail and a sob from the hostler's bench drew both men thither.

"It was a story to tear you apart," Rhoda's daughter, Salome, used to reminisce. The bundle was the girl's stillborn infant. Temporarily insane with grief over the loss of her first child, young Mrs. Clark had risen from her bed the preceding evening, as soon as her husband had fallen asleep. Setting forth, she knew not where, she had gone in search of a "granny woman" who might breathe life into her little one. Exhausted by the two-mile walk from the home into which she and her husband had recently moved, she had seen the light of the hearthfire reflected on the window panes of the Inn. Terror and fatigue compelled her to seek shelter here. Through the ensuing years, the Moores and Clarks, including the children of both families, became close friends.

During the half century that Seth and his wife kept the Inn, Rhoda's dream of having a family was fulfilled. Six times the borning-room resounded to the cry of a newly arrived little one: Merritt and Calvin, Salome and Rhoda, Bradley and Seth Jr. in turn added to the joy and the cares of her household. After the death of Seth's mother in 1824, she found the work particularly heavy so was glad that the girls were old enough to help, and increasingly so year after year until they went to homes of their own.

Both Salome and Rhoda were married, however, the year before their mother's last child was born. That fall she was happy to welcome a new pair of assisting hands when Calvin brought their neighbor Oliver Harwood's daughter, Ruby, home as his bride. Seth also was glad to have his son assume more and more of the Inn and farm responsibilities, since he himself had become involved in numerous town offices, including state representative and constitutional convention delegate.

Cattle drovers; peddlers; teamsters hauling cheese, butter, grain, and other produce to the Troy market, all were increasing the work of inn-keeping. Daily the brick oven in the wall beside the kitchen fireplace was crammed with the crooked sticks, that would not fit around the crane kettles, to heat the interior. Daily, Rhoda and Ruby raked out these coals to thrust in the iron basins of corn bread and beans, the rows of pies and loaves of bread, until the long-handled iron shovel (called a slice) seemed never to be quite cool.

Two of the almost daily standby sweets were Pumpkin Cake and Green Gooseberry Fool. From her grandmother in Connecticut, Mary Moore had brought the "receit" for the Cake. It directed: "Pare the pumpkin and cut it in large squares; set it to cook with very little water; stir & bruise it until it forms a paste, rather firm, and let the mass evaporate until it ceases to appear watery. Melt some butter in a spider (frying-pan); turn the pumpkin into it; salt it a little and add plenty of sugar (white, brown, or maple); let it simmer some time and put it in a dish; cover with shaved or powdered sugar, and with a red-hot shovel make a crust on the surface. The pumpkin diminishing a great deal in cooking, considerable quantity is needed to make a presentable dish. This is an elegant aid to the digestion."

The recipe for the "Fool" instructed: "Top and tail (Cut off the stem and blossom ends) the gooseberries, and then fill wide-mouthed bottles, shaking them down till no more can be put in; then tie them down with damp (not wet) pieces of bladder (pig or beef), and place the bottles, surrounded by hay, in a boiler or kettle of cold water, over a slow fire; let them simmer till reduced about one third, then take the "boiler" off the fire (in the arch) and let the bottles remain in it till quite cold. Keep in a cool dark place, such as the cellar, and you always have a supply on hand for baking, from one summer till the next.

"Line a tart dish with rich pie crust. Beat up a quart of the gooseberries with eight ounces of sugar, three ounces of fresh butter, the yolks of three well beaten eggs, and the grated crumb of a stale roll. Pour the mixture into the tart paste and bake from half to three quarters of an hour."

During the months of May through October, Rhoda and Ruby continued the annual battle against the flies that "seemed possessed" to come into their immaculate house whenever so many comers and goers only half closed the doors. Ruby one day happily found a "receit", which can still be read in her hand-written cookbook. "To Destroy Flies—To one pint of milk add a quarter of a pound of raw sugar and two ounces of ground pepper; simmer together 8 or 10 minutes, and place it about in shallow dishes; the flies attack it greedily, and in a few moments are suffocated. By this method, kitchens and other rooms may be kept clear of flies all summer, without the danger attending poison."

Ruby could supply no substitutes for much of the Inn work though. An old family diary describes the general routine: "Ladies hold on zealously absorbed in housecleaning, whitewashing, laying down carpet, &c. Sweeping and sleeking up without as well as within doors. The geese have been picked and quilled by our ladies (The feathers were annually removed by hand at moulting time from the live geese.)—they numbered 37 & yielded rather more feathers than they did a year ago."

Tedious toil though it was, the Moore ladies conscientiously kept their pillows and bed ticks filled with the feathers from their flock of geese that fed along the meadow brook and in the poultry house. They firmly believed in a prevalent superstition of the period—that anyone who slept on a bed or pillow stuffed with wild fowl feathers would himself go "wild" or insane.

At least twice a year, fall and spring, and oftener if necessity demanded, those feather beds were laid out on benches in the yard for a thorough sunning. Bedsteads and the cords that laced the frames together lengthwise and crosswise, were then scalded with boiling water and scrubbed with homemade soap, to kill any possible vermin left by a traveler. At harvest threshing time, the tick that was always laid under the feather tick was emptied and freshly filled with clean oat straw. Through the years the Moore ladies capably kept a check on any vermin.

When the *Vermont State Banner* in 1851 announced a certain remedy, they were thankful that there would be no need to use it in any of their chambers. It advised: "Many persons complain of being pestered by bedbugs; it is easy to avoid the inconvenience. On going to bed, strip off your shirt and cover yourself from head to foot with boiled molasses. Let every part of the body be thickly covered with it. On coming to bite you, the bugs will stick fast in the molasses, and you can kill them in the morning."

Although Mary, Rhoda, nor Ruby ever found boiled molasses on a single feather bed, Ruby's daughter Louisa once had a harrowing experience with something else that had been left on one.

That young lady, along with her two brothers, Henry and George Albert, had been "keeping Grandma Rhoda young", ever since their respective arrivals in the 1830s. Louisa began making beds when she was ten, and from the first she could pat a feather tick into shape with surprising proficiency. One sunny morning, she decided that the bed, which had been occupied by a young couple and their two small children the night before, was due for a thorough airing. Bundling the feather tick up in the light blanket which covered it, she threw it out the window. With a thud, it landed on the grass directly outside the screen door of the common room. There at the table, the transients were just topping off their hash, fried eggs, and corn meal mush with doughnuts and baked apples, preparatory to their departure in their buggy. The mother jumped to her feet with a cry of distress, nearly overturning the table and spilling coffee in all directions. Beneath the blanket on the feather bed was her two-month-old baby. Much to everyone's relief, the balloonlike descent had not even wrinkled the little one's pinning-blanket nor upset his slumber.

The spring of 1852 marked the coming of the railroad through Rupert. No longer would stagecoach or stage sleigh be sheltered in Moore's shed. No longer would teamsters heading for the Troy market bait and lodge at the Inn. Fewer transients would likewise be staying there, so Seth and Rhoda Moore, Calvin and Ruby decided to close their Inn and enjoy their dwelling as a home only.

Their ell chamber would continue to be used as a Publick Hall for Town and Freemen's Meetings, but the common room, kitchen, and bed chambers would no longer be a hostelry. With considerable satisfaction, Ruby arranged her parlor in the common room. The other front room and bedroom behind it were now a separate apartment for the parents.

Seth and Rhoda's fiftieth wedding anniversary occurred that fall. Many of those who had formerly assembled at Moore's Inn to digest the news of the day, to vote in the ell chamber, to "Muster" in the adjacent meadow, and a few who had here celebrated Vermont's joining the Union, as well as two who had helped with the "Raising" in 1786, decided to give the Seth Moores a Golden Wedding party. The guests would this time provide the viands, but Rhoda and Ruby insisted upon supplying the Seed Cake for which they were famous.

As the date of the Party drew near, happy anticipation filled the Moore house. Bed ticks were emptied, sunned, and refilled. Out came the handsomest coverlids and quilts, the best tablecloths, silver and china, all freshly "done". Carpets were taken up, beaten with a rod out on the board fence along the meadow, and re-laid, each on its 4-inch mat of clean oat straw. As Rhoda bustled about, putting a final polish on the balustrade, she observed to Seth, "My life has always been a happy one. I've had plenty of wood, water, and work. What more could a body want?"

A similar complacency shone from her black eyes beneath her snowy matron's cap, as she donned her best black alpaca dress, her string of gold beads, and her small, fringed black silk "house shawl" to greet her guests that October evening in 1852. Beside her stood Seth, his ruddy face beaming in its frame of hoary side-whiskers above his black broadcloth suit and his stiff-bosomed and collared white shirt. Ruby, Calvin, and the children crowded close behind, Ruby in a new rose-sprigged challie and her husband in his "best seal brown"; the girls in ruffled white muslin frocks, and the boys in long white trousers and closely buttoned blue short jackets.

The small-paned windows gleamed with candle flame; the yard and the edge of the meadow were studded with the lights of countless lanterns. And up the marble walk, amidst the rustle of crisp fallen leaves, came the Moore relatives and other friends from far and near. Each bore an offering for the Golden Wedding feast. These were deposited by the bearer on the three long trestle tables, including the one from the Publick Hall, each now resplendent with creamy white linen cloths and numerous tallow candles in burnished brass holders.

The children romped up the stairs for a game of "Blind Man's Buff" in the great upper hall. The older men clustered around the hearth in the kitchen, where the ruddy flames licking at a five-foot apple backlog and forestick provided sufficient light for their reminiscing and their whittling. Recollections of the 1791 Union Day, of "the boys" long gone from the "Muster Roll," and amazing tales of horse-swapping, sickle-races, and "champeen crops" were accompanied by the whittling of sundry goose quill pens, butter molds, and husking-pins.

In Rhoda's sitting-room, a dozen or so matron's caps, very little whiter than the coiffures they covered, bent above the ladies' knitting of socks and mittens as they exchanged news of grandchildren and great-grand-children, household helps, and recollections of their bridal days. Rhoda's recalling her experience with her first mince pie that she served at the Inn set off a gale of laughter. "Driver Dodge said," the bride of 50 years before recalled, "that my pie was so heavy that it set his stomach snarling. And Seth laughed. I almost never forgave him."

Uncle Bijah's violin notes sounded from the common room and adjacent bedroom, where the bed had been moved out for this event. "Balance your pardners all," rang through the house. Young and old scrambled for their places in the "figures" and the "changes". The aging walls and floors throbbed to "Money Musk", "Old Zip Coon", "Irish Washerwoman", "Pop Goes the Weasel", and many another favorite tune, as reel, quadrille, and minuet sped the hours till midnight.

Then came the feast. All stood reverently around the tables laden with tempting dishes as they sang "Old Hundredth" and the "Doxology". White bread and plum butter sandwiches, sliced pink ham on rye bread, shaved turkey on brown; elderberry chutney with watch-shaped crackers; pickled peaches, pears, and tiny tomatoes; baked beans and cold sliced corned beef, along with raised biscuit and dill butter, golden brown doughnuts, cheese, hickorynut cake, and spiced cider—most of the community favorites were there.

And so was the Seed Cake, for which none but the Moore women knew the recipe. This was set up on a smaller table in the corner of the parlor, where the tables were assembled. Calvin helped Ruby cut and serve the rich sweet loaves until every one of the more than seventy guests had had a piece. Laughter and gay voices filled the "sun line house" long after midnight and then accompanied the clatter of hoof and rattle of wheel out of dooryard and meadow and away on the road.

Every woman who so chose carried with her that starlit night the heretofore secret recipe. Great-Grandmother Vesta and Grandmother Mary Ann were among those who took a copy of it, written by Rhoda on "slips of foolscap", which were stacked in a pink willow bowl on the "Seed Cake Table." The Rule may still be read in the family cookbook.

"Seed Cake – Beat one pound of butter to a cream, adding gradually a pound and a half of sugar, dried and sifted, beating both together for a quarter of an hour. Have ready the yolks of eighteen eggs and the whites of ten beaten separately to a solid froth; mix in the whites first and then the yolks and beat the whole for ten minutes. Shake in with the left hand an eighth of a peck of best flour, add two grated nutmegs and mix them gradually with the other ingredients. When the oven is ready, beat in three ounces of picked-over caraway seed (fresh or dried). Bake it about an hour in a moderately hot oven. (The bricks should be a little less than white hot.)"

Landlord Moore's descendants continued to operate their dairy farm after the house was closed as an inn, until it was sold to the Gilbert Croffs in the 1930s. Their daughter, Wilma Batease, now cherishes the old home. Only legend remains of stagecoach and market wagon, of guns that announced the admission of Vermont to the Union, of the fifes and drums of Muster Day, and of the brick oven that fed countless travelers that tarried at Moore's Inn.

But the lilacs, roses, and clematis, rooted from those that Mary and Rhoda and Ruby Moore first planted in their dooryard, still pour their profusion of foliage, bloom and fragrance along the tight stone wall that Seth and Calvin laid more than a century ago. And the hand-hewn timbers of the "sun-line house" stand as square and true as they did on Raising Day in 1786.

6

ALONG THE TURNPIKE

From 1806 to 1867, Rupert Turnpike was only a tiny capillary in the national arterial traffic system that provided for the farm-to-city transportation and communication of agricultural New England and its neighboring states. Even so, it carried a share of the joy and sorrow, the hope and despair, the law-abiding and the lawless, as well as many another element characteristic of the constant struggle to build and maintain an emerging nation.

"The Turnpike Committee ran a line through our land this P.M." Great-Grandfather Joseph's fingers tingled with a sense of adventure and high hope as he recorded these words in his diary one day in early May, 1806.

A decade before, his brother Abel had brought his family from Bennington to Rupert over a trail where, he reported later, "We were momentarily in danger of being swallowed up by the Slough-holes."

Joseph had required two days to make the same thirty-mile trip behind his floundering, straining ox-team, when he brought his bride and their first household possessions to Windy Summit the fall of 1801. By then, however, there had been some promise of better travel routes throughout the area.

Ever since the first Turnpike Company had been incorporated in the Green Mountain State in 1796, Rupert citizens had been debating the formation of a turnpike of their own. All recognized the need, but men were cautious about investing so much money, time, and labor as would be required in such a corporation. When would they ever recover their investment by tolls charged the public The cost would run high, probably unpredictably high. Finally, four of the most prosperous men of the township decided to undertake the risk.

The Town Records state: "A Survey of Rupert Turnpike road granted the last session by the Legislature of the State of Vermont to David Sheldon Esq., Josiah Graves Esq., James. Moore (Jr.) & Lyman Dewey Surveyed agreeable to the directions of William Jenkins & Thomas Hammond a committee appointed by said Legislature to lay said road bounded as follows:—

"Beginning at a stake standing on the town line where we left Pawlet Turnpike road said road being four rods wide running from thence....to a stake in the road by Samuel Danforth's....thence S. 40 W. 54 rods to a stake Then S. 55 W. 862 rods to the line of York state or Salem 110 rods SW of a stake marked M. G. J. W. K.

Rupert May 31st 1806   Surveyed by

                             Thomas Hammond   Committee
                             William Jenkins
                             Thadeus Smith   Surveyor"

Two helpers, Isaac Hay and Eusebe Wolf, lugged the Gunter's chain by the handles on the ends throughout the survey. That 100-link standard measuring device, invented by the English mathematician, Edmund Gunter, in the early 1600s, had been used to measure all the township lands. Twenty-five links, a "quarter chain," signified a rod; eighty chain lengths a mile. At each mile interval, the surveyors set up a stone marker or milestone. On the new road, distance would no longer be measured, as it had been heretofore, by the number of turns of the right front wheel of a wagon, 320 turns in a mile.

Standard wheels they had used, 16 feet 6 inches in circumference, for the measuring, with the axle 6 inches in diameter to insure an approximate 10 to 1 ratio of weight to power. Always the axle was kept well greased to avoid friction. Joseph had rigged up an effective counter on the right front wheel of his wagon. It consisted of an iron wire projecting from the right front end of his wagon box and an iron pin placed on the inside of the rim of the wheel. Each time the pin would click against the flexible iron wire,

Great-Grandfather Joseph or his rider would record it by means of a slate pencil on his slate thus: ⌐⌐⌐⌐. All agreed that the milestones along the Turnpike way were a great improvement in time and labor.

Since most of the way the turnpike would follow the course of the earliest main route through town, only the trees along the margin had to be felled to make a highway four rods wide. Crosswise the rough stone and earth roadway, logs were laid closely side by side to provide a smoother, firmer foundation. In the marshes, whole trees were pressed into the slimy depths for a stouter fill. Over this wooden road bottom, the brawny arms of David Sheldon, Josiah Graves, James Moore, Lyman Dewey, and their hired helpers then spread the seemingly endless shovelfuls and cartfuls of dirt, which they rounded up in the middle to promote drainage, and packed down firmly with the aid of their heavy-footed horses and oxen.

Undulating breakers they spaced along the way to aid drainage by transversely channeling off to the side the rivulets that would course down the roadway in wet weather. The dip after the hump of each of these water bars likewise served to ease the loads of the animals used in hauling. Even as late as the early 1900s, more than a hundred of these "thank-you-ma'am's" (so named since they often caused the heads of those who lurched over them to nod violently as though expressing gratitude) were still in existence on that twelve-mile stretch, known in earlier days as Rupert Turnpike.

By 1840, hewn planks were replacing logs for the turnpike base, each alternating plank projecting four to six inches out at the side of the road so wagon wheels that slid off could turn back on. Otherwise, the wheel would slide or drag along the edge. These 4-inch-thick planks were well covered with gravel, which was also rounded up in the middle of the road and bordered on each side by a deep ditch for water run-off.

For many months in 1806, Township Turnpike Company and the men whom they hired at $1 a day, or $2 with a team, toiled early and late to lay and fence the new highway. Its required four-rod width was spanned by barely one-and-a-half rods of actual road, the balance being used for ditches, "margins", and fences.

A diary entry by one of those who labored on the highway the summer of 1806 gave some of the typical fencing details. "We fenced with wall 3 feet thick, 41/2 feet high. Jonas lays 2 rods per day. Estimated price $1 per rod. Wall along Turnpike stones dug from ledges or picked out of the earth—ledge more durable and stronger. Large drawn on stoneboat, smaller on ox-cart. Just before we finished drawing stone our Boat broke asunder, but it can be mended again. We had a large quantity of Tackling to take home, I returned Mr. Brown's cart, all were wearied with the labors of the day."

Finally, by November moonlight, the pike pole was erected as a barrier across each terminus of Rupert Turnpike. This pole was fastened to, and turned by, an axle set atop a pair of three-foot posts. In a boxlike enclosure beside it sat the toll gate keeper, who would turn the pole to permit passage of all who would pay admission to the appropriately named "Turnpike". From the collected fees, the Company would in time recover their expense of construction and maintenance, plus approximately ten per cent on their investment, as audited by the State Legislature, before the road would revert to the town, county and/or state. Sheldon, Graves, Moore, and Dewey estimated their expense for building and fencing the twelve-mile highway at approximately $600 a mile, or a total of approximately $7,000.

Rates of toll were posted on a signboard beside the axle-turned pike:

A four-wheeled pleasure carriage drawn by two beasts .... 50¢
Each additional beast .... 4¢
A two-wheeled pleasure carriage drawn by one beast .... 25¢
Each additional beast .... 4¢
A wagon drawn by two beasts .... 25¢
A horse wagon drawn by one beast .... 20¢
Each additional beast .... 4¢
A cart drawn by two oxen .... 20¢
Each additional beast .... 3¢
A pleasure sleigh drawn by two horses .... 20¢
A pleasure sleigh drawn by one horse .... 10¢
A sled or lumber sleigh drawn by two beasts .... 121/2¢
A sled or lumber sleigh drawn by one horse .... 8¢
Each horse and rider .... 6¢
All horses, mules, or neat cattle, each .... 2¢
All sheep or swine, per dozen .... 6¢

For those drivers who were going only short distances on the turnpike, fees were often adjusted according to mileage, for example: One-horse pleasure carriage, per mile .... 1¢

Military service men were exempt from paying the turnpike fee. No man need pay toll either if he were on his way to the grist mill or to Sunday meeting. If he were on the turnpike on Sunday, however, it behooved him to be going to meeting. During the late 1700s and early 1800s, some Vermont laws were Puritanic in severity. One stated, "No person shall drive a team or droves of any kind. or travel on the Lord's Day. except it be on business that concerns the present war or by some adversity they are belated and forced to lodge in the woods, wilderness, or highways the night before, then only to the next shelter."

Even the wife of a minister in a neighboring town was once arrested for walking along the turnpike to see her daughter's baby born that very morning. And her husband unprotestingly paid the five shillings fine for his miscreant wife.

The town's tything-men had a way of appearing at various points along the turnpike on the Sabbath and of inquiring from the traveler why he was not in church.

Great-Uncle Abel was once apprehended, much to his own family's amusement. He had seen two of his young cattle licking the pasture bars beside the turnpike when he returned from the village one Saturday evening. He decided that his animals were needing salt more than he was needing religion, so the next morning he prepared to take care of the more urgent need. To avoid suspicion (he briefly thought), he poured salt into the basin designed for live coals in the foot warmer that he and his family habitually used in the unheated church in cold weather. With sanctimonious expression, he then briskly set forth on the turnpike, foot warmer in hand. Near his pasture bars, whom should he meet but Daniel Weed, his own church tything-man for this district!

"Carrying a foot warmer to church in May?" Weed inquired with considerable surprise.

"Drafty near the door," Great-Uncle Abel explained hopefully, tightening his grip on the punctured wooden box with its enclosed basin.

"Might's well walk a piece with you," Weed drawled, as he fell into step with the recalcitrant Abel.

Both men knew the law; they knew each other, and they knew that Weed held the advantage. Together they went to church, and Abel received religion on that Sabbath Day. His cattle received their salt on Monday.

The question of payment of fee when going to mill became a controversial one at times, because of the wear and tear upon a Pike when heavy loads were hauled thereon.

The journal of one of Great-Grandfather's nephews on a September day in the early 1800s relates one of his experiences: "I told the woman at the Turnpike gate the distance I wanted to go to get lumber on the nether side of the first ridge of the Mountain for my cider mill. Inquired the amount of fee—she could not exactly say— referred me to Esq. S— who was working on the road a few miles ahead—so I passed on but said nothing to him about it as I went by. Passed up to ridge & piled on wagon a few hundred feet spruce boards & on to mill a rough half mile off Turnpike. Was even obliged to cut out the top part of a tree which had broken off during a recent storm & fallen across the road a few rods from mill yard. Loaded 2 yellow birch planks 11 feet by 1 1/2 feet by 5 inches making me a pretty snug load with which I returned thundering over the hardheads (boulders) & splashing through thick and thin to the Turnpike, which itself was none too smooth but compared with these public roads seems to be a race ground. Stage passed. Came on down Mt. & questioned Esq. S— respecting what to pay at gate. Said for passing twice it was rulable to pay 25¢—he being a proprietor I tried to get him to say 12 1/2¢ since I passed once with an empty wagon but he stuck for the whole. When I came to the gate I settled with the lady." (Frequently a woman was appointed to sit in the boxlike shelter at a turnpike entrance and collect the tolls. When traffic was slow, she could employ her time in knitting socks, in hemming sheets, or in stitching the seams of family garments, all of which were then done by hand.)

The score regarding the payment of fees was reversed once shortly after the diary-writer's settlement "with the lady". Solomon Moore was keeper of the tollgate one day when Deacon Farthingale's sixteen-year-old daughter, Mercy, came blithely riding up to the turnpike entrance. When he requested the customary six cents, he and his three cronies who were helping him to while away the hours with tales of their hunting prowess, while they whittled shoe pegs, were considerably taken aback by her retort.

"The signboard states," said she, " 'Six cents for each HORSE and rider!' I, Sir, am riding a MARE." Dumfounded, the men made no move to halt the saucy miss as she merrily urged her steed past the only half-closed pike.

Mainly, however, no one protested payment of toll, since the "Shunpike," or "public road" extended around the Turnpike, much of the way, providing a highway for those who preferred not to pay. This was generally used for traveling short distances only, since its hardheads and slough-holes considerably reduced its popularity.

One who was about to travel the shunpike rather than use the taxpayers' money for toll was Simon Stone, the Pawlet Constable. One evening in 1810, he came galloping along the Pawlet Turnpike on horseback and was about to enter the Rupert Shunpike when the keeper of the Rupert gate turned the pole and urged him to enter the toll road without payment of fee.

The man attending the pike that day was Aseph Sheldon, a former constable in Rupert, and he believed that common sense was of the essence of the law. Riding on the horse behind Constable Stone's saddle was one 16-year-old boy, Amasa Buckingham, whom Stone was returning to his father's home in East Rupert. Sheldon recognized the youth as one who had long been known as an undisciplined big bully. Recently he had been infrequently working as a farm hand in Pawlet. This morning, he had over-refreshed himself from the customary jug of hard cider in the hayfield. When the elderly Mrs. Darling went to the field with doughnuts for the haymakers' mid-morning lunch, he had threatened to disembowel her with his sickle. The Herculean Constable Stone, riding past at that moment, forced the young scoundrel into his saddle and took him before the Justice of the Peace. There the boy was sentenced to the whipping post which faced the Pawlet Congregational Church on the village green. Escorting him hence as soon as he was sober, Simon Stone tied the delinquent to the stout oak post and vigorously applied the whip, which Amasa had earlier stolen from the field and secreted in his pantaloons.

Having completed the chastisement, Stone admonished the half-limp boy, "Now you're going home, where we hope you'll learn to be a man instead of a savage."

Amasa may have learned from that day's experience. When a Vermont Law, passed in November of 1816, deprived justices of the peace of authority to sentence any person to be whipped, young Buckingham commented, "Maybe this law should be passed, but what Simon Stone did to me was what brought me to my senses. I'd always been let do as I damned pleased, and I hated everything and everybody, including myself. Then, between Stone and my neighbor Sheldon, who hired me to work, and I do mean *work* on the Pike right after that, I built my self-respect. I HAVE become a man instead of a savage."

Perhaps another incident on Rupert Turnpike near the Salem terminal helped also to promote better attitudes and human relations. A local *Journal* of December 12, 1828, reported: "Hannah Westbury was recently attacked on the Turnpike by a half-starved, squalid looking fellow, rather below the middle size, who seized a basket hanging on her arm and made off with it. Not relishing this kind of treatment, the girl, after deliberating with herself a minute or two, determined to regain her basket. She followed, overtook the fellow, and commenced an attack. He struck her on the back with a stick, which she wrested from him, and beat him with it till he cried for mercy. He then alleged that distress had led him to the commission of the deed. The girl's compassion being awakened by this tale of woe, she took a threepence out of her pocket, gave it to him, and pursued her journey without further molestation."

Comparatively little banditry occurred on the New England turnpikes of those days, however, since goods and services were mainly obtained by barter, and little money was carried. Besides, the majority of the people were so absorbed in the work of building homes, roads, bridges, and the rest of the foundations of America that they had more of a desire to help than to injure one another.

Along both sides of the Rupert Turnpike from Salem terminus to the Pawlet line, the results of hard work, love for the home, and civic pride were apparent. Numerous great white clapboard houses of Georgian style architecture or of American Colonial design were erected on the productive farmsteads. Interspersed among these on both sides of the Mountain was an occasional red or grey saltbox house, including Great-Grandfather's on Windy Summit.

A broad green dooryard surrounded each, with lilacs, syringa, pink blush and yellow Martha Washington roses, blue verbena, sweet peas, bachelor buttons, and other floral favorites lending color and fragrance, each in its season. Near each house, too, was the orchard of apple, plum, and pear trees, giving bloom and fruit as priceless gifts to the community.

Beside nearly every domicile was the walled-up well sweep with its waterbucket suspended from one end, many replaced later by a bucket on a chain, wound up by a windlass, the whole covered with a wooden roof, often painted red. At first, these wells supplied the water not only for the farm or village homes, but also for the thirsty teams of horses or oxen hauling stagecoaches or other wagons along the Pike. Later, these were supplemented at two-mile intervals by great black cauldrons or huge hollow log troughs, to which water was piped through slender bored spruce tree trunks called pump logs, from the hillside springs.

A row of sugar maples, of elms, or of white oaks was planted on each side of the road along these dooryards and often considerably farther along the highway. Shade and water for man and beast were essential in those day of turnpike travel.

So, too, were a strong hitching-post and carriage block near each house, as well as one of the latter at the meeting-house steps, and one of the former at the blacksmith shop, where each faced the village green. At the nearby general store, the steps provided a place for alighting from the wagons, and a row of posts paralleling the end of the building supplied a tying-place for twenty teams or more.

In the broad sweep of fields between pike and wooded hillside, flocks of sheep and herds of cattle grazed, called to one another, and lent the cadence of their bells to the rustic quiet.

Six of the most spacious of the farmhouses along the Pike were operated as inns, the most popular ones being kept by the Jenks, Moore, and Eastman families. Moore's Inn, since it stood at the center of the township, was likewise for more than a half century used as the Town Hall. Across the road from this home also appeared one of the first of the big frame barns, some painted red, others left to weather to a silvery grey, that soon loomed up beside the farmhouses along the Pike.

Near them stretched broad fields of hay and oats, of barley, wheat, and rye, of corn and potatoes. At harvest time, the stacks of grain were topped by protective covers of homespun towcloth so that they resembled snowcapped knolls. Often they were neighbored by shocks of corn with round-bellied pumpkins clustering near. And at this season, the air was pungent with the fragrance of ripened apples piled in red and gold heaps amidst the orchard trees, awaiting transportation to cider mill or cellar.

Because of wear from its steady flow of traffic, and because of damage by storms and by frost upheaval, the turnpike was in annual need of repair, supplemented by general maintenance. A *Vermont Gazette* of the early 1800s carried frequent advertisements stating: "The Turnpike Company wishes to employ some person who has two yoke of oxen, cart & plough and who will take charge of a set of hands to repair the turnpike the ensuing season, or they will hire it repaired by the job as the party may choose."

To prevent disputes respecting the price of labor on the highways a law had been enacted in 1787, asserting that "the price of labor shall be 4 shillings a day, the person boarding himself from May 1 to October 1, and any other season 3 shillings a day (a shilling being figured at 12 1/2 cents or 16 cents, according to whether it was a Vermont shilling or a York shilling)."

Gradually, prices of labor had risen so that by 1809, one of Great-Grandfather's nephews noted in his diary: "Our highway captain or pathmaster this year is E.F. He gave out orders last week—to me on Sat. Orders for 3 days only—$8.75. Ate dinner at nearest house. Team & stoneboat drew earth into gullies..."

For sixty years, Rupert Turnpike bore townsmen and out-of-towners on countless journeys of business, pleasure, and exploration. During most of that time, the Manchester-Salem stage, an extension of the Bennington line, twice a week thundered east, twice a week rumbled west over this highway. Leaving freight, discharging and picking up passengers, it bugled announcement of its arrival, as its sweating horses were reined in at the doors of the inns along its route. At every open door where an eager, questioning face appeared, the driver called out his latest items of news as he wheeled past. "Madison has been elected president." "Our boys are marching on Plattsburgh." "The War is ended." "The pound party for the preacher is tomorrow night." "Prudence Graves has got twin boys."

Numerous peddlers with "mountains of goods on their backs", with horsedrawn carts of wooden dishes and brass kettles, or with brightly painted big wagons, also thronged the road to inn and farmhouse. Tin-ware, brooms and rags! Clocks from Connecticut! Chairs from Massachusetts! Patent medicines from New Hampshire and New York State! All did a thriving business along the Pike.

The village doctor on horseback, on foot, or in his side-sagged buggy made his daily rounds to patients confined in their homes.

In winter, gay belles and beaux frequently flashed along the Pike en route to a New Year's ball, a skating party, or other merrymaking. Their "Rogue's March" or "Sleighing Song" echoed gaily along the valley from their sleighs, piled with straw, buffalo robes, and homespun blankets. Tin horns tooted, galloping hoofs clicked off the miles, sleigh bells jingled, and laughter rang out under the moonlit, starry skies, as the six- or eight-horse teams conveyed twenty or more of the young people in long sleighs to an inn or home where the gala was to be.

A wide variety of smaller conveyances likewise kept the toll keeper busy. Again one of the Harwood boys noted in his diary: "Aug. 19 18—: Father and Mother rode over on the Turnpike to the first gate in the yellow buggy. Saw a chaise and horse with silver tipped harness."

"Feb. 3, 18—:A fire red cutter on the Pike, also a fine covered sleigh drawn by a span of handsome greys superbly harnessed with a string of open silver bells."

"Today I saw a cutter with trim in gold leaf for $28, without the gold—$26."

Numerous solemn-countenanced older citizens drove their plodding nags along the Pike to revival meetings, to funerals, or to watch with the sick. Others in sulky, chaise or phaeton, buckboard or democrat, hurried to the "Raising" or other "bee" which was a frequent occurrence, to town meeting, election, or other community assemblage.

Pedestrians flocked along the way also. These were allowed to pass the turned pike without paying a fee. Men and women, riding single or double, often with a child perched behind the saddle, likewise frequented the highway at all seasons. Regardless of the number of riders on a single horse, the toll fee remained 6 cents.

Many of those who streamed along the Turnpike were "just going visiting." This custom of spending a day at a time in one another's homes was the main social and recreational activity. Great-Grandfather and his family were among those who frequently visited back and forth among their brothers and families. For Great-Grandmother's comfort in travel, he kept a square-framed, sturdy-legged and well-braced armchair, with a stout splint seat, to place in the wagon or sleigh whenever they set forth. Around the chair, the children were settled on piles of straw and blankets. In cold weather, a supply of billowing buffalo robes provided a warm nest into which to snuggle against whipping wind and biting cold. Great-Grandfather himself would ride at the front of the vehicle, if it were a horsedrawn one, to drive the team. If his brothers or other men were riding with him, as they often did, they huddled around him, so as to enjoy conversation along the way. When the oxen were used for transportation, Great-Grandfather, like all other ox-drivers, walked in the center of the road beside the shoulder of the "near ox"—the one on the left side of the team, facing forward. Two drivers meeting were then in better control of the animals, as they were between the two teams. Numerous yokes of the sure-footed beasts were "Geed" to the right, "Hawed" to the left, and "Whoaed" to a stop along the pike, or urged on with a sharp "Giddup."

Whether walking or riding, short distance or long, the travelers of the day enjoyed conversation—reminiscences, philosophical discussions of politics, religion, family relations and events, inventions, national expansion; exchange of information regarding crops, recipes, child care—all supplied meat for intellectual and verbal savoring along the turnpike.

During its early days, the Turnpike was often traveled by a representative of a Land Grant Company, who threw out his advertisements at the inn doors. These told of the amazing farm lands that were readily available in the northern and western plains of New York State. Two of Great-Grandfather's nephews were fired with the desire to help open the advancing frontier.

In February of 1807, Jonas and his family, along with a neighbor, set forth for Hopkinton in the St. Lawrence Valley. His long sleigh was loaded with three beds and bedding; table, chairs, cooking kettles and pans; wooden dishes, and a supply of dried meat, apples, pumpkin, corn, and berries; potatoes, turnips, beans, and flour. A 600-pound potash kettle completed the load. The whole weight was estimated at a ton, so both

Jonas and his neighbor hitched on their ox-teams, and Neighbor Robinson drove. His son followed the load driving the four cows, two for each family. Jonas hitched his team of horses to the "big sled", tied Robinson's team behind, stowed his wife, two small daughters, Mrs. Robinson, and her four-year-old twin boys among blankets, robes, and straw, and all were ready for the new adventure. Stoically, the parents of the emigrating couples bade them Godspeed and watched them out of sight along the Pike. The gilded buttons on the tips of the ox-horns glowed in the wintry sunlight, seeming a beacon for the caravan.

Isaac Godfrey, another pioneer in the St. Lawrence Valley, who returned to help his brother move out there, a month or so later, brought a report of Jonas' journey, to his uncle.

A few miles along the way, the men found that their load was too heavy for the oxen, so they hitched one of the led horses on ahead. Stopping overnight at another uncle's fifteen miles further on, they were consternated the next morning to discover that Jonas' oxen had gone lame from the unaccustomed travel. There was nothing to do but unload the potash kettle, leave it, and send for it later. The two lame oxen were unyoked and driven with the cows. Twelve days later, all arrived in Hopkinton and "went into a comfortable (log) house", which neighbors had prepared for their coming. Jonas sent word that "it was very good crossing the lake." Lake Champlain was frozen unusually smooth and hard that winter.

A family diary tells of another migratory expedition a few years later. "April 10, 1814: Uncle Ira, with Elisha Smith and Luther Smith, off to Attica, Genesee County, N.Y. on March 1st now returned in eve. Had purchased a small farm, 45 acres half of which was under improvement, including a log house and a small framed barn—paid $127—took a deed and gave back a mortgage—when wholly paid would amount to $500. Uncle appeared highly pleased with the country and its inhabitants.
"March 6, 1815: On Feb. 6th, Uncle Ira and family set forth in 2 sleighs, escorted by Uncle Sam. Their traveling expense under $30 they arriving Feb. 16th, the day news of Peace arrived there on the wild frontier where Indian warfare had raged. They did not see their Smith friends—state of weather and roads forbade. Uncle Sam returned today and brought the report."

One of the most valuable aspects of the Turnpike was its promoting commerce. Loads of ashes from woodlot and household were conveyed along the highway to the local asheries. From them, subsequently went forth along the same road barrels of potash, of pearlash, and of soap. Marble from the Dorset Quarry went also along the Pike toward Troy and thence to far markets.

Regularly, twice a month and sometimes oftener, teamsters delivered the township produce to the river market in Troy and brought back the essentials and sometimes the luxuries, that were otherwise unobtainable in the more remote communities.

Again an old family diary gives an account of some of these typical expeditions.

One Sunday evening in January 1818, young Harwood and a neighbor teamster loaded their wagon with about 22 bushels of wheat and set forth for Troy about half past ten. (No tything-men would be on the road at that late hour.) A full moon lighted the "track of wheels as smooth and hard as iron." Through some windows they saw "several couples enjoying the blissful hours of courtship and almost grudged their happiness."

Arriving at a roadside inn around half past four in the morning, the men halted, hoping to take a nap. However, so many other young men on their way to Troy with their loads of wheat were just getting out of bed and making such an uproar over their breakfast and their teams that Harwood and Montague could only get a meal for themselves, and "bait" their horses before going on to Market.

Arriving in Troy in the late afternoon, they opened their load for inspection by the merchants. They complained of finding rye mixed with the wheat and argued over the price. The best grain was bringing 17 shillings per bushel, but Harwood finally had to settle for 13 shillings 9 pence, bringing a total of $36.91.

Although he was greatly disappointed by the return, he was somewhat mollified by his subsequent trading-success. Prices on the broom, buttons, codfish, nails, salt, sugar, tea, ginger, barrel of tar, and 38 pounds of wool that he had had carded at the woolen factory were lower than he had anticipated. Cheerfully, he started homeward in the late afternoon, with a balance of $22.14 in his pocket.

Six miles outside the city, the men stopped to "bait" (feed their horses). "The landlady," Harwood reported, "thought that we planned to tarry only until moonrise. She grew cross, said we might either go to bed or go along, for she was not going to find us in wood and candles. We slept over."

After their first sleep in 36 hours, the men enjoyed their drive home "over good waggoning." They were greatly interested to see on the road "a portable building containing a family and furniture—an Ark—moving to the West, drawn by 3 yoke of oxen—they had the same number behind to change." (Who says that mobile homes are a modern development?) The Ark was making slow progress as it mingled with a throng of horse and other ox-teams from Vermont, Massachusetts, and New York, most of them traveling to or from Troy Market.

All too many of the teamster days along that route were far less enjoyable. An old family diary reported one such in late November of the 1820s. Hiram and his wife Sally left at "10 A.M. with 15 casks of cheese on their great lumber waggon." The warm, thawing day made the road so muddy that "waggoning was very bad." Having stopped for the night at Wadsworth's Inn, the next day they were stormbound there. Heavy rain and wind beat upon the land until noon, when a roaring snowstorm swept in. Hiram and Sally "did not stir from their snug retreat". Now and then they saw a team pass, "a melancholy spectacle."

Loath to resume their journey in the teeth of the storm, they still felt compelled to do so at daybreak the next morning. The clouds packed in, black and low; the Northwester whistled, roared, and caused even the "great waggon" to sway behind the almost balking horses. The River waves lashed their banks, sending frigid spray across the Pike. Men and women who had braved the elements tied their hats on with what strings they could clutch, often winding the cords around their coat collars to hold them high, and cocooned themselves into their blankets and robes.

In spite of the fury of the storm, the throng of teamsters battled their way to their delivery points and unloaded their wares. Hiram and Sally then stabled their team and ate dinner at "Cousin Sam's". Directly afterward, they went on their "trading tramp." Twenty yards of calico at 25¢; numerous yards of mull and ribbon, bobbins of lace, spools of Clark's floss, and 2 pairs of suspenders headed the list. Then came "4 yards cotton for shirtees at 1 shilling, some table crockery, 2 toys—13¢, sole leather, 1 sheepskin—50¢, & 1 calfskin tanned." Weary and so laden with packages that they could barely move against the battering gale, they returned to "Cousin Sam's" a little before 10 o'clock. Hiram was kept awake most of the night by the incessant roar of wind and water and by his anxiety over the next day.

Much to their relief, morning brought calm, so husband and wife completed their purchases of spices, buckskin mittens at 41¢, cake cutters, and sundries. Returning to Wadsworth's Inn that night, both felt deep satisfaction in their trading, in spite of their having had to grapple with the "Worst storm ever." But their journey's struggle was not yet ended.

Early the next morning, they set forth for the last 25 miles homeward. That Friday, December 1, challenged all travelers every inch of the way. Snow choked the Pike more and more as traffic thinned. Hiram's horses waded heavily and slowed to a crawl. Though the wagon was but lightly loaded, the wheels could barely turn. The storm had ceased, but it had left its freight of woe.

As dusk blotted out the road line, an insurmountable drift blocked the way. The floundering horses tangled in their harness and could move in no direction. Despair and terror of being imprisoned in the unyielding drift for hours of freezing helplessness gripped man and wife.

Suddenly a lantern light bobbed out of the black wall of night. Dr. Swift was plodding home from delivering a baby at a remote farmhouse. Together, with "monstrous tugging", the men extricated horses and wagon. The doctor then guided the close-to-exhausted team and driver through the adjacent meadow, wind-swept clear of snow, and back into a "tolerably clear" stretch of pike that brought the travelers to their home dooryard.

Thereafter, Hiram and some of his neighbor teamsters formed a wagon train when making the Troy trip in any but the summertime. If an "ex" (axle) broke under a heavy load; snow, mud or other hazard developed along the way, assistance was assured.

On such trips, the men cut travel expenses by carrying with them their own johnnycake, cheese, fried sausage, and frozen cakes of bean porridge or cups of baked beans to eat at some "landlord's inn". Haynes' was a frequent stopping-place. He charged 47¢ apiece for keeping a span of horses, including oats and hay, lodging and cider for the teamster over night.

On one occasion, he charged nothing, however, for lodging and feeding a devoted little dog. Skip, a shaggy brown and white pet of no special pedigree, had happily shared the driver's seat with Uncle Benjamin when he carted thirteen barrels of cider to the Troy market one November day. Dog, master, and team were housed at Cousin Sam's in Troy for the night. As Uncle Benjamin drove his team up Spruce Knob Hill, en route home, two days later, he suddenly became aware that no warm little body was snuggled close beside him, no loving pink tongue was occasionally licking at his hand. In his concern for loading numerous barrels of flour on his wagon for the home trip, he had forgotten his dog. Ruefully, he decided that his heavy load would not permit him to return to Cousin Sam's to retrieve Skip. He comforted himself with the thought that his pet would be safe and well cared for until his next trip to market a week later.

Halting for the night at Haynes' Inn, he had barely unharnessed his horses and settled down to his beans, cider, and cheese, when he heard a scratching and a strangely familiar whine at the door. When Landlord Haynes opened it, in limped a bedraggled, small, mud-covered dog.

Wearily, he dropped to the floor at Uncle Benjamin's feet, rolled, and licked his master's boots in an ecstasy of reunion.

"'Twas worth a free bucket of milk," Haynes observed later, "to watch that shrewd old Benjamin try to swallow his Adam's apple as he huggered his dog up in his coat. Smart little critter never'd been over the pike but that once before! Ben sent word in to Robinsons by another teamster, about the 'runaway.' "

Two other runaways, who followed Rupert Turnpike not long thereafter, were of a completely different character. The notice of their disappearance, published in a Bennington newspaper, was posted in every inn along the pike and in many other areas. It told its own story.

"Whereas Salla my wife did on the 6th day of June inst. desert my bed & board without any just cause on my account; and took with her a brown horse, saddle and bridle, which are my property; and also took from several stores a number of articles of clothing on my credit, amongst which are silk for a gown, shawls, etc., to a considerable amount: These are therefore to forbid all persons trusting her on my account. She is supposed to be gone to the westward with one Mr. John Williams, who has lived in Dorset for more than a year last past, as a Baptist preacher, and has absconded and left his wife with four small children in distressing circumstances.—He is about six feet high, dark complexion, and thirty years of age—Said Salla is about twenty-seven years old, light complexion, and of middling stature.

"To prevent this 'wolf in sheep's clothing' from again imposing on any of the good people of the United States, this notice is given, with the desire that it may be as public as friendly presses can make it.

"Dorset, June 16, 18—.   Daniel Gray"

Reportedly, no one in the county ever heard of the culprits again.

Seven years after their disappearance, Daniel Gray escorted his neighbor's flaxen-haired and pink-cheeked recently orphaned, 18-year-old daughter, Hope, up the Turnpike to Windy Summit. There he requested Grandfather Seymour, a Rupert Justice of the Peace, to perform the marriage ceremony. Since seven years' desertion following the "adulterous act" of Salla had canceled that marriage contract, and since the County Court, having "advertised", had received no "petition of contest", he had been released from any legal obligation on that score.

Following the ceremony, witnessed only by Grandmother and the two hired men, bride and groom joined the others in their midafternoon refreshment of gingerbread and milk. Then the carriage wheeled briskly down the Pike, past the red schoolhouse, Moore's Inn, village store, blacksmith shop, the meetinghouse, and all the other familiar township scenes, as bride and groom turned also "westward" there to establish their pioneer home.

In 1867, "following considerable debate", the Rupert citizens obtained a ruling by the State Supreme Court Commissions. Just as in numerous other townships, such action permitted them to abandon the Turnpike and build a new public road. This served to improve several steep grades and numerous sharp curves. The cost of rebuilding the one most controversial mile of the new highway totaled $1927.42. Costs had escalated since 1806, when the entire expenses of the 12-mile Turnpike had been approximately $7000.

A wide blacktop road, devoid of waterbars, now extends from "Pawlet Road to York State line." Motorized vehicles smoothly bear their often many-ton loads where ox-teams floundered through the "Slough-holes" a hundred-and-eighty-odd years ago.

Into those ageless miles of snow and mud and hard-packed earth of former Turnpike and present State-Town Highway have been impressed innumerable records of a mobile America.

7

ON BENNINGTON STAGECOACH LINE

Interstate buses today roll smoothly along U.S. Route 7 from New York to Montreal. Commercial travel along this road from New York to Bennington, Vermont, and its environs was not so smooth, however, for many years after its rugged beginning in the 1790s. Part of that story appears in some old family diaries and newspapers.

Great-Great-Grandfather Zechariah strode vigorously into what is now the Walloomsac Inn at Old Bennington one early March morning in 1798. He was filled with happy anticipation, for he was about to have his first ride in a stagecoach, a vehicle so named because it progressed from place to place by stages, with overnight stops between. Usually, about 15 miles comprised a day's journey.

With his usual expression of composure, in spite of inward excitement, he handed one half of his fare to James Hicks, current owner of the Inn, that had been built in 1764 by one of the first pioneers, Captain Elijah Dewey.

"Looks if you'll have a fair day for your first stage ride," Hicks observed genially.

Zechanah nodded and watched the proprietor record on the Way Bill under "Names" - "Mr. Harwood"; "No. Seats"-1"; "Where From" - "Bennington, Vt."; "Where To" - "Williamstown, Mass." "D" (for dollars) - "0"; "C" (for cents) - "60"; and left the space at the bottom for the stage driver to sign his name after he had collected the balance of the fare. Sixty cents was a high price to pay for going twelve miles to visit his sister Mary, but the 56-year-old Zechariah had a desire to find out about this modern mode of travel, that had come to Bennington the year before. Now at a little past five o'clock, the morning stars patterning the sky promised a pleasant day to come.

He settled his coonskin cap more firmly on his greying head, squared his broad shoulders in his dark blue woolen greatcoat, and reached into one pocket. Drawing forth a chunk of tallow candle, which he habitually carried, he lighted it from an ember on the hearth, and lifted it to read the page from *The Vermont Gazzette* posted on the wall.

Hick's advertisement there announced: "THE NEW YORK AND VER-MONT LINE OF STAGES respectfully inform the public that their stages run from Bennington to Pownal, Williamstown, ...Pittsfield, Lenox, Stockbridge...Danbury...White Plains, and Kingsbridge to New York & return regularly on the same route to Bennington. The Vermont Stages will leave New York every Monday, Wednesday, and Friday morning at eight o'clock...arriving on the fourth day at Bennington in Vermont. The stages start from Bennington on Monday, Wednesday, and Friday mornings at 6 o'clock. They reach New York the fourth night at 6 P.M., extraordinaries excepted, making a route of 184 miles. The fare for a passenger is 5¢ a mile, 14 pounds of baggage gratis; 150 weight of baggage equal to a passenger. The fare through is nine dollars. The proprietors not accountable for baggage unless receipted. The proprietors having made every arrangement in their power to accommodate the public, the inns they put up at being good, their drivers careful, & the road equal or superior to any in the vicinity, they flatter themselves with receiving the patronage of an indulgent public. In behalf of himself & fellow proprietors

James Hicks

Bennington   October 18 ,1797"

It was understood by all concerned that no one traveled on the Sabbath in the Green Mountain State except "from necessity or charity," until the law to that effect was repealed nearly a century later.

The musical notes of the coach horn sounded through the dawn-streaked dusk. The ponderous-wheeled yellow and black stage wagon, drawn by four spirited bays driven by young Story Brown, clattered and rumbled up to the tavern door.

The other six men and three women in voluminous cloaks, who had just finished their ham and eggs, hash, baked apples, buckwheat cakes, and hot cider, trooped forth from the breakfast table. Some clutched valises, some stout linen bags, and one a small cowhide-covered trunk. Candles and fireplace logs shed their light through the small-paned windows and wide doorway, considerably facilitating the departure.

"Whoa!" commanded Story Brown, bringing his team to a sharp halt. He leaped down over the right front wheel and rolled up the heavy leather curtain enclosing that side of the stage. The three women, assisted by their husbands, climbed up by means of the wagon step serving the driver's seat and the front bench, crawled over the two backless benches, and settled themselves on the one at the rear. There the tail board and another leather curtain provided that seat with the only back support in the vehicle. Three men followed and occupied the middle bench, after which three more filled in the front one.

Story Brown smiled broadly at Great-Great-Grandfather as soon as he saw him. Though less than half the older man's age, he greatly admired this one of the patriarchs of the township. "You're not going so far," he observed as he collected the balance of the fare, "so you can ride up front with me."

Zechariah welcomed this chance to visit. He climbed up to the left end of the driver's seat and shuffled his feet to a comfortable position on the dash board.

The nine passengers on the benches stowed their luggage beneath their respective seats. One by one, they paid the balance of their fare to Driver Brown, who carefully stowed Waybill and money away in his hat to carry them to the proprietors at the other end of the line. Dexterously he then lowered and buckled down the side curtain, and the conveyance was ready to start.

Light and air entered the stage interior only from the front this breezy March morning. The three leather curtains, one on each side and one at the rear, were rolled up only when the weather was warm and winds not brisk. No baggage was allowed on the top, since the light roof was supported only by four slender pillars on each side of the vehicle.

Although Zechariah was well clad against the weather by his own flannel underwear, his homespun woolen short coat and breeches under his heavy greatcoat, by his sheepskin moccasins, and by a three-yard grey woolen muffler wrapped around his neck and chest, he was lightly dressed in comparison with the stage driver.

Story Brown, equaling Zechariah's six feet in height, was even more powerfully built. And even more ruddy of face. Although spring was near, he took no chance on shedding his winter garb yet. He yanked his shaggy buffalo skin coat close around himself, over his several homespun woolen shirts and pairs of breeches, and pulled down the earlappers of his fur cap. His feet were encased in thick leather boots into which his trousers were tightly tucked. Over these were drawn a pair of enormous bright red stockings, that reached well up his thighs and over which were laced a pair of light leather shoes. Three pairs of mittens covered his powerful hands. Wool for the hip socks and mittens had been carded, spun, dyed, and knit by his bride, Sophronia, who had likewise raised the sheep that provided it. Story was well fortified with both physical and mental comfort as he set forth on his long daily drives, even though a bitter cold journey lay ahead and no place to warm till he changed teams and ate dinner at Reed's Hollow beyond Pownal.

He lighted the candle in his lantern and placed the punctured tin cylinder at his side of the front of the vehicle. He adjusted the reins on the necks of the lead horses, Dan and Prince, settled the collar on one wheel horse, Deak, and patted the nose of the other sleek bay, Ned. Then swinging himself up to the right end of the high unsheltered seat, he clutched the reins, clucked to his team, and the stage wagon thundered away from Landlord Hicks' Inn.

A rhythmic clank somewhere in the rear caused Great-Great-Grandfather to inquire whether something were amiss. "Oh, no," Driver Brown assured him. That was only the wooden chamber pot that he had chained beneath a removable cover which he had cut out in the back seat. He knew one driver who provided the hole and cover without a pot, but Story had a thought for public sanitation. As well as for the comfort and convenience of his passengers.

Dawn soon cast a shadowed light along the deeply rutted stage way. Story recalled that this trail (known now in the 1970s as U.S. Route 7) was first used by the Mohican Indians, the "Wolf People", who had been driven by the hostile Mohawks from the Hudson Valley into the Hoosic Valley in the 1600s and had settled near Pownal and northward to Arlington. It was still the natural route for travel between the Taconic and Green Mountain Ranges Great-Great-Grandfather agreed.

He doubted inwardly though that the Mohicans had ever been bounced around as he was being jounced. "Never saw the ruts much deeper," Story observed. "Thawed last Sunday so when we left on Monday, the wheels went in pretty deep a lot of the way. The driver from Lenox on never got into New York till Saturday night, two days late. More than one place everybody had to help lift the wagon over some stumps—good thing they were all men—first time the wheels wouldn't straddle those stumps. None much over a foot high, but in the deep mud we got hung up on them. Well, you always know that spring brings mud."

He chuckled. "Not so bad as summer at that. When the bees and flies and dust come, how the riders do quarrel. Some want the curtains down to keep off the insects. And some want 'em up to let in the air and breeze. Then they all want more room because they're hot. And some of those la-de-da women don't like the horses' hair on their dresses nor the smell when the teams lather up with sweat or stop to empty themselves. What do they expect of a horse anyway?"

A sudden lurch of the stage over some upjutting rocks amidst the hubs and ruts brought a bass growl from the seat behind. Zechariah turned and peered toward the source. The tall gentleman in a broad-brimmed, high-crowned hat was clutching his head gear in one hand and trying to reshape it with the other. "Near cracked my skull on that jounce", he grumbled, "and smashed my hat besides."

Story looked worried. Every stage driver was held responsible for the safety of his coach, his passengers, and the freight entrusted to his care. Paying for a smashed hat would considerably deplete his wages of $12.50 a month. How well he remembered that one of the other drivers had lost a keg of cider brandy off his stage last December, and it had taken all the money for his family's winter shoes to make up for the loss. He glanced back again and was mightily relieved to see that the high crown was regaining its height.

"One time last winter, when the stage was going on runners," Brown reminisced, "we got into a northeast blizzard. Took three days to go 17 miles—stayed at farmhouses over night. Good thing nobody was hurt when we got overset in some of those drifts.

"Fellow driving on Spruce Knob down near Peekskill was thrown into a gully, stage and all. Wagon rolled over once and lodged against a tree. Hold-back strap had broke when the wheel horse slipped going down a steep hill. Only one hurt was the driver and he not bad. His ear was torn off close to his head but he picked it up and carried it along in his pocket." Great-Great-Grandfather looked startled. "Healed up good," Story added. "I understand he can hear as well as ever and never lost a day driving stage.

You never know what extra-ordinaries you'll meet on the road." Great-Great-Grandfather nodded in grim agreement.

The stage was just grinding its way to the top of Pownal Mountain, beyond which the road curved down a sharp descent. Story braced his feet more firmly against the dash board, clutched the two pairs of reins wound around his hands in a tighter grip, and yelled at his team. Stage wagons were not then equipped with brakes, so it would be disastrous to try to hold one back on a steep down grade. Besides, the down hill runs were where the drivers picked up their speed. The four bays broke into a gallop. The rear wheels of the wagon barely missed the edge of the precipice. Groans erupted from the seats behind. Story's powerful hands bulged beneath his reins. His sharp black eyes focused on the lead horses' ears, and his jaws clenched his teeth in a rigid row. Zechariah braced his feet also and gripped the edge of the seat with both hands. His muffler whipped in the wind, but he still clung to the seat. Would his wife, Lovina, be able to milk their young Jersey cow when she freshened next week if—? A strange hard lump wedged itself into his stomach—much like the one he had felt when he looked down Bennington Battlefield Hill at the rows of bayonet-drawn British and Hessians that August day a score of years before. But that day had ended well. So must this. Some familiar Bible verses coursed through his mind: "He driveth like Jehu, for he driveth furiously." "Be strong nor be affrighted." "Jehovah thy God goeth with thee—He will not forsake thee."

"I'm always glad to have that hill behind me," Story observed above Great-Great-Grandfather's muffler. Right now the main rut holds the wagon. I hear there's some talk of improving both the road and the stage. Good thing!

"I understand there's a straighter hill road maybe not quite so steep as this down near New York, where a couple of drivers raced their teams one day last summer. The doctor that was called said, 'They were under the stimulus of ardent spirits', and when one put his horses in full speed to pass the other, the stage was overset with a crash which just about shattered it. The wounded passengers were in a dreadful dilemma but the driver could do nothing to help them because it was all he could do to hold the horses. They took such fright that they would have dashed down the hill and destroyed the other stage, team, and passengers, too. I understand they both lost their jobs. I don't drink myself—too risky!"

Zechariah rode inside the stage wagon when he returned to Bennington Center two days later. That is, he rode part way. As the horses strained to tug the heavily loaded vehicle up Pownal Mountain, Driver King from

Massachusetts solicited help from the passengers, as he led his team up the thawed and almost impassable slope. The ten men, all of "sturdy build", with shoulder shove and with rails from a nearby fence, practically carried the coach through the deep muck of the roadway.

Landlord Hicks' supper table had to wait that evening, while the passengers scraped a crust of mud from themselves, and the driver performed similarly on himself, his horses, and his stage. Another case of "extraordinaries excepted."

Zechariah was relieved as he alighted at the tavern steps. His first trip by stage had been strenuous both ways. But it had been exciting also. And he had found Mary and her family all well. Story Brown could tell more hair-raising road tales than anyone else he knew. But he was a skillful driver, too. One of the best. In spite of numerous hazards, he had never had an accident.

Great-Great-Grandfather felt himself a part of a whole new universe that spring evening. This Inn was the headquarters, the meeting place, the central point of change for passengers and teams, as well as a hostelry for the stage travelers and horses from Rutland, Vermont; Adams, Massachusetts; Troy, New York; and all the towns along the way and farther. He was exhilarated by his mingling and conversing with men from the east, the west, the north, and the south; and by his access to newspapers brought to the Inn by stage. Yes, this stagecoaching was a wonderful means of transportation and communication. Even though it had its hazards! It would contribute to American progress and unity as nothing had ever contributed before.

When his nephew Benjamin soon came to the Inn with his 10-year-old son Hiram to convey Zechariah to his home out toward the Shaftsbury Hills, the conversation of the two men so much impressed the boy that he resolved to ride the stage all the way to New York as soon as he was "a big man." By the time his dream came true in October of 1836, the Bennington Stagecoach had played an increasingly vital part in the social and economic development of the country.

A branch line was soon afterward built to Troy through Hoosick and another to Boston through Brattleboro. During the summer, after the Green Mountain Turnpike was built in the early 1800s, the stage would leave Albany at 11:00 P.M., Troy at 1:00 A.M., and would arrive in Bennington by 6 or 7 o'clock in the morning. Hence it would continue over what is now Vermont Route 9 to Brattleboro, arriving there that evening. After May 31, 1814, this coach was authorized to carry the mail twice a week.

The Green Mountain Turnpike Proprietors "spared no pains to keep this road in repair", as it was considered "the most safe route from Boston to Albany." During the summer, five coaches a day traveled this scenic Bennington-to-Brattleboro route.

"Most safe route" though it really was, a tragic accident occurred thereon one early morning in the summer of 1817. A local newspaper reported: "The mail stage from Boston was overturned before daylight Tuesday morning on the Green Mountain Turnpike. The driver was instantly killed and two other drivers in the coach were thrown out. The skull of one was fractured; the other was seriously injured. The accident was attributed to the oversight of some men in the Turnpike company's employ who placed a pile of stones intended for repair of road in the center of the carriage way." Thereafter, the carriage way was meticulously patrolled each evening for impediments.

From 1800 to 1814, before the stagecoaches on the Bennington line were authorized to carry the United States mail, they were carrying other media of communication, in the form of newspapers, posters, and various types of "Notices".

One of these, brought in by Story Brown, and posted in James Hicks' Tavern announced:

TAKE NOTICE

"Ran away from the subscriber last Sunday evening an apprentice boy named Daniel Spenser. He had on when he went away, blue long coat, butternut colored pantaloons, striped vest, new wool hat, and new thick shoes. He is about 5 feet, 10 inches high, of light complexion, with a guilty, down cast, sour look; and he chews tobacco. Whoever will take up said apprentice may be entitled to half a cent reward. but no charges will be paid by me.   John Stanton Jr.
Pownal, March 4, 1810

The notice excited considerable local interest, but no action to secure the "Half a cent reward." According to some of Great-Great-Grandfather's papers, the runaway was never captured but subsequently joined a group of first settlers in the St. Lawrence Valley and established his home there.

Regularly, the stage brought news on a national level also. Two such communications brought in by Story Brown concerned events in the War of 1812. Zechariah's nephew reported these in his diary.

"Monday, Aug. 29, 1814—Walked about farm to see the operation of the great flood Sat. and Sun. which indeed was strikingly melancholy. Late P.M., at Stage Time, visited town (Inn)—heard the mortifying intelligence that Washington City was captured on the 24th inst. A great hue and cry throughout the land. Our rains Sun. came from S.E. British rains I conclude. God save us from any more such. "

"Mon., Feb. 13, 1815—A hand bill arrived by Stage from Albany announcing the glorious & heart cheering intelligence that a treaty of Peace had been signed at Ghent, ratified by the Prince Regent & transmitted to our executive for the finishing stroke. They fired the iron (cannon) 64 times to celebrate the occasion. Father went."

According to other reports, the stage that brought that "glorious & heart cheering intelligence" had had a struggle to cover its route. It had been delayed nearly three days by "poor sleighing night and day—runners screeching and groaning all the way." But Story Brown was accustomed to struggle.

Sometimes his struggle was with his patrons rather than with the elements. Soon after his stage began carrying the mail, a family diary noted: "S. Brown came in from N.Y. City trip with trunk for—. Long dispute at P.O. over it and over a cent for pamphlet postage."

Although after May 31, 1814, letters could be sent by stage for 60 miles at an 8-cent fee, the receiver must pay the postage. This fee increased according to mileage. Frequently there were heated arguments over letter, as well as pamphlet, postage, so that all the stage drivers found carrying the mail somewhat arduous. Even so, it was generally agreed that it was a valuable service.

One of the most important roles of the Bennington Stagecoach about this time was the transportation of a local man and his wife on the first leg of their journey toward promoting civilization on the other side of the world. Hiram Bingham was the fifth son of Calvin Bingham, who owned a farm at North Bennington, a part of the present Bennington College campus. Born in 1789, Hiram had early shown a greater interest in books than in farming, though he did work diligently for his father and did develop ingenuity and skill in "farm labors". Although his family did not help him with expenses, they did encourage him to "become a scholar". With much pride, they had watched him board the stage at Hicks' Inn as he set forth to Middlebury College shortly after his twenty-third birthday anniversary. They had stood there proudly also to greet him, when he had returned as a graduate in 1816 to visit them.

Stoic acceptance was mingled with the pride in the hearts of the Bingham Family the October day in 1819, when they again stood on the Hicks' Inn steps to bid farewell to Hiram and his bride, Sybil. They had just emerged from the First Congregational Church across the green (appearing much as it does now) where Calvin Bingham was one of the deacons. Here Hiram's faith had been nurtured from earliest childhood. And here the parishioners had assembled that day for a farewell communion service for the young couple as they left for a strange land.

Above his high white collar and black broadcloth suit, Hiram's deepset eyes burned with eager purposefulness. His long dark hair hung smoothly in front of his ears, his clean-shaven face glowed with vitality, and his firmly set mouth gave an austere but not unkind expression to this handsome, sparely built, six-foot missionary.

Sybil's brown curls were almost hidden under her deep-visored, close-fitting green bonnet above her brown bombazet cloak. A steel-like purpose gleamed also in her shining eyes and radiant features. The dream of being Pioneer Missionaries to a "heathen land" filled man and wife with a powerful urge to be on their way.

Reports brought in subsequently by stage gave an account of their progress. In spite of the extensive postage due on these letters, no recipient protested.

At 10 o'clock the evening of the day they left Bennington, they arrived at Brattleboro, 38 miles over the Green Mountain Turnpike, having paused for refreshment and change of horses at Wilmington Inn. After tea and a two-hour rest in Brattleboro, Hiram, Sybil, and the other passengers were called a half hour after midnight. At 1:00 A.M., they were ferried across the Connecticut River and were on the last lap of their stagejourney to Boston. The $5-fare each for the Binghams, as well as the $3-fee for their "tea-and-lodgings", had been provided by the Bennington churchmen.

The night of the fourth day they slept in Boston. The next morning, Hiram and Sybil joined several other faith-inspired men and women at a meeting in the Park Street Congregational Church of that city. There the band of young people formed a mission group for the purpose of evangelizing the Sandwich Islands. The Congregational Board of Missions had been inspired to this endeavor by a young Hawaiian, Henry Opukahaia. This enterprising youth had come to America some years before, had been converted to Christianity, and had become convinced that this would be the salvation of his people. Although he died of typhus before he saw his dream fulfilled, the Board of Missions went dauntlessly forward.

On October 19th, the sailing vessel *Thaddeus* bore seven young couples, including the Binghams; five children; and four Hawaiians who had come to America as seamen, out of the port of Boston toward Cape Horn. After a nearly six-months' voyage, all arrived in the Sandwich Islands. As the first missionaries to arrive on the Island of Oahu, the Reverend Hiram Bingham and his wife faced an almost overwhelming task. Their family and neighbors in Bennington avidly shared with one another the newspaper reports and the infrequent letters from the Islands as fast as the stagecoach brought the messages in.

With considerable relief, they learned that the Great Chief Boki, Governor of the Island, had, upon their arrival, granted permission for the Binghams to stay one year to evangelize his people. With equal relief, they later learned that the permission had been extended indefinitely after "Father Bingham", on April 25th, 1820, preached the first sermon ever delivered in Honolulu, from the text, "Fear not, for behold, I bring you glad tidings of great joy."

On that epoch-making day, the Missionaries had presented their message for brown and white, kings and commoners alike, in the spacious home of the American merchant, Captain Isaiah Lewis. Governor Boki, with his retinue, led the gradually assembling natives. The Hawaiian Honoli, who spoke English, translated the sermon for his countrymen. All seemed deeply impressed by the words of peace and good will.

With much satisfaction, too, Benningtonians read that Sybil had opened the first school near Honolulu in May, 1820, and that Hiram was preparing the manuscript for the first printing ever done in the Islands. Hiram's letter later stated that "On the 7th of January, 1822, a year and 8 months from the time of our receiving governmental permission to enter the field and teach the language in order to give them letters, libraries, and the living oracles in their own tongue, that the nation might read and understand the wonderful works of God," the printing project was accomplished. This consisted of a language written by the Reverend Hiram Bingham from the oral explanation of the Island natives. The Bingham letter added that "It was like laying a cornerstone of an important edifice for the nation." Little did the missionaries dream that they were "laying a cornerstone" for the Fiftieth State of their own much greater nation.

Consternation filled Bennington, as well as much of the rest of New England, however, when somewhat later the stage mail brought a less welcome report from Honolulu. An entry in a family diary of that time noted: "The outrage committed by the American Sailors of the *Dolphin*, Captain Percival U.S.N., on the Missionaries & Authorities of the Island of Oahu has been among the most important articles in the papers. The Mission and Authorities I think were abused, but I also think they were imprudent in enforcing obedience on a population...so long used to such habits as were attempted to be done away in such haste."

The "articles in the papers" had reported that the preceding January, the U.S.S. *Dolphin* had arrived in Honolulu as the first United States warship to pay a visit to that port. Captain "Mad Jack" Percival was infuriated by discovering that by then the Missionaries had instituted tight control over the troupes of native girls who had previously followed the custom of boarding the ships, that docked in the Hawaiian harbor, to entertain the lusty sailors. The tabu had aroused bitter resentment among shipmasters of other lands also, but "Mad Jack" took action against the new moral reform. He gave his men rum and unleashed a savage attack on the Mission church, home, and head Missionary himself. Only the equally vigorous action of the natives saved Father Bingham.

In the pandemonium of 150 rioting seamen and the several defending Hawaiians, "much glass was shattered in the Prime Minister's fine hall and much damage done to mission buildings." Order was restored and some damages repaired when "Mad Jack" and Governor Boki finally reached a compromise that permitted "the violation of the tabu in the harbor of Honolulu."

Missionary Bingham concluded his report of the event by philosophizing that the interlude of violence and licentiousness really served to strengthen and increase the subsequent acceptance of the Gospel teachings in the Sandwich Islands.

Some months later, Bennington Stagecoach brought more gratifying news from the other side of the world. Boki, after having taken daily instruction in reading the Bible from "Father Bingham", had given his teacher "the land of Punahou", including Rocky Hill stretching from Round Top to King Street, with fish-ponds, salt-beds, and coral flats, all valuable. This is the tract of land that is now the endowment of Punahou College. A memorial boulder in Honolulu states: "ON THIS SPOT STOOD THE HOME OF THE REV. HIRAM BINGHAM, WHO GAVE THIS BROAD ESTATE TO THE CAUSE OF CHRISTIAN EDUCATION."

Although Chief Boki died on a fatal expedition to the South Seas that same year of 1831, without ever joining the Christian church or giving up his habit of "strong drink", he had let it be known to the very last that he revered his instructor.

Some years after the Reverend Hiram Bingham and his wife returned to America in 1841 from their "valuable mission" in the Sandwich Islands, Sybil died. In 1854, Hiram remarried and shortly thereafter returned to Bennington for a family reunion with his six brothers and three surviving sisters. The brothers had, like Hiram, ridden the Bennington Stagecoach line out into "positions of learning and responsibility", although they had majored in the practice of law in various parts of a well-established United States. Upon their return in that year of 1855, the Binghams rode only a short distance, the few miles between Bennington and their early farm home, on the old stagecoach. Its former long "runs" had been replaced by the railroad.

For the two decades that the people of Bennington were finding satisfaction in reports of their "native son's" contribution to the development of education on the other side of the world, they were likewise promoting the same cause at home. Here again the local stagecoach played a vital part.

It was the stage drivers who for many years delivered the advertisements for a Bennington Boarding School. These announced: "Mrs. Mulholland Respectfully informs the public, she has opened a School in Bennington, a few doors from the Meeting-House (now known as the First Congregational Church) where young Ladies may be taught the following branches of education viz.—Reading, Writing, Geography, English Grammar, plain Needle Work, Ornamental on Muslin, Print Work, & Embroidery. Those Parents and Guardians who will please to commit young Ladies to her charge may rest assured that strict attention will be paid to their morals and behavior.

"N. B. Young Ladies may be accommodated with genteel Boarding by Mr. Hull in the same house with the school."

Numerous Young Ladies annually rode to this Boarding School via the Bennington Stagecoach.

Mrs. Mulholland was not so specific in advertising living costs at her Boarding School, however, as were the administrators of Union College. When Great-Great-Grandfather's nephew, Eleazer, rode the Bennington Coach to Albany one fall in the early 1800s, on his way to Union College in Schenectady, he carried in his coat pocket a notation that had been circulated on the stage lines by the College authorities for many years. It stated: "The annual expenses are estimated thus, viz: College bills, $42; board from $1 to $1.50 per week; fuel and light from $5 to $7 (for the year); washing from 12 to 20 cents per week."

From such opportunity offered at Union, Amherst, and some other nearby colleges, many a teacher, dentist, and other professional was prepared for helping to build a better nation.

Many a young man, too, and some not so young, through the first five decades of Bennington stagecoaching, rode the line to various metropolitan centers where attendance at a winter course of lectures at some "medical school" would earn the candidate a certificate to practise as a physician. One old diary noted: "Nov., 1819—Friend Ashur set forth to New Haven, Conn. for Medical lectures—expected next spring to come out an M.D." The profession "played it by ear" in those days before a demanding A.M.A.

About the same time that "Friend Ashur" was coaching off to Yale University, the Bennington stage line was cast in a kind of mystery "whodunit" miracle role. About seven years before, in May, 1812, Russell Colvin had disappeared from Manchester, about twenty miles north of Bennington. He and his wife, Sally, in their early 30s, and their sons Lewis and Rufus, aged 10 and 7, lived with Sally's parents, the Barney Boorns, and "came and went" as they pleased. Sally's brothers Jesse and Stephen bitterly resented Colvin's living so irresponsibly with their parents, while they themselves had to work much harder for a living. Consequently, they often quarreled with their brother-in-law.

The townspeople paid little attention to Colvin's absence until three years later, when it became apparent that Sally was pregnant. According to Vermont law, she could not "swear the child" onto its natural father as long as she was a legally married woman, no matter how preposterous the legitimacy of birth would be. However, if she could not otherwise arrange for its support, she could "throw herself and infant on the town", and the taxpayers would have to provide for them. This Sally declared she would do, after she had searched unsuccessfully for her husband. The townspeople were incensed. They strongly opposed the further tax burden and agitated against it. What had become of Russell Colvin anyway?

Sally told the local lawyer that her brother Stephen had said that she COULD swear the child on its father because he knew that Russell was dead. He also had declared, and was confirmed by Jesse, that Russell "had gone to Hell and was buried where potatoes wouldn't freeze." This statement immediately gave rise to the belief that the Boorn brothers had murdered their brother-in-law, though empty-headed Sally had intended only to convince the town authorities that her husband's death had released her from marriage. Suspicion ran wild, but there was no arrest, although most of the population believed that the Boorns were guilty. Reportedly, the infant was stillborn and hostility in the town considerably abated.

Then the spring of 1819, Sally's uncle dreamed on three separate nights that Colvin appeared to him as a ghost and told him that he had been murdered and buried in the cellar hole of the field where he and his brothers-in-law had been picking stone the day that he disappeared. Believing this to be a sign from God, the elderly man revealed his dream.

Suspicion and the desire for justice flared anew. Neighbors flocked to the old cellar hole where the Boorns each winter stored their potatoes in a deep pit so they "wouldn't freeze". Industriously plied shovels and pickaxes produced some incriminating evidence—a jack-knife, a pen-knife, a button, and a mouldy hat, all of which Sally recognized "for a certainty" as Colvin's. Also there were some small bones that MIGHT have been from a man's fingers. A nearby barn was burned about that time. The townspeople were convinced that Colvin had been murdered, his body buried at the cellar hole, dug up, and burned in the barn-fire. They were equally convinced that Jesse and Stephen Boorn were guilty of the crime.

The two suspects were jailed, and, in the hope that a confession of guilt would mitigate their sentence, as their numerous callers at the jail led them to believe, they finally "admitted" that Stephen, with Jesse's assistance, had committed the murder.

The brothers were finally brought to trial before the State Supreme Court sitting in the old Congregational Church of Manchester on October 26, 1819. Colvin's son Lewis testified that he had seen his father and Uncle Stephen fighting in the field with clubs that May day in 1812, but that he himself had run to the house. He had not seen his father again.

In the light of evidence presented, and of the men's own "confession", the jury gave a verdict of "guilty of first degree murder", even though both brothers immediately and vehemently protested that they were innocent and revealed the reason for their "confession".

Both were sentenced to be hanged on January 28, 1820. Stephen collapsed. Nevertheless, there was general approval of the sentence throughout the State, where the stagecoach line carried the news south, east, north, and west.

There were a few, however, who believed that Jesse was only an accessory to the crime and that Stephen had struck only after being struck first, so a petition for long term imprisonment rather than death, signed by many Manchester citizens, went north by stage to Montpelier, where the General Assembly was then in session.

A few days later, Governor Galusha, riding the stage south to his home in Shaftsbury, brought the grim decision following "a spirited debate" by the Legislature. Jesse was to spend the rest of his life at Windsor State's Prison, but Stephen must be "ignominiously hanged". Jesse was overjoyed at his own commutation but deeply distressed by the rejection of the petition for Stephen.

Leonard Sargeant, counsel for the defense, visited his unfortunate client in the Manchester jail and found him extremely despondent. He wept frequently and bitterly and begged Sargeant to place an advertisement in the newspapers in an effort to obtain information regarding Colvin. Sargeant was startled. This was his first convincing evidence that Stephen's confession was false. He asked his client whether he did, in the eye of his Maker, actually murder Colvin. When Stephen vehemently declared, "before God," that he did not, the lawyer was greatly concerned and proceeded to prepare the advertisement.

This he reportedly sent to *The Rutland Herald* and to the *Albany Daily Advertiser*: "Murder. Printers of newspapers throughout the United States are desired to publish that Stephen Boorn, of Manchester in Vermont, is sentenced to be executed for the murder of Russell Colvin, who has been absent about seven years. Any person who can give information of said Colvin may save the life of the innocent by making immediate communication. Colvin is about five feet, five inches high, light complexion, light colored hair, blue eyes and forty years of age. Manchester, Vermont, Nov. 25, 1819".

Great-Great-Grandfather Zechariah was among the innumerable readers of this advertisement in the many newspapers throughout the Northeast that carried it, as soon as the stage brought in the request. He had not attended the Boorn trial at Manchester Church, but he had conversed with the beloved black pastor of that church, the Reverend Lemuel Haynes, and he felt a deep sympathy for the unfortunate prisoner.

Regarding him, Pastor Haynes had reported, "He says to me, 'Mr. Haynes, I see no way but I must die: everything works against me; but I am an innocent man; this you will know after I am dead.' He burst into a flood of tears and said, 'What will become of my poor wife and children; they are in needy circumstances, and I love them better than life itself.' I told him God would take care of them. He replied, 'I don't want to die. I wish they would let me live even in this situation, some longer: perhaps something will take place that may convince people that I am innocent.' I was about to leave the prison when he said, 'Will you pray with me?' He arose with his heavy chains on his hands and legs, being also chained down to the floor, and stood on his feet with deep and bitter sighings."

Great-Great-Grandfather Zechariah shook his head. Much as he would like to have "something take place" to prove young Boorn's innocence, he shared the belief of everyone else that no such miracle could possibly occur. Even though Stephen and his Pastor clung desperately to the hope.

In the meantime, strange circumstances were developing. The notice that the Bennington Stagecoach had carried to the Albany *Advertiser* was shortly thereafter reprinted in the New York *Evening Post*. By a miraculous coincidence, among those who had congregated in one of the hotels of that city to hear the news when the stagecoach came in, were two men who became dramatic figures in the Boorn case. After hearing the Sargeant advertisement read from *The Post*, James Whelpley who had grown up in Manchester but had left to serve in the War of 1812 and thereafter settled in New York, was deeply disturbed. Strangely enough, he happened to become engaged in conversation with another who was also profoundly impressed, Tabor Chadwick, who lived near Dover, New Jersey.

Chadwick related the story that about seven years before, a man who then identified himself as Russell Colvin from Manchester, Vermont, had come to Shrewsbury, New Jersey. At that time, in November, 1819, he was working for Chadwick's brother-in-law on his farm at Dover. At the time of his arrival, Colvin had appeared somewhat mentally deranged and had become increasingly so, even to the point of changing his name. However, he had frequently mentioned the names of the Boorns and of several others whom he knew in Manchester.

Chadwick described him as "a man of rather small stature—round forehead—speaks very fast, has two scars on his head, and appears to be between 30 and 40 years of age."

Whelpley and Chadwick agreed that he probably was the one who was supposed to have been murdered but was so mentally confused as not to be able to give a satisfactory account of himself. However, the men decided that if he and those who had known him in Manchester could meet, some identification for "the cause of humanity" might result.

Consequently, directly thereafter, James Whelpley went to Dover and encountered the man who had earlier given his name as Russell Colvin. Whelpley was sure that this was the one whom he had known as Colvin, but the other man gave no sign of recognition. He also declined the invitation to go to Manchester.

Whelpley finally lured the reluctant "Another Man" to go to New York on a date with a girl who lived nearby and whom the farmhand very much liked. Arriving in the Big City, she immediately slipped away home, and Whelpley finally persuaded his companion to board the Bennington Stagecoach, which the confused man thought was conveying him back to Dover. The driver of the stage that left New York a day ahead of the one that Whelpley was taking, carried the incredible news to James Hicks' Inn, whence it was relayed to Captain Black's Tavern at Manchester by the driver of the "Northern Coach".

Up and down the County and across the State, the news was shouted by stage drivers to all who came to their doors to hear: "Colvin is alive! He is coming home!"

Pastor Haynes hurried from the stage stop to the Manchester jail where he conveyed the "Miracle Word" to Stephen Boorn in his cell. Overcome, the haggard prisoner dropped to the floor, among his chains, in a dead faint.

On December 22nd, Story Brown reined his four-horse team up to the Hicks Inn door. He needed no toot of his horn to announce his arrival. A knot of townsmen, including one of Zechariah's nephews, was already clustered around the steps. One of the men dashed up the street to the nearby Court House where the County Court was in session.

"Colvin has come!" he shouted hoarsely to the assembled men, some of whom had helped to convict the Boorns. A mad scramble ensued, some of the younger men pushing one another over the sills of the windows that they jerked open while others crowded through the doorway. Along the snowy walk they rushed to the Inn. A Manchester man grabbed his horse, leaped into the saddle, and dashed off to carry the advance news to his townsmen.

When the stage drew up at Captain Black's Tavern in Manchester, pandemonium broke loose in the even more excited crowd waiting there. Stephen Boorn, dragging his chains, was borne from jail on the shoulders of four of the churchmen and set down beside the big old cannon on the village green. Trembling so that he could barely accept the honor of firing the first of fifty huge balls from "the iron", he nevertheless sent a roaring discharge echoing up and down the stageway.

In confrontation, Colvin and Boorn instantly recognized each other. As the cannon shots and sundry musket shots died away, Colvin asked Boorn why he was in chains. "They say I murdered you," Stephen replied.

The astounded Russell exclaimed, "Why you never even hurt me!"

Although Colvin almost immediately recognized and talked warmly with his sons and many others whom he remembered, in spite of his mental deterioration, he turned his back on Sally and refused to have anything to do with her.

When Pastor Haynes had finally quieted the crowd sufficiently to be heard, he led them in a prayer of thanksgiving for this miraculous prevention of a horrifying tragedy. As Stephen Boorn stood beside his wife, with tears streaming down both faces, he told his minister that he believed that the shock of this actuality would have killed him if he had not had the previous warning.

A few days later, James Whelpley and Russell Colvin boarded the stagecoach for Bennington, and thence to New York. Reportedly, Story Brown was the driver as far as Albany, but his friend Zechariah had grown too feeble to share his seat and hear his tale of this most astounding event of the century so far.

The Rutland-Bennington Stagecoach on January 8th, 1820, brought the State Supreme Court Judges into Manchester. There they rendered their decision that very night, it being Saturday, to void the sentences of the Boorn Brothers and to liberate them.

The following Monday, Stephen boarded the Bennington coach for Rutland and thence to Windsor, where he met Jesse as he emerged from the State's Prison, a free man. The brothers clung to each other, racked with sobs of wordless relief, in the knowledge that neither would any longer face life in a confining cell nor "ignominious death by public hanging", which had been set for a fortnight hence.

As events transpired, the same man who drove the stage to convey the Boorns back to Manchester, a few years later brought news of their settlement with their families "Out West" in Ohio. The letters that he delivered at intervals at the Bennington Post-office came from other settlers in the same area. One young couple reported to their parents that the Jesse and Stephen Boorn families were hard working and highly regarded citizens in the Western community.

Although Great-Great-Grandfather Zechariah had by then "passed into eternity", numerous other early settlers frequently voiced the fulfillment of his thought of 1798, that the Bennington Stagecoach Line would exert a powerful influence upon the nation and upon humanity.

By 1828, those, who patronized the Line, were riding in coaches far more elegant than was Story Brown's equipage of the earlier days. That was the year that the wonderful new Concord Coach made its appearance. This vehicle, manufactured by Messrs. Downing and Abbott of Concord, New Hampshire, was a tremendous improvement upon the previous stage wagon. Its tightly enclosed body, rounded at the bottom, was suspended in thoroughbraces, which were several layers of wide, heavy leather straps used as slings between the two axles. No other form of springs could have been used as they would have broken on the rough roads. These thoroughbraces eased all jolts by giving the riders a rocking, springlike motion over the humps and hollows. The driver, however, found that the added comfort posed some problems. He had to adjust the motion of his own body to the sway of the coach or his arms would pull on his horses' reins so forcibly as to slow speed or even to injure the animals' mouths. Passengers, too, sometimes became sick from the backward-forward rocking, especially after a particularly sumptuous meal.

Nevertheless, travel *was* improved. With the Concord Coach spinning along the fast-developing turnpikes, in 1828 speed was almost doubled. Amazingly, a four- or-six-horse team could now cover seven miles an hour on the level, as well as three or four on a considerable pitch when weather was favorable. Two or three miles an hour had been a good average for a team hauling the earlier stage wagon.

Besides being a more comfortable vehicle, the Concord was a handsome one. Its exterior was painted red with black and gold trim. The four-and-a-half-foot wide body had been fashioned by a skilled joiner from well seasoned ash and all sections smoothly fitted together. The huge, iron-tired wheels, 5 feet and 1 inch in diameter at the rear, 3 feet and 10 inches at the front, had been constructed from woods yielding the utmost strength and least weight possible: elm for the nave, oak for spokes, ash for felloes, and black locust for hubs. These, too, were well seasoned and meticulously fitted together. Heavy red mohair upholstery added comfort as well as beauty to the two seats facing each other inside the snug enclosure, and to the backless seat in the middle, extending from the hinged and latched door on one side to a similar one on the other. The ends of the latter seat were hinged to turn up, thus permitting passengers to move directly from the step at each door to the back, front, and then middle seats. There would be no more clamoring and crawling across other seats in order to reach one's own. A hinged window beside each front and back seat, and in the upper half of each door, provided additional comfort. So, too, did the "blinds" attached thereto, when sunshine was unbearably hot and bright. The $2400, 2400 pound Concord Coach was generally pronounced a marvelous invention.

True, those who must ride on the driver's seat behind the dashboard up front or on the jump seat at the rear were still exposed to the elements, but they traveled for a cheaper rate, which was some compensation. Luggage was carried on the coach top or on a rack under the jump seat, so limbs were less cramped, but nine travelers inside the Concord were still a tight fit if any were above medium size.

The Concord also continued to carry the mail, including both letters and publications, as well as packages. One of the most eagerly read accounts of correspondence and freight carried by the local stage appeared in *The Journal of the Times* of May 6, 1829, published at Bennington Center and edited by William Lloyd Garrison:

'The following correspondence received by Mr. Doolittle, agent of the Iron Works in this town, from Isaac Cox Barnet, Esq., American Consul at Paris, has been handed us for publication: 'Paris, March 16, 1829

To Isaac Doolittle
Bennington Iron Works

'My dear Friend:- You will see by the annexed letter how I have disposed of the bear skin you so kindly sent me. If you don't approve of my thus bestowing your gift, why send me another. But you will approve. You will rejoice that our illustrious friend has done us the honor to accept it; and that it has furnished the occasion of such grateful reminiscences, such flattering recollection of the heroic Green Mountain Boys. Tomorrow evening I shall take the General by the hand. I wish I could reach yours!

Signed, I. Cox Barnet'

'Paris, 14th March, 1829
To General Lafayette

'My Dear General:- The snow that has just fallen will hardly serve as apology for my offering you so late in the season the cub bear skin which was sent me last year by my friend, Isaac Doolittle, but the dilatoriness of the leather dresser is the cause of this tardy offering.

The animal was killed in the mines of the Bennington Iron Works (Vermont) of which my friend, nay our friend, is the director. Like the other progress in civilization, liberty, and prosperity of every kind which your labors have so pre-eminently contributed to advance—this one of the primitive inhabitants of the Green Mountains—affords a new item for grateful meditation.

'I pray, my dear General, to allow it to be placed at your feet— under your desk. It may also prove an antidote for the gout, which unfortunately, is of all seasons.

Most respectfully and affectionately,
Your humble friend,
Signed, I. Cox Barnet'

'Paris, March 15, 1829

To Mr. Barnet,
My Dear Friend:—I beg you to receive my affectionate thanks for the beautiful and comfortable present you have been pleased to confer upon me.

'Its coming originally from our friend, Mr. Doolittle, gives it an additional price and so does the remembrance of Bennington and the Green

Mountains to which I am bound by more than a half century of patriotic attachment. My fellowship with the Green Mountain Boys goes back to he year 1777.

'I hope before long to be able to offer in person the grateful acknowl-:dgment of your long obliged and most

Sincere friend,
Signed, La Fayette'

Needless to say, Isaac Doolittle found great satisfaction in sharing the above correspondence with his fellow townsmen. And they, especially the few remaining Green Mountain Boys, whose fellowship with General LaFayette going "back to the year 1777" was still a treasured memory in the fight for American independence, found an equal satisfaction.

By 1835, a friend of Story Brown's, Daniel Alvord, was one of the drivers for the Bennington Stagecoach Line. He was particularly impressed by fragments of news regarding York State, which he occasionally heard from his passengers and passed on to his friends. Among these was Great-Great-Grandfather Zechariah's nephew, who had been so much fascinated by his uncle's account of his stagecoach ride in 1798. Nephew Hiram noted some of Alvord's details in his diary for 1836.

"Lewis Chandler—in from Troy—told of Hudson and Delaware Canal on which one summer he had executed some considerable jobs at building toll houses, by which he had become well acquainted with the country. Some good farm land still to be had.

"Cousin G. H. came through Buffalo since the great storm of Nov. 11th, 1835—most furious ever known in that place. Canal frozen up with great quantities of flour afloat, in consequence of which the article has risen vastly in market—worth $7 a bbl. in Troy.

"Samuel Scott into town on the Southern Stage said last summer when at Saratoga Springs he improved an opportunity to ride in one of the cars attached to the engine employed on the rail-road in that vicinity—traveled over the space of 8 miles in 25 minutes, found it as great celerity as he could bear.

"S. Brown came in from New York City trip with trunk. Never saw such wonderful sights. (National Institute being held there as a National Exhibit of current inventions)."

Inspired by Story Brown's report and by his own childhood resolution to go to New York when he was "a big man", Hiram prepared to visit the metropolis that fall. Jottings from his Journal tell something of his trip and of the current American scene.

"Tuesday, Oct. 17: Overnight at Worthington's Inn"

Wednesday morning, Hiram was up at 4 o'clock, having been awake most of the night in his excitement over his trip. After a fortifying breakfast, he boarded the Troy-Albany stage and "was off lively on the rumbling McAdam way which hardly admitted of much conversation among the passengers."

Aboard the steamboat *Dewitt Clinton*, he met three friends, Bloss, Robinson, and Patchin. The two-day trip to New York, "with very good meals", was pronounced a great comfort and convenience, as well as a scenic pleasure. Patchin recalled having taken the trip previously on a sailboat, which had consumed three weeks because of "poor winds".

The Atlantic Hotel provided them with a room for two nights, meals included, at a total cost of $3.12 1/2 each.

Friday was spent at The National Institute in Niblo's Garden— "admittance 25 cs." The four men from Vermont were overwhelmed by the "noblest specimens of the inventive and mechanical powers of our countrymen", "everything made in America." The mechanical churns, cheese presses, grass and grain mowers, cider-making equipment, post or rail sharpeners, iron plows and glass beehives astounded the Bennington farmers. So, too, did many another invention, the use of which was unknown to them.

"Just before candle lighting", they "entered the Grand Saloon where enchantment itself reigned." Porcelain dishes, silver cutlery, cut glass, luxurious carpets, colorfully dyed and patterned fabrics— words failed Hiram as he wrote his diary that evening. The four friends marveled until late at night over the wonders that they had seen that day in Niblo's Garden.

"Let out to the great world in Broad Way", the next day they visited the Battery, which they rated "the finest"; looked at new Astor Hotel"; and saw many other "amazing sights."

That afternoon, they again boarded the boat for their return trip to Albany, arriving there at "6 A.M.—Monday." After doing some business in Troy, Hiram returned home Tuesday, having ridden "the 3 A.M. stage north at a cost of $1.75 to Bennington."

Needless to say, Hiram's family and friends listened eagerly to his account of the wonderful sights in the Great City and of his comfortable stagecoach ride.

Hiram was no longer living when, late in 1840, Fayette Shepherd of Albany wrote to Charles Hicks, who was then managing the Hicks Inn (now the Walloomsac), concerning sanctuary for black fugitives from the

South. Hiram's son, Hopkins, however, and his Grandfather Benjamin took a keen interest in aiding these runaways who were seeking freedom from slavery by entering Canada.

Hicks reported that during one period of two weeks Shepherd had sent him twenty-two such refugees. One stagecoach brought in thirteen, the entire passenger list composed of Shepherd's "guests". Hicks observed that some of these were of "noble bearing". He confided to his men patrons that one of these females was so nearly white and so beautiful that her master had been offered $1200, $1500, and even $2000 for her, "for foulest purposes." It was even rumored that Thomas Jefferson had sired her and that she possessed "high mentality" as well as physical beauty. Consequently, she was given prompt conveyance in a sleigh, well equipped with buffalo robes, along the least traveled road toward Rutland. Reportedly, Hopkins was one of those who drove the sleighs, provided by Dr. Wilcox of Bennington, to the station of another "underground operator", Daniel Roberts of Manchester.

The passage of the Fugitive Slave Law in 1850 greatly increased the hazards of the underground, even in Vermont, from pursuit by slave hunters. A white-haired friend of Benjamin's, who had driven many a load of hay or of shocks of corn, freighted with weary runaways, toward "Freedom Land", narrowly escaped capture himself. That was on a glorious autumn day, when the Northern countryside was bright with scarlet maples, golden birches, and crimson apple orchards. "Old Dave" was, to all appearances, conveying a half dozen barrels of apples on his lumber wagon to the cider mill. As he turned out of the carriage-way to let a stagecoach bound from Bennington to Rutland pass his slow-moving vehicle, he heard the driver, a "new hand" from New York, comment to the sullen-looking gentleman on the seat beside him, 'That old man's one of the underground runners, I'm told. They say he's always carting something, most of it alive."

"Stop!" commanded the sharp-eyed stranger.

Old Dave's heart thumped against his ribs. Then inspiration saved him and his precious cargo. His intermittent tetter was troubling him, so that his face was badly blotched. As the stranger leaped down over the coach wheel and started toward him, Old Dave shrieked in a distressed voice, 'The Pox—Stay away! I've got the Pox!" Fear of the dread disease, which was then in epidemic in parts of the country, sent stagecoach, driver, and rider into a hasty resumption of their journey.

Dave slapped the nearest barrel, where the punctured head was loosely topped by orchard "seconds", and croaked with a chuckle, "Best gol-darned case of pox I ever heard of. Hee-hee! God forgive me!"

A few years later, one of Zechariah's grandsons was among the last to patronize the Bennington Stagecoach Line. Like numerous other venturesome men of the day, he had been seized with the Gold Rush fever. Consequently, early in the 1850's, young Silas joined a half dozen of the other prospectors from the County and set forth for California.

Over the Green Mountain Turnpike and out of the port of Boston they went with high spirits and high hopes. Around Cape Horn they sailed to the Gold Fields. There they encountered banditry, near-starvation, dysentery, and a bitter shattering of their dreams.

With more adventure tales than gold, Silas and the other three surviving prospectors returned via the Western Vermont Railway, connecting with the Troy and Boston, a couple of years later.

"I missed our old stagecoach almost as much as the gold nuggets," Silas used to tell his children in later years.

The Western Vermont Railway coaches, that superseded the stage, have now in turn been superseded by motor buses, that daily speed along the smooth macadam of Route 7. No tangible trace remains of Story Brown's four-horse stage wagon, in which his innumerable passengers lurched over rock and stump and gully in the early days of its opening the way to progress.

Nevertheless, the tales that are recorded concerning those coaching days reveal an increasingly amazing portrait of infant America to each successive generation. And an increasingly impressive one!

8

UP ON APPLE HILL

"There is scarcely anything in America that is esteemed so useful and valuable as the orchard. A single tree has been known to bear ten or a dozen barrels of sound winter apples. A single tree has also been known to produce in one year apples enough for six or seven barrels of cider. He that plants an apple tree, grafts it with a Roxbury Russetin or Rhode Island Greening and takes good care of it, has provided an inheritance for his son."

Great-Great-Grandfather Zechariah Harwood, who harvested his first real crop of apples in October, 1774, fervently believed those words, which may still be read among his papers.

His own orchard, begun the spring of 1767, brought him lifelong satisfaction. It also did, indeed, "provide an inheritance for his son" and for three succeeding generations of sons. In 1949, Zechariah's land was sold to the present owners, the Paul Bohnes, again passing from father to son and grandson. Again it has proved itself "useful and valuable."

Zechariah's first two acres of orchard land is now a section of the 60-acre piece under modern apple culture, currently known as both the Harwood Hill and the Apple Hill Orchard.

The great barn, which Zechariah, his sons, and neighbors raised in 1785 to shelter his horses, oxen, sheep, and cattle, and to store his hay, grain, cider, and apples, now houses a cider-press, stores apples, and serves as a sales barn for the farm produce.

The Bohnes' current brochure states: "The huge timbers which make up the construction of the barn are all hand hewn and a tribute to the Vermont craftsmen of nearly 200 years ago.... We grow 40 varieties of apples which include many of the older ones."

As we paused at that barn a few miles north of Bennington, Vermont, one fall day, we found the cupolaed old red structure pungent with the fragrance of ruddy-cheeked McIntosh and Wealthy apples, the Wolf Rivers and Cortlands, some Red Delicious, and the Four-by-Fours.

Near the entrance, a more-than-a-century-old Pound Sweet tree spread its branches, still bearing a few scattered yellow apples.

"We keep it mainly for its lovely blossoms," Mrs. Bohne commented. "Each May it puts forth a mass of fragrant pink and white bloom, but there never are many apples on it these last few years."

Nostalgically, I recalled the Pound Sweets, Tolman Sweets, "Punkin Sweets" and August Sweetings, which used to provide our customary New England Sunday evening supper of baked-apples-in-milk.

"We enjoy having people browse through our barn and watch our cider press in operation," Mrs. Bohne added. "Our newest venture is homemade apple pies. They're baking over there in the oven," she explained, as we inquiringly sniffed the enticing aroma.

After watching a gold and crimson pile of freshly washed "drops" cascade into the wide-mouthed hopper in one corner of the barn, we went down the stairs to watch further. There the fruit catapulted into an electric-powered grinder. The mash poured out at the bottom of this mechanism into a press cloth of stout burlap, which lined a two-inch-deep and four-foot-square wooden frame. An alert, blue coveralled attendant smiled his welcome as he busily spread the juicy pulp in the quickly filled frame, folded the burlap over the top, and slid it under the elevated press. Lifting the frame from the bundle of pomace, he laid a barred wooden rack on the burlap folds and returned to the grinder, where another frame was filling. He repeated the procedure until a half dozen of the racks were stacked directly under the hydraulic press. Then a 2000-pound pressure was gradually applied to the stack. Within 10 or 15 minutes, over a hundred gallons of orchard ambrosia had streamed into the huge oak trough set to receive it. From this receptacle, it was electrically pumped into wooden barrels and thence through plastic pipes into gallon or half-gallon glass bottles.

"A bushel of apples should make a little more than three gallons of cider," the press-hand remarked, as he sealed a bottle. "Here we never pasteurize any of it. We sometimes freeze it, but most generally we press the apples fresh from the orchard or from storage according to demand, the year around. That way our cider is always fresh and full of goodness.

"The best cider needs seven kinds of apples in it. Or even better, eight," he continued. "My father used to like Baldwins and Northern Spies, Blue Pearmains and Snow Apples, Gravensteins and Winesaps, Pippins and Seek-No-Farthers. We still use some of those and they are prime. But those homely old brown Russets that come later give it the best flavor of all." As he concluded, he handed each of us a cup of sparkling elixir to sip.

As we drove away from the Harwood-Bohne barn, I recalled the family legend of this Apple Hill. The spring of 1767, the 25-year-old Zechariah brought his 16-year-old bride, Lovina Rice, from Hardwick, Massachusetts, to his newly acquired farm "out toward the Shaftsbury Hills". With her and her dowry chests, he also brought saplings from her father's orchard: Rambos, Nonesuch, Winesaps and Spice, Tewksbury, Black Gillyflowers, and Hoary Mornings. All were well wrapped in a worn homespun blanket, which Zach kept wet at the fording streams.

On one of the roughest pitches along the trail, the precious freight was jolted off the top of the ox-cart load down into a rocky glen. Risking torn buckskin breeches or even a broken leg, Zach plunged down the steep embankment. There he braced himself against a scrub pine, clutched the mud-caked bundle, and hoisted it up to Lovina.

"As he scrambled back up by grabbing hold of tree trunks and roots, we most keeled over into the ravine ourselves," Lovina used to tell her grandchildren. "But your Grandpa was dead set on raising those trees. He remembered Pa's last words to us when we left home. 'Cider is the wholesomest drink of all for hard-working people and everybody else,' sez he. 'Some day mebby you'll be setting up a mill of your own.'"

Together, Zach and Lovina dug ample root beds and planted their trees in their newly cleared meadow near the top of the hill.

Zach's older brother Peter brought them a seedling from the first apple tree that was ever planted in the Bennington Grants, then growing in his orchard. It had been a stout whip from near the Massachusetts line and had served as a riding crop for Peter and Zechariah's mother, Bridget. As the first white woman to arrive in the Grants, she had firmly set the switch in the moist ground beside a brooklet where she alighted from her horse that June day in 1761. There the shoot had taken root and flourished. The little tree had borne its first few apples the fall of 1765. From the seed came Peter's orchard offering. This throve, as well it might, having come from stock so sturdy that it belied horticultural assertion that an apple whip could not root as Bridget's had.

Zechariah's great grandson, who subsequently inherited the place, noted somewhat more than a century later that the parent of one of his orchard trees had been uprooted by a "fierce gale" in early September, 1870. He added that this pioneer apple tree at "Uncle Peter's old place" had been bearing its usual "good crop of very sour apples." The matriarch tree was so highly esteemed by Bridget's descendants that several of them cut sections from the fallen trunk and limbs to fashion into inkwells, trinket boxes, and sundry other keepsakes.

By then, the daughter tree at Zechariah's orchard had been grafted and was providing sturdy base stock for a prized Twenty Ounce Pippin. However, it had come into its original "common fruit" bloom for the first time in May, 1774.

Like it, most of Zach's other orchard trees were canopied with blossoms that spring. Sunny days favored the bees, so Harwood Hill promised an abundant crop.

Throughout that summer, Zach, with the help of Brother Peter, labored all his spare time from farm work to build a cider mill. Neighbors, whose young trees were likewise beginning to bear, contracted with him to grind their apples with his own. His first son John was nearly seven years old and would be able to drive the ox-team on the sweep as well as a man. By utmost diligence and with hope for a profitable business, Zach finished the cumbersome mill in mid-September.

The sweep was an eight-inch-in-diameter, thirty-foot-long pine log. One end was equipped to be hooked to an ox-team. The other end of the timber was attached by wooden spikes and nuts to the tops of a pair of "hump and hollow" rollers set upright in a circular trough made of peeled oak logs. These hickory rollers stood three feet high and so close together that they almost touched. Zechariah had adzed one roller so that its surface bore five diagonals of three humps each. The surface of the companion roller he had gouged into corresponding hollows.

As the oxen, Duke and Turk, plodded along the circular path surrounding the trough, the moving logsweep caused the rollers to rotate and crush the apples poured upon them. Often the resulting pomace clogged the hollows and so halted the grinding until Zach or his helper dug it out with a pointed stick kept near at hand for the purpose.

From this trough, the pomace dropped into the cistern, a great hooped cask, from which it was scooped by means of a wooden shovel onto the press.

The press foundation consisted of two hewn oak timbers, fifteen inches square and ten feet long. Set a foot or so apart, they rested horizontally upon heavy wooden blocks a foot and a half above the ground. A timber of equal size was bolted perpendicularly to each end of each horizontal beam. A log, nine or ten inches in diameter, was screwed into place a little more than a yard above the crossbeams and parallel with them, the whole providing a lever and fulcrum.

Upon the two base timbers, Zechariah and Peter placed a slatted wooden tray, four feet wide and six long. On this, they spread a layer of freshly flailed wheat straw, shoveled on a thick layer of pomace, and covered it with another layer of straw, the stalks laid at right angle to the first, thus producing a mesh for drainage. They repeated this procedure until the alternating layers of straw and pomace were piled three feet high. The men then laid a cover formed of two two-inch thick, two-foot wide oak planks, a little more than six feet long, over the top of this "cheese". Zach pulled the press log down as tight as he could upo.. the plank cover. He then helped Peter chain a 200-pound boulder, dug from the edge of the orchard, on to the free end of the horizontal log as a dragload.

Amber juice poured, under the two-ton pressure, into the hollowed log trough set beneath the press. John and his two younger brothers, Silas and Perez, squealed gleefully and brought their noggins to be filled from the keeler, into which the trough emptied. The dozen or so men who had congregated to watch the new mill work, sampled the cider, voiced monosyllabic approval, wiped their chins, and went their separate ways. A 63-gallon receptacle, adzed from a tree trunk, placed near the trough, was filled before sunset.

Throughout the ensuing years, countless barrels were filled with cider from that hill to go forth into the community.

Zechariah was a member of the local Council of Safety, and this group sometimes met at his home. Among those who first assembled there were the fiery colonial hero, Ethan Allen, and his brother Ira. Since they lived only a few miles away, they frequently came also to Harwood Hill to obtain the fortifying beverage that aged throughout the year in barrels filled at the orchard press. The older the liquor was, the more powerful was its effect on a man's spirit.

From the hill press, the Allen Brothers annually produced their own specialty known as Apple Jack. Storing a barrel of cider in their root pit until the content was thoroughly fermented, the men awaited the Green Mountain winter. When the 30 or 40 below zero cold set in, they rolled the barrel out into their backyard. By the time the water content of the cider had frozen to a six or eight inch depth along the surface of the barrel, the alcohol was driven into the center. Ethan would then pull the plug from the bung hole and thrust a poker, heated red hot in the fireplace, through the ice to the center reservoir. From this, he and Ira would siphon the "jack" or brandy through the thawed outlet into a keg. Daily draughts from this keg no doubt fortified the Allen Boys to meet "Yorkers", "Red Coats", Hessians and every other colonial menace with the valiant defense for which they were noted.

The Harwood barrels were likewise credited with helping to win the Battle of Bennington the summer of 1777. According to legend, a troop of Colonel Seth Warner's men, commanded by Lieutenant Colonel Stafford, that had been stationed in Manchester, several miles to the North, came marching southward in the torrential rain and whipping wind of August 15th. Too exhausted by the storm, wash-outs, and fallen trees to press on to the Henry Farm overlooking the Walloomsac to join General John Stark's forces that were facing Colonel Frederick Baum's for a fight to the finish, they camped out on Harwood Hill.

From their host's cornfield, those weary, half-famished soldiers gathered arms full of roasting ears, and from his barrels of year-old cider, they drew invigorating drink. Beside the embers that roasted their corn, they dried their rain-soaked gear and snatched a few hours of sleep. The next day, having filled their canteens with more of the fortifier from the cider barrels, they struggled over the six flooded miles to arrive at the battlefield just in time to turn the previously outnumbered partriots' retreat into a rallying victory.

Back on Harwood Hill, Great-Great-Grandmother and her four small boys had grimly choked back the tears as they watched Great-Great Grandfather march away with the troops. Throughout the early part of the day, the five brown homespun clad figures busied themselves with gleaning the early apple "drops" in the orchard and with sundry other tasks around the home.

When, in mid-afternoon, the din of battle became louder and louder, they sought refuge in the woods down over the hill. The cannon roar from the several miles away battlefield pounded in their ears. Trembling with fear and anxiety, they repeated together the Twenty-Third Psalm and awaited the outcome. At suppertime, the juicy golden August Sweetings, with which they had filled their pockets, brought them their only comfort.

Late that night, they heard Zach's "Halloo", signaling his safe return. Weak with relief, they hurried to the house to meet him. Exhausted, but unscathed, he rejoiced to find his wife and little ones unmolested by wandering marauders. The reunited family knelt beside their hearth and gave thanks to their Maker that the Battle had brought some promise of future freedom.

Zach's cider mill diligently continued to renew the community beverage. Often the operation was marked by some verbal feuding between the owner and those with whom he contracted to use his mill. Many of his neighbors proclaimed, "You need a few rotten apples in your grinding to give spunk to the cider."

Zechariah did not care for that kind of "spunk" nor for some other pollutants that his neighbors brought with their apples to be ground. Therefore, when a *Farmer's Almanac* of the late 1700s published an article stating what he also believed, he posted it on a beam of his mill.

"Pshaw, pshaw, Mr. Draggle, this is no way to make cider," the *Almanac* asserted. "I would as soon drink from a duck pond as to take a draught of your liquor, thus made of rotten apples, animal's dung, and tobacco cuds and your cask too smells as stenchy as a he-goat. Now the rules laid down by Farmer Snug are these: 'See that your mill, press, and all the materials are sweet and clean and the straw free from must. The fruit should be ripe but not rotten, and when the apples are ground let the pomace remain from 12 to 24 hours, according to the heat of the weather, and the cider will be richer, softer, and higher-colored. Place the juice in a vat as it comes from the press, for fermentation. When the first fermentation is over, draw the liquor off immediately into clean casks and fumigate it with sulphur; thus, viz. take a strip of rag 2 inches by 12, and dip it into melted sulphur; and when a few pails of worked cider are put into the cask, set this match on fire and hold it in the cask till it is consumed; then bung the cask, shake it well, and then fill it up and bung it.' So says Captain Snug."

For nearly a century, much of the cider was used for barter. In the family daybook appear such random entries as: "For Blacksmithing - 8 Barrels of Cider; For Carding - 1; For Preaching & Burying our Little Boy - 3 Barrels & 1 Watered; For Making Shoes - 2 Barrels; For Ramsay's *Life of Washington*, in boards, valued $3 - 1 Barrel; and to Jonathan Hunt, In Some Way or Other - 1 Barrel. To which may be added 20 for our own drink and for making our apple sauce. Made in all about 130 barrels from our orchard. Had a good stack of pomage from our own and others' grinding to spread on meadows and orchard with barn manure and ashes. Kept 90 bushels of apples for our family use. We harvested around 1500 bushels—a rather poor year."

Apples for family use from 1774 to 1785 were stored in a pit dug deep into the hillside "below the frost line", at the foot of the orchard. Barrels of cider were kept in a shed attached to the house or in a nearby shanty. Then, in 1785, the Big Barn was built. One section of the basement, apart from the animals and their fodder, housed the apples. Water from a never failing spring on the hillside above was piped into this area to provide cold storage in warm weather.

By 1800, young Perez had discovered that a pound of honey added to a gallon of cider would, within a few months, produce a "powerful vinegar." The previous year he had set some beehives in the orchard to promote pollination of the blossoms and subsequently had been experimenting with the honey.

This vinegar from Harwood Hill was frequently in demand for remedies for numerous ills during the next three quarters of a century. During the earliest 1800s, Zechariah was elected to keep the Bennington Pest House, a forerunner of the quarantine hospital, for the treatment of smallpox. Although he had never had any formal education in medicine, he was widely noted for possessing a "peculiar skill in the management of the disease."

His "management" included a rigid schedule of exercise, fresh air, a vegetable diet, plenty of drinking water, rest, and cleanliness. To soothe the "pocks", he employed light sponging of the skin with equal parts of vinegar and water at room temperature.

The Bennington Stage Proprietor often came for a remedy for Burnt Tongue, a frequently occurring ailment among his coach horses. Perez had worked out this remedy: "Take Borax, Alum, and Saltpeter each one ounce; Honey two ounces; Vinegar one pint. Pulverize and mix the ingredients and simmer them on the fire till the mass is reduced to three gills. Swab or syringe the mouth with the mixture."

Numerous citizens of the town credited another of these vinegar remedies with saving their lives. Andy Robinson from a nearby farm was helping to grind pomace on the hill one day when a flying stone from among the apples gouged him near the temple. In spite of cold applications, the bleeding continued. Finally Perez applied a thick paste of rye meal and vinegar. Like magic, the red stream ceased to flow down Andy's face. Thereafter, many local woodsmen carried the meal-and-vinegar paste with them when they went to chop logs on the mountain.

Reportedly, a poultice of the same many years later stopped the hemorrhaging from a bayonet wound that one of the Bennington boys received at the Battle of Gettysburg.

Throughout the early 1800s, Perez was mainly in charge of the cider making on the Hill. Although for several years, a wooden screw set above the press beam had been supplying the ton-pressure formerly provided by the 200-pound boulder as a dragload, much of the rest of the equipment was unchanged. Then, in June, 1826, "after much figgering and callating", Perez contracted with a neighbor, Mr. Atwood, to put up a "frame cyder house, 36 feet by 24." By then, both Lovina and Zechariah had "passed into Eternity", but their orchard was still "useful and valuable" for their son.

Perez had not planned to build until later, but on the last day of pressing in November, 1825, one of the posts gave way at the bottom, when "the boys were screwing down the cheese". After many years of service and weathering, it had rotted off.

By October 5th, 1826, the cyder house was finished, and the men "graveled the horse path around the mill." Perez was determined to eliminate as much as possible the clouds of dust that had always accompanied the oxen as they plodded along the old dirt path in dry weather. A family diary reported some of the incidents of that 1826 cider season.

"Oct. 6th: Hiram drove round our horses attached to the sweep. Friend Levi here, seemed to think he had formerly been a person something on the Herculean plan. Never saw a cider press screw turned so far down but that he could start it immediately after the stoutest man he ever saw handle one had laid out all his might in so doing it. He thought his bleeding at the lungs was in the first place occasioned by pulling at the screw. Took two men to start ours off today. We expressed 15 bbls. of cider—about 150 bus. apples from the orchard.

"Oct. 19th: Governor's man brought 100-101 bus. very rotten apples and ground them. He dismissed his apple cheese after getting out 10 1/2 bbls. This week Cousin Stephen helped make cyder for me from apples brought here by Col. Hill, M. Dewey, and J. Swift. All ground and pressed together. Each man took out his share of cyder according to what apples he put in.

"Nov. 10th: I am so perplexed about this cyder-making business that I don't sleep much more than half the night. Some hard apples thrown into the hopper along with a couple of stones mixed in caused the sweep to split almost from end to end. Our pile of Little White Apples, Rustings, Greenings, Black Gillyflowers, and Seek-No-Farthers especially good this year, may freeze before we get the whole fixed. Mr. Kent came on, and our men worked all day.

"Nov. 13th: Resumed grinding and pressing. Col's casks were in bad odor so smoked them out with burning straw and brimstone.

"Dec. 1: Made cyder from apples gathered before Nov. 13th. 130 and more bus. took all day to grind as surface of heap was so frozen had to break out ice pieces to throw away. Bad business grinding and laying up pomace. By 9 in eve - 10 bbls strong cider expressed. A long season now ended. Have ground for many neighbors."

In poor year and good alike, the cider made from Harwood Hill orchard with no other apples included, was in great demand because of its special flavor and clarity. Frequently it commanded $5 and $6 a barrel, when the regular price was $1.50, and so showed a satisfying profit. The income from his orchard enabled Zechariah to rear his ten sons and two daughters in what was locally termed "comfortable circumstances." It likewise enabled his son and grandson, who in turn inherited the farm with its orchard, to rear their eleven children and nine respectively not only in comfort but also with extensive educational advantages.

Several of Zechariah's great grandsons attended Williams College a few miles south on funds that they earned for themselves in the orchard. Two went on to help found Drury College in Springfield, Missouri, and Pomona College in Clearmont, California. Some served on the Board of Trustees for numerous educational institutions, some as bank presidents in California, and some as heads of sundry industries in the Republic of Mexico.

Yes, the orchard was providing a generous inheritance for Zach and Lovina's sons and succeeding generations of sons. The inheritors, in turn, were carrying its benefits into far fields as well.

To insure a good crop of fruit annually, the Apple Hill men had a persistent struggle against the "caterpillars that infest our trees." Among the family papers of those 1800s is an account of the method used for scores of years.

"I provided a long pole and a sponge at the end of it. This I dipped in spirits of turpentine and conducted it to the nest and with a small touch of the sponge, thus charged, the spirits penetrated the nest, and affected the vermin to such a degree that, in sundry instances, on cutting off large nests, I found that in 15 minutes they were wholly destroyed."

Other insect pests for many years were treated according to instructions in *The Medical and Agricultural Regiserter the Years 1806 and 1807*. It advised:

"In the month of February or before frost is out of the earth, prepare the trees for reception of insects by applying in a most convenient place on the trunk a strip of old linen cloth three inches wide and so secured with clay or tow that insects cannot pass underneath, also tow should be twisted in the form of a rope and tied around the trunk at the lower edge of the cloth to prevent tar from running down, which would injure the tree.

"When the earth begins to thaw, apply tar to the cloth with a brush just before sunset and sooner if the weather be cloudy. The tar should be thin; it may be necessary to warm it so it will run free. This should be applied every day during the season of the insects' going up; and if they are numerous, it may be necessary to apply tar twice in an evening.

"After the season of tarring is over, remove the cloth &c, scrape the trunk below the place of tarring, and apply four or five inches of earth round the trunk to keep the eggs, deposited below the tarred service, from hatching. In six weeks, this earth may be removed from the trunk as the eggs will by then be destroyed for the want of proper heat and air."

Although by the late 1800s, the demand for cider as the year-round beverage had greatly diminished, the women on the hill continued to use many gallons annually for their apple butter, their mincemeat, and other delicacies. By then apple butter was mainly cooked in the home kitchen. However, even today, Lovina's descendants treasure the 200-year-old instructions for making this family staple.

"On October 10th or the first fair day thereafter, unless it be the Sabbath, prepare to make the Apple Butter. The best sweet apples should then be ripe and some good cider made."

Previously, Lovina would have scoured and burnished her 15-gallon brass kettle ready to hang it on a cross-pole erected between two of the apple trees nearest the house. "Never use an iron kettle," she admonished, "for it will turn the apples black.

"Early in the morning," she continued, "clarify the cider. Mix together one quart each of lime and clean ashes, all dry, and two quarts of new milk; pour these into a hogshead of cider just from the press. In two hours it will be fit to rack (draw off the dregs)." Lovina knew that even with the greatest care, dust, leaves, and insects "were bound to get into the pressing."

"Set a slow fire to burning under the kettle of cider," the instructions continued. How well she knew that a brisk fire would "scorch the boiling." "Pare, quarter, and core your apples. Many hands are needed for this, and even the children can help. Add as many apples as you need to the cider, and cook all day until the sauce is done."

By experience, Lovina could tell how many apples to add to the cider, and "by squint" she knew just when to remove the kettle from the fire. An old rule in a later recipe called for four gallons each of prepared apples and new cider. This one of Grandmother's, written a hundred years later than Lovina's, estimated that "One bushel of good sweet apples should make one gallon of butter." Since the family required 25 or 30 gallons of apple butter each year, Lovina usually prepared three batches on her "fair days" in October.

As soon as the pungent concoction was removed from the fire, Great-Great-Grandmother would ladle it into her crocks. It must not be allowed to cool in the kettle, as it might then taste of metal. These crocks she would cap with pieces of bladder, saved from the butchering, and "stoutly tied on" with a heavy homespun string.

Apples from the orchard provided numerous other favorite dishes for the families who tended it. Among these was the Marlborough Tart. The recipe can still be read on the yellowed pages of an old, handwritten cookbook. "Quarter and stew tender some juicy tart apples. Sieve and mix 1 teacupful with the same amount of maple sugar and of boiled cider. Add 1/4 teacupful melted butter, juice and grated rind of 1 lemon, 1 cup rich milk or cream or a mixture of both, 4 eggs, and 1/2 nutmeg grated. Mix all well and pour into deep plates lined and with high rim of rich paste. Bake 30 minutes in a medium oven."

During the 1870s, Perez Jr. and his son Albert, who had by then inherited Harwood Hill Farm, discontinued using the cumbersome cider-making equipment. They replaced it with a hand-operated mechanism patented in 1859 as Hickock's Keystone Cider Mill. Operating on the same principle as the earlier and as the present mills, it occupied a space only three feet square, stood only four feet high, and weighed less than 400 pounds. Amazing contrast though it was to the 1774 mill, it did prove to be a highly satisfactory all-in-one piece of equipment for the current comparatively small demand. It would make 6 to 12 barrels of cider a day, any time that it was needed. And in any kind of weather, as it was enclosed in a part of the barn! It could also be used to prepare berries, cherries, currants, and other fruits for cordials, jelly, and jam. (Similar mills are still sometimes obtainable at country auctions, or from a special manufacturer).

In 1894, upon the death of his father, Albert, Zechariah's great-great-grandson Everett came into possession of Harwood Hill. Under his management, the orchard became only an incidental operation. His main interests were his Guernsey herd and his flock of sheep. Razing the last of the long disused cider mill, he fenced the 22-acre orchard away from pasture and meadow and relegated its care to the sun, the wind, the rain, and the frost. Although the crop deteriorated, it did not disappear.

As Everett developed an extensive dairy, famous for both the quality and the volume of its production, he regularly included cut apples in his cattle feed. His sheep, noted for the fineness of their wool, likewise received apples in their winter rations. Zechariah would have been convinced that the apples accounted for the excellence of both the dairy record and the flock production. He had always "tonicked" his animals for lambing and calving time by mixing chopped apples with their hay and grain for several weeks in advance.

After Everett's son chose a career that took him to California, he had no interest in the orchard and farm for his inheritance. Finally, the Harwoods persuaded their close friends, the Paul Bohnes, to buy the homestead that had been in the hands of the first owners for five generations.

Since the Bohnes are professional horticulturists, they soon had the orchard vastly extended and producing thousands of bushels of first quality apples annually.

Today, Paul Bohne III has made the most radical improvements of all on Apple Hill. Dwarf trees, bearing three or four bushels each, set 450 to the acre, are gradually replacing the lofty, spreading-branched ones of earlier years. However, the modern nursery stock has been grafted to bear many of the longtime standard varieties.

Where Zechariah and his descendants climbed ladder and boughs or "gleaned" with a long pole to harvest their crop, the present owners stand on the ground and gather the fruit directly into its receptacle. The sheepskin shoulder strap with a half bushel basket hooked to it has been replaced by canvas belt and much smaller bucket. Where the ox- and horse-drawn wagons moved formerly about the orchard to load the gold and crimson largesse heaped beneath the autumn trees, a tractor-propelled flat rack brings in the carefully packed boxes of freshly picked apples these latter days.

Today's orchard is annually treated against disease and insects by a commercially prepared pesticide applied by mechanized sprayers. No pole with sponge and turpentine patrols the trees these twentieth century springs. No bands of linen, tow, and tar have bound their trunks for many decades. Phosphates, too, have replaced the barn manure and ashes of those earlier years, but pomage from the cider mill is still spread upon the orchard soil to help renew its nutrients, just as it was in Zechariah's time and throughout the intervening years.

The orchard product is as highly esteemed in America today as it was two hundred years ago. The present owner, like the one who set the first trees in his meadow, looks upon Apple Hill as providing "an inheritance for his son", who at the age of six already helps to gather the apples.

9

A BRIDGE FOR ROARING BRANCH

Roaring Branch is the main tributary of the Battenkill River, the nationally famous trout stream in Southwestern Vermont and bordering New York State.

The first settlers in the Benning Wentworth Grants in the early 1760s sought out this fertile valley for its fine farm land. Throughout a full century, however, a permanent bridge for Roaring Branch in Sunderland seemed as impossible to achieve as it was essential to community life.

Then, in 1869, a local builder made a promise that has been completely fulfilled: "I'll build you a bridge there that'll never wash out. Taken care of, it'll last a hundred years and more."

The story of the series of bridges for Roaring Branch is a chronicle of the rural New England way of life.

During the years from 1761 to 1779, when the Vermont settlements were extending the early American frontier northward and westward, rough logs were used to bridge this obstructing stream. All too often, those logs were soon rotted by weather and water, causing great inconvenience and hardships at the ford, especially for those who were transporting loads to and from Remember Baker's Grist Mill a mile or so away.

Sometimes misfortune at the ford unexpectedly revealed current philosophies, personal resourcefulness, and promotion of human relations.

The story was told that one day in the early 1770s, a man who was said to be an atheist was crossing the Branch, when the log beneath his feet gave way and tumbled him into the mud along the bank. Unable to extricate himself, he yelled, "Help! Help!" with all the power he could muster.

The devout Episcopalian, Matilda Brownson, peered out of her kitchen window a rod or so away. Recognizing the wretched man floundering in the muck, she sauntered toward him and asked pointedly, "Are you not Tom Peters, the atheist?"

Knowing that his life might depend upon his answer, poor Tom hastened to cancel her doubt of his worth. "Oh, no, " said he, "I am no atheist. You mistake me."

"Then say your belief," Mrs. Brownson commanded.

"I believe in God....." Tom's voice quavered as he desperately worked his way through "The Apostle's Creed." His gratitude to his grandmother for having taught it to him as a child mounted fast. The mud sucked at his knees, and his voice almost broke on "the resurrection of the body and the life everlasting." Earthly life had never seemed more precious.

Convinced that Mr. Peters was, indeed, a Christian after all, Mrs. Brownson charitably threw a stout fence rail down the bank to him. She further obliged him by sitting on the end of it, while the mud-coated traveler writhed and tugged himself up onto dry land.

A few years later, one of the logs in current use had been washed out in a fall freshet. A townsman's diary reported, "Harmon and Philip barely got across the Branch on the sagging bridge. Had 2 feet of water in their sleigh box and lost 12 lbs. tallow, entire batch for the doctor's candles. Came home pretty considerable wet."

That same year of 1779, the community doctor nearly lost his life at the same crossing. Spring thaws, sending a torrent of water along the gorge, had immersed the bridge logs. Dr. Littlefield's horse, carrying his master one dark night to the farmhouse where a dozen or so Revolutionary soldiers lay stricken with camp fever, lost his footing on the slippery logs and pitched headlong into the icy stream. Beast, chaise, and the nearly drowned doctor were barely hauled ashore by neighbors who heard the hoarse cries and wild whinny mingled with the roar of the rushing water and grinding rock.

Necessity demanded that the town provide a bridge immediately. The resultant stout plank one had to be replaced within a few years. So did three successive ones at frequent intervals. Storm, flood, snow and ice accumulation, and the severe heat of summer, all heaved and weakened the base timbers and plank overlay.

By the early 1830s, Sunderland Selectmen had become convinced that a covered bridge, such as several that were appearing about that time in various sections of the Northeast, and which they had been reading about as used in Switzerland for over a half century, was the best hope for spanning the Branch. Together, they finally convinced their fellow towns-men. Together, also, they persuaded one of the most prosperous of these, Major Brownson, to go to Philadelphia and there inspect the famous Permanent Bridge. This massive, roofed structure, designed by Timothy Palmer of Newburyport, Massachusetts, had spanned the Schuylkill River at the Quaker City for more than three decades, and it was still sound. The steeply pitched roof shed snow and rain, thus protecting the timbers from excessive weight of ice and snow. It also insulated them from the cracking heat of the sun's rays.

Returning to Sunderland, Major Brownson stopped to look over the "Burr Truss" bridge which had been built across the Hudson River at Waterford, New York, according to plans by Theodore Burr of Connecti-cut in 1804-1805, about the same time that the Palmer Bridge had been constructed over the Schuylkill. Thoroughly impressed by both master-pieces, the Major hardly knew which design to recommend for Chiselville, as this section of the township had been named, shortly after a "chisel factory" was erected there.

While riding the stagecoach back to Bennington and conversing with a fellow passenger, however, he learned of another type of bridge, which seemed best of all. The designs of Palmer and Burr, who were then deceased, were being rapidly displaced by the design of an Ithiel Town, an architect in New Haven, Connecticut. In 1820, Town had secured a patent for his bridge plan known as the Town Lattice Truss.

This type of bridge consisted of a crisscross lattice-work of heavy, slantingly upright planks, pinned together and fastened at the top and bottom ends respectively to heavy longitudinal timbers. These were spliced lengthwise to form the horizontal girders or chords to cross the stream. Every plank was pegged, or "pinned". at every point where it crossed another. The whole structure, thus rigidly formed, provided tremendous strength, never shaking under even the heaviest loads, as long as the wood was sound. Town's Lattice Work Truss Bridge had proved to be an outstandingly strong one for its time.

It differed from the Palmer and the Burr bridges in that it required no heavy framing timbers, as it could be completely constructed of planks. Since these were easier to handle, they involved less expense for labor. Also, the Town Truss was of simpler design and construction, so it could be built by any handy man who could do rough carpentry. The average cost was approximately $2,000. The Palmer Bridge across the Delaware River at Easton, Pennsylvania, was reported to have cost $61,000 by the time it had been completed in 1807, having been under construction nearly two years. Small wonder then that the Town design was increasing in popularity.

One factor not to be overlooked was that Town charged a royalty for his designs and specifications which he furnished to prospective builders. If the fee were paid in advance, he demanded only one dollar per foot of span. If he had to collect after the construction was started, he doubled the fee. The shrewd Sunderland Selectmen paid the $117 royalty the day their plans were delivered.

Hayden's meadow in 1841 soon became the scene of major activity. Towering piles of spruce planks, pungently seasoned in the sawmill yard, reared tawnily against the greening hillside. Blue-frocked men, amidst resounding hammer and saw, geed and hawed their ox-teams with heavy load chains clanking at their heels.

In a matter of months, the wonderful new bridge was assembled, the timbers firmly pinned by hundreds of trunnels (wooden pegs called tree-nails), and the gigantic truss (framework) was erected to a vertical position by brawny men straining at their raising poles. Sides were locked into place by well-braced roof beams, shingles nailed on, and the hundred-ton masterpiece was ready to be pulled into position across the Branch.

Hardwood rollers on a track and "cribbing" of heavy beams set the stage for action. The strongest team of oxen in the township, Duke and Prince, raised and trained by William Landon, provided the power to turn the wooden capstan. Around this upright windlass was wound the two-inch-in-diameter rope which was attached to one pair of pulleys on the bridge and to another pair on its far abutment across the Branch from Hayden's meadow.

The powerful, sleek, red and white beasts strained at yoke and cable. The capstan turned. The throng of men and boys who had assembled for this history-making event sent loud cheers against the mountains as the giant-in-wooden-achievement inched toward its destination. Three days later the feat was accomplished. The Branch was bridged for the citizens of 1841, and, all firmly believed, for posterity as well.

A few weeks later, the Town Board of Authority voted to paint the bridge. From a copy of *The New England Farmer*, they obtained instructions for making their own paint. The rule called for: "2 quarts Skim Milk, Buttermilk, or Whey; 8 ounces of Newly Slacked Lime; 6 ounces Linseed Oil (Obtained by grinding flaxseed); 2 ounces Turpentine; and 1 1/2 pounds Pulverized Ochre."

Along the banks of the Branch were extensive beds of yellow ochre, or clay containing iron ore. When this clay was baked dry in the sunshine and then in the slow heat of a brick oven, the resultant hard red lumps could be crushed fine to produce a rich red pigment.

Six of the men who had helped to build the bridge now shoveled and baked and pulverized the required amount of ochre; ground the flaxseed, expressed and strained the oil; and mixed their buckets of paint, using the whey from their cheesemaking.

Bobolinks and bluebirds flitted and piped their songs above the meadow; the Branch babbled serenely among its stones where water was low at this dry season. And while the men spread their paint on clapboard and beam, they entertained themselves and one another with stories of their individual, and often amazing, prowess in fishing, in horse-racing, and in winning the women.

One of the younger men who helped with the painting reported that he and his brother induced Deacon Billings, another of the painters, to take a swig from the group's frequently used rum jug. Believing that the drink was switchel (a popular concoction of ginger, molasses, vinegar and water), the elderly deacon, who was a staunch temperance man, gulped down a generous quantity of the refreshing drink, which had been kept cool in the shady edge of the Branch.

After he resumed his work, one of the men noticed that he was applying the paint with sporadic flourishes. "Don't you feel well, Deacon?" he inquired.

"Feel well?" the Deacon guffawed, "Why I feel as if I'm a-sittin' on the roof of the bridge and every shingle is a jew's harp."

In spite of tall tales and long draughts, or perhaps because of them, the men finished their job ahead of schedule.

Grandfather Seymour, a youth of nineteen in that summer of 1841, recalled that the covered bridge stood handsomely forth among the forested hills and ripening fields, its ruddy bulk, against the surrounding green, mirrored with white cloud puffs and blue sky in the placid pool at the Mill Dam.

One of the first to cross the 1841 Covered Bridge, "a hayload wide and a hayload high", was Dr. Littlefield, the same community physician who had nearly lost his life in Roaring Branch sixty-two years before. The clop-clop of his faithful old brown Morgan Ned mingled with the clack-clack of his phaeton wheels as the ancient equipage rolled along the plank floor. He was on his way to his once-a-year meeting of the Bennington County Medical Society of which he had been elected president in 1840. The honor had been conferred upon him as the oldest member (aged 90-odd years) of his profession in his county. And as one of the most venerated. His well-brushed black long-coat had become shiny at the seams, and his pockets bulged into shapelessness with his perpetual cargo of favorite medical standbys for his patients. But his smooth shaven face glowed with vitality, and his piercing blue eyes still twinkled with the humor as well as the wisdom for which he was famous. He ruminated aloud to Ned that this was the finest bridge that had ever spanned the Branch. Wonderful growth in a Free Nation!

Reportedly, Dr. Littlefield was walking across the bridge a few days later when he met a Mrs. White who was noted for her persistent complaints regarding her ailments. Since the good man seemed unimpressed by her "Doctor, I have a racking pain in my left side," the determined woman grabbed his coat lapels with both hands. Her shackling grip belied her words proclaiming frailty.

"Ah, " said the doctor, "shut your eyes, put out your tongue, and press with both hands on the seat of your pain." The would-be patient complied with alacrity.

Stepping briskly through the farther arch, Dr. Littlefield called back, "What you need is a good dose of pickled walnuts. Those up there in the meadow are just right to gather now. Mrs. Hill has a good receipt."

According to legend, Mrs. White gathered green walnuts, known usually as white walnuts or butter nuts, from the Bridge Meadow and started her pickling that very afternoon. No doubt the activity was beneficial to her complaint.

So popular was this recipe for pickled walnuts that it had been copied by many from an early issue of *The Vermont State Banner*. It declared: "The fact is, walnuts, when properly prepared, are an excellent medicine and alterative, and this is the way to prepare them: get the green walnuts, fit for pickling; put them in a stone jar filled up with sugar, in the proportion of half a pound to a score of walnuts; place the jar in a pan of boiling water for about three hours, taking care that the water does not get in, and keep it simmering during the operation. The sugar when dissolved should cover the walnuts; and if it does not, add more, cover it close, and in six months it will be fit for use. The older it gets, the better it is. One walnut is a dose for a child six years of age as a purgative; and it has this great advantage over drugs, that while it is an excellent medicine, it is at the same time very pleasant to the palate, and well esteemed by the young folks as a treat."

Each summer and fall for many years numerous local residents flocked across the bridge to gather the desired walnuts for pickles, and later for cakes or candy or sundry other purposes. Some of them also gathered the bark of the trees, "at the proper season", to brew a tea for "inveterate coughs."

Although there is no record of the use of this tea in the case of one Elijah Welch in the mid-1840s, it would seem that the potion's preventive effects might well have been tested thereby.

A Bennington newspaper, a local inn wall, and the Arlington Church door all carried the notice:

"ONE SHILLING REWARD:

"Runaway from the subscriber in Shaftsbury on the 13th inst. an apprentice BOY by the name of ELIJAH WELCH, about twelve years old, dark complexion, had on and carried away with him, a bear skin short jacket and overalls, grayish colour, two flannel shirts, a black felt hat, one pair of taps to his shoes; whoever will take up said boy, and return him to the subscriber, shall have the above reward, and no charges paid. All persons are forbid harbouring or trusting said boy on penalty of the law. William Matteson

Shaftsbury, January 14th."

According to legend, young Elijah was most unhappy in his apprenticeship to Matteson, a blacksmith and farmer of Shaftsbury. After serving eleven months of his 10-year term as "bound boy" to his taskmaster, he resolved to go in search of his parents who had moved seventy or so miles northward.

Plodding as fast as he could through the snowdrifts, he arrived just before daybreak at Chiselville Bridge. A barn loomed up in the adjacent meadow. Shivering with cold and exhaustion, the boy crept inside. There he found a basin of milk that had been left for the cats, and this he drank ravenously. Then wriggling himself into the haymow, he found heavenly respite in its soft warmth from his long night's battle with the zero cold and whipping wind. But not for long!

Suddenly, he was startled out of his half-sleep by lantern light's ruddying the panes of the stable window. Terrified by the thought of being captured and returned to his master, young Lije slid down the hay chute at the other end of the barn. Grabbing an apple that had rolled out of a cow's manger, he squirmed through a wide crack in the prop-closed back door and plunged through a snowdrift toward the bridge.

Daylight was brightening the eastern sky. Farm teams must be on the road by now. He must hide. But where? Cautiously he edged his way down the ice-patched timbers of the bridge and worked himself to a timber brace that offered sanctuary. There he clung, chilled, hungry, and almost too weary to clutch the friendly wood. Sleighs creaked across the planks above his head. Families' voices made music with the jingle of sleigh bells. Would he ever be part of a real family? Drowsiness crept over Lije, and he lost all desire for anything but sleep.

When he awakened, he started up with a hoarse cry. Two terrified black eyes were staring at him from a pinched white face, blue around the edges.

"There, there, take a sip of this and then you can go back to sleep." A woman's warm hand patted him on the cheek, as she removed the mirror which she had held in front of his mouth to detect his breath and in which Lije had glimpsed the reflection of his own face.

The boy swallowed some of the steaming broth and then sank back into the comforting depths of the feather bed. Even the welts and bruises from his master's cane found relief here in the home of the Sunderland Justice of the Peace.

A few days later, Lije learned that these two men, who had long known each other well, had arranged to transfer his apprenticeship to the miller who had found him as he checked his mill wheel further down the "Crick". In his new situation, the boy found a kind and patient master, with whom he worked in the sawmill even after he "came of age" and was free nine years later. Often, during those years, he was sent to the bridge, that had been his refuge, to check the weathering of the timbers. Always he found them sound.

Elijah Welch was only one of many fugitives whose freedom was implemented by Chiselville Bridge. Across its reverberating floor numerous black men, women, and children were sped on their way to legal liberty in Canada. From 1820 to Civil War days, runaway Negro slaves were materially aided by the residents of Sunderland who placed "God's Law" above any "man's decree". After the Fugitive Slave Law was strengthened by the Compromise of 1850, the rugged Vermonters were more determined than ever to assist the victims of moral injustice.

As early as January 22, 1820, the legal voters unanimously directed the Selectmen of Sunderland to build and maintain a house (hostelry) for Negroes on a lot near Roaring Branch bridge. To this "Negro home" came scores of fugitives, who entered Arlington (the neighboring town) from New York State at the west and from Albany by way of Bennington to the south.

Fragmentary notations in the local town records tell some part of the "Underground Story". "March 9, 1831—to E. Parsons Ploughing Negro land—$4.50; H. Lathrop for whiskey delivered the Negro house—$1.62; Reuben Salisbury, ditto—$.62.

"March, 1842—The Poor Master has drawn from the Treasurer to order to J. King for boarding Black Woman—$10.63 (at 50 cents a week).

"March, 1851—To A. Judson for Drawing &Housing Negroes— $1.50; to Pierce Hill for ditto—$4.50; to John P. Roberts for wood for Negroes house—$4.82; to Elizabeth Brownson, cloathing Negroes—$5.67. "

Guided by the North Star only, and walking the road as though going to work with an axe, a hoe, or a fork; sometimes carrying a small or weak child in a sack on his back, many a black man and woman trudged into the Negroes' hostel. Exhausted from having swum rivers, waded canals, plodded rough woodland roads, and existed on scanty rations grubbed from garbage or any other available source along the way, the desperate seekers of freedom would drop to the floor and sleep. Sometimes they stayed two or three weeks, restoring their hunger-and-work-ravaged bodies with the generous stores of food from the valley of the Battenkill, "the Fertilizing Stream." Then, with rags replaced by stout homespun suits and frocks and overcoats, old sores healed by elder salve, coughs relieved by walnut bark tea, and spirits buoyed by human kindness, the black transients resumed their journey.

The remaining 100-odd miles to the Canadian border were traveled in comparative comfort, although somewhat under cover of secrecy. The latter was mainly a matter of avoiding the inconvenience of controversy rather than of punishment by law. Slavery had been constitutionally prohibited in the Green Mountain State from the day of its organization in 1777.

Then, in 1843, the State Legislature passed a law banning any action against fugitive slaves. Any State Magistrate who violated the law was subject to a fine of $1,000 and a prison term of five years. This Act was the legal expression of the doctrine voiced by Judge Theophilus Harrington about 1800. After trying the case of a fugitive slave in the Town Hall at Middlebury, Vermont, that year, he refused to remand the runaway back to slavery. He defended his decision by stating that nothing short of a "bill of sale from God Almighty" would be sufficient evidence for him to recognize any ownership of slaves as valid. This doctrine prevailed in general throughout the State.

So, for several decades, wagons bearing loads of corn, potatoes, hay, and other produce, as well as vehicles well equipped with blankets or fur robes, bore blacks and mulattoes across the Roaring Branch bridge northward in relays from station to station, in a system called the Underground Railroad. Mainly this operated with little or no molestation, due to the prudence of the liberators. Most of the emancipation-dissenters throughout Vermont were known and shrewdly avoided.

Nostalgic memories of the Underground and of other traffic across that bridge surged through the minds of Sunderland residents one disastrous day in 1869.

Grandfather Seymour's diary for October 4th stated: "Very rainy, there was quite a flood today—done some little damage."

Considerably more than "some little damage" was wrought by that "flood today" in the land of the Roaring Branch, a few miles from Grandfather's home.

Accompanied by crashing thunder and jagged bolts of lightning, a raging gale funneled down the valley, bringing a deluge of rain and hail from a cloud-black sky. In the onslaught, hen houses, fences, and haystacks were hurled to the ground. Out-houses and uprooted trees, rakes and plows, cattle, pigs, and horses, wagons and shocks of corn were all precipitated into the tangled mass of wreckage which was being sucked into, or tossed upon, the tawny, savage current of the swollen Branch.

Amidst the screeching, crackling roar, men, women, and children watched in frozen horror as their chimneys toppled from shattered roofs, their fields of potatoes and barrels of apples disappeared into the fast-deepening sheet of water, and great gullies furrowed their hillside meadows.

At sunset, the wind subsided; the torrents of rain and hail were spent. But as the citizens of Sunderland looked toward the Branch crossing, sick dismay surged through them. The covered bridge, that they had struggled to erect with such high hope somewhat more than a quarter century before, was now a shapeless stack of timbers against which the thwarted stream was grinding rock, tree, and animal carcass in its wild rush toward the 'Kill.

The Selectmen, who had been appointed to superintend the building of the 1841 bridge, had known that the water, originating in several large ponds among the Green Mountains to the East, poured with frequently violent velocity over the huge boulders along the gorge, thereby giving Roaring Branch its name. Nevertheless, they had directed the building of the 1841 bridge close to the surface of the mill dam there in the Chiselville hamlet of the township. The approach at either end was down the steep bank of the Branch, the road at one end bending in a sharp curve to follow the valley.

On that flood day of October 4th, much of this road was torn out along with the bridge. As Needham Knight, Reuben Webb, Hiram Bacon, and E. A. Graves gazed sadly at the wreckage, their minds were weighted with memories. They were the ones who had argued vehemently for the building of this now demolished bridge, at the special Town Meeting in January, 1841. They were the ones who had pushed through the vote for the necessary tax money, "four and a half cents on the Grand List of 1840". This had been a major achievement, following ten years of a negative vote for covered bridge funds. Selectmen Webb, Bacon, and Graves had also planned and supervised the bridge construction. They had likewise labored with their own hands and with their ox-teams to assemble, join, and raise the timbers, as well as to build the stone, log, and dirt road leading to it. Now all was a mass of ruins.

A few days later, the Sunderland Selectmen, a half dozen other townsmen, and one Daniel Oatman assembled near the site of the destruction at the "ford".

"I'll build you a bridge THERE that'll NEVER wash out." Oatman, the local contractor and builder, grimly pointed to the 40-foot high cliffs which flanked the mill dam. "Taken care of, it'll last a hundred years and more."

Dubious though such a possibility half seemed, as all surveyed the scene at the Branch, Oatman was given the contract. He immediately set to work at fulfilling his promise.

A town record for the present Chiselville Bridge across Roaring Branch is a hand-written and yellowed paper, preserved in the Dr. George Russell Library of Vermontiana in Arlington. It is headed: "Expenses of High Bridge—Chiselville from Malcolm Canfield's Journal as Selectman of Sunderland, Vermont, then owning and living in the house and on the farm formerly owned and occupied by Ira and Ethan Allen. December, 1869 - Friday, 24th.

"Bill of Timber for Lattice Bridge at Chizzleville as given me by Oatman on Sunday last."

Materials included approximately 710 pieces of Cut Timber, 3 to 10 inches thick and 4 to 10 inches wide, totaling 34,479 board feet; 1800 Pins and Wooden Pegs, 1 1/2 inches in diameter and ranging from 9 inches to 21 inches in length; 22 bunches of Shingles; 140 Keys (pieces to hold parts together) for Braces; and 250 pounds of Nails.

Labor was performed by various townsmen, who also brought in bills for oil, Brandon red (ochre found farther north), White lead, 60 loads of stone, powder & fuze. Broken windows, aqueduct spikes, and land damages. The last item was figured (amazingly enough today) at $160. The total cost was $2307.31, of which Oatman received $1750.

So, at approximately the same estimate as $2000 for the 1841 Bridge, another Town Lattice Truss was set at the much higher elevation across the Roaring Branch in 1869.

The construction operations were similar. In both instances, the center of the bridge was arched so that it was twelve inches higher there than at the ends. As traffic beat down the hump, the action tightened the lattice struts. Although the joints had already been made as solid as possible with wooden pins, they were pounded even tighter by the weight of hoof and wheel.

A four-ton load of marble from Dorset Quarry, drawn by a two-ton team, provided the first severe test for the bridge. With satisfaction, Daniel Oatman noted that the timbers showed no sign of strain.

Somewhat later, the township added to their investment in the bridge by voting "$33.16 for Insurance on school buildings and Chiselville Bridge."

One of the animals that early contributed to the tightening of the struts on that bridge was Amos Chapman's Jersey bull. As Amos drove his prize Champion of the herd into the dark interior, the beast bellowed, pawed, and swung his head savagely. Probably infuriated by believing that he had entered a barn devoid of hay or grain, he wheeled and knocked Amos flat on the bridge floor. Before the man was back on his feet, Mr. Bull lunged up the hillside. Bolting through Mrs. Sargood's front doorway, he toppled her into the cheese vat and splintered his way out through her kitchen door. There the stone wall around the back yard impounded him. And there, an hour later appeased by a bucket of oats, he meekly surrendered to being LED home across the bridge.

Another recalcitrant animal whose hooves pounded across the abutments was Isaac Greene's pony. In the mid-1870s, 11 year-old Ike was riding down from his home near Manchester on his roan Tim, when the Western Vermont locomotive came roaring south. Railway and road ran parallel and not far apart at that point, so Ike was seized with an impulse to race the train. With a sharp yell, a crack of the whip, and a kick with his heel, Ike urged his aging pony to his topmost speed. Iron wheels thundered; galloping hoofs clattered and the shriek of the engine mingled with the shouts of the boy. Past the point where road and railroad became widely separated, Ike was still possessed by the spirit of speed. Tim's eyes gleamed white and his nostrils red under his forelock. His pony heart was filled with resentment of his rider's whip and heel.

Just as they dashed through the bridge exit, a woman wearing a flapping white shawl and leading a goat appeared beside the road. "Ma-a-a," bleated the startled goat.

"Ugh-h-h," wheezed the equally startled woman.

This was too much for the already maddened pony. He snorted, shied, kicked, reared, and sent Ike somersaulting into a yawning puddle of wet mud and clay.

As Tim wheeled and went galloping home toward Manchester, Ike pulled himself to his feet, dripping and plastered with mud. Vowing revenge, he brandished his whip at the woman, goat, and pony that were fast disappearing beyond the far arch of the bridge.

Malcolm Canfield happened along at that moment and was somewhat astonished to be greeted by a muddy apparition who was loudly threatening to sue the Railroad, the Sunderland Selectmen, and the woman with the goat.

Canfield persuaded the irate young man to be bundled up in the carriage laprobe and "ride a piece" with him. Halfway to Manchester, they met Ike's father, who was an acquaintance of Canfield's, out looking for his son. Since Tim had returned riderless to the barn, Mr. Greene had feared for his son's safety. By then, the youngster had become considerably mollified by Canfield's stories of his own boyhood. He managed to smile wryly through his mud mask when his rescuer parted from his passenger with "Better luck to your next race!"

Three sheep men of the township likewise drove their animals across the bridge once a year. On a warm, sunny day in late spring for many decades, the flocks were brought to a "dipping pool" in a nearby meadow. The hordes of small hoofs tapped in brisk rhythm along the resounding planks where shafts of sunlight filtered through cracks between the side timbers. (Later, top sections of this planking were removed to admit more light. The removal incidentally exposed the interestingly pinned crossbeams of the lattice truss.) The grey of bobbing woolly backs blended with the grey of the timbers in the shadowed interior, smelling of hay, horse manure, and damp wood. Robins and barn swallows chirped from the overhead beams, their calls mingling with the patter of feet and the baaing of the ewes separated from their young lambs.

The high-booted men who drove their flocks went into the pool with their sheep. There each grimy woolly coat was thoroughly scrubbed and thickly sprinkled with snuff or powdered tobacco leaves to kill the ticks lurking in the matted growth. When all were scrubbed and powdered, they were driven back to their barns to await their next day's shearing.

Old Shep, a black and tan collie, devotedly attended the Brownson flock for many years. He and his charges walked together along the road the entire distance between barn and pool, with never a side excursion. Their coordinated discipline won much admiring comment. Shep understood flock politics, and so he always trotted near the lead sheep, known as the bell-wether, and barked all essential instructions to that one, knowing that the others would follow.

A pedestrian who frequently used the High Covered Bridge during the late 1800s was Sig Weinberg, a pack peddler who lived 30 miles or so away in South Granville, New York. Having left his boyhood home in Hesse Cassel, Germany, to avoid compulsory service in the Prussian Army, Sig had settled in this upper New York hamlet. Investing his slim resources in a pack that weighed a few pounds more than his own 125, he periodically made his sales rounds throughout the area. The Manchester-Arlington run was one of his regular routes. His nimble figure, bearing the huge canvas sack fastened to his body with heavy leather straps, was always a welcome sight to the housewife who seldom went to town. From the stores his pack revealed, when spread wide on the kitchen floor, she could choose numerous essential "notions". Pins, thread and needles; brooches, scissors, combs, and lace handkerchiefs; brushes, pencils, hand mirrors, harmonicas, and even jew's-harps, as well as babies' rattles and pacifiers, all spelled shopping delight for the homebound wife and mother.

When Sig took a bride after several years of back-packing, he also acquired a peddlers' wagon and team of horses. His first trip with wagon and wife took him across the Chiselville Bridge. There the newlyweds paused to rest the team and cool themselves beneath the rafters where Sig alone had so often found respite from the heat of sun, the force of wind, or the beat of snow and rain, with his pack a pillow for his weary back.

"It's a 'kissing bridge,' " Sig told his bride, as they started on their way again. And following the usual custom, he collected two expressions of affection before emerging into the open road.

According to legend, another bridal couple started their courtship inside the Branch Bridge. A bashful twenty-year-old, Joe Stone, had finally mustered the courage to invite a new arrival in town, Helen Brown, to go with him to the Valentine dance in Grange Hall. Helen's eighteen-year-old beauty was fast establishing her as the belle of Sunderland. Almost overcome by his good fortune in winning her for the occasion, Joe became tongue-tied as soon as he had tucked her into his cutter. The only response that he could make to her efforts at conversation was "Is that so'?"

Helen was beginning to wonder how she could ever get through the evening on such limited verbal fare. Suddenly, as the sleigh entered the bridge, an owl's "Who-o-oo" sounded from the rafters. Momentarily startled, boy and girl then lost their tension in a burst of laughter.

"Did you ever see an owl?" Joe asked. Helen never had. "One swooped right down over where I was chopping sap-wood this afternoon!" Joe exclaimed. "A big fellow he was. Brown and white feathers almost like a checkered shirt, and his head all eyes and beak. At first I thought he was coming at me to peck my face, but the old boy was just floundering around because he couldn't see very well. I'd jolted him out of his hollow tree and he was flapping around to find another place to light. I finally grabbed him with both hands and stuck him into another tree, where he blinked and settled down, gentle as a kitten."

Helen then recalled her frightening encounter with a bat that came down the chimney and out of the fireplace into her family's sitting-room one day the preceding summer.

One story led to another until both were surprised to find themselves at Grange Hall. And both found it so enjoyable to share remembered experiences all evening that they began sharing new ones from then on.

Years later, Helen Stone often recommended the question, "Did you ever see an owl?" when her own bashful sons were going out on a first date with a new girl.

By then, the young men were doing their courting in an early model Overland. The oldest one, George, out in that automobile, had a harrowing encounter with his neighbor, Charlie Parks, one bright Sunday afternoon, as both approached the High Bridge. Charlie was driving his spirited pair of bays, Ben and Fan, hitched to a surrey filled with a half dozen guests from the city. George had his sweetheart, Cindy, on the open seat beside him, her broad-brimmed white leghorn hat swathed in a voluminous pink veil, and both of them wearing crisply spotless tan linen dusters. Car and surrey approached the bridge simultaneously, but George waited for the team to come through the arch first. With tossing heads and redly dilated nostrils, Fan and Ben pulled hard at their bits and began prancing sidewise when they caught their first glimpse of the coughing, chugging, strange-smelling Overland. "Get up! Get up!" commanded Charlie, lightly slapping the reins.

'Get up" they did, in one leap into the open road. There Fan lunged forward just as Ben haunched back in his breeching, bracing his front feet, stretching his neck, and baring his teeth. The straps tangled, the wagon tongue creaked warningly, and every passenger in the surrey screamed and gripped her seat. Charlie sprang down over the front wheel and grabbed the bit straps of his recalcitrant steeds. Their nostrils grew redder and their eyes rolled white. The Overland engine snorted along with the horses while belching black smoke and gasoline fumes.

"If you'll shut off that damned stinker of yours, mebbe we can pass," Charlie shouted. The stinker went dead. As both vehicles left the bridge behind, George observed, "I'd ruther see an owl!"

Horses and drivers soon became reconciled to frequent encounters with "the horseless carriage", and by World War I days, with motorized trucks as well. In those trying years, sacks of grain from Arlington Depot to the neighborhood dairies; loads of milk, potatoes, maple syrup, and other local produce to help feed the "rationed people", all were conveyed on wheels and runners across the seasoned planks that demanded no repairs. The scene was repeated in World War II. Boys in khaki, boys in navy blue and boys in Air Force and Marine uniforms, girls to serve in the Red Cross, the WACS, and in other volunteer forces all mingled in the busy traffic line. And the aging steeds that were often pressed into service, especially during gas rationing, no longer snorted and reared. They, too, accepted change.

As the cavalcade has continued across the bridge during the twentieth century, the mail carrier has been one who has made his daily rounds along its way. The sheltering timbers frequently brought relief to him and his horse as late as the 1930s. Thereafter the Branch Road was kept open throughout the year so he no longer had to resort to "runners" in the ruggedest part of the winter. His Model-T, Model-A, and models of a later vintage have unfailingly served R.D.2 out of Arlington even on days of freshet and gale.

One of the teamsters who hauled produce along the route for many years recalled that he had sometimes had to tie his team to a bridge brace and shovel a "monstrous lot" of snow onto the planking before he could drive his loaded sleigh across. In his estimation, the bridge timbers could be too protective at times.

A few years ago, a family from the other end of the county attempted to drive their U-Haul through the arch. Piled high with household goods, the load was topped by a three-year-old surrounded by pillows, on a mattress packed into an inverted kitchen table. After much maneuvering, the young parents unloaded table, mattress, pillows, and child into a snowdrift.

Driving the rest of the carryall through the farther arch, they then lugged the table with its freight across the bridge, reloaded, and went blithely on their way. The rosy-cheeked youngster crowed and waved merrily as he peered up at the lattice beams. Interestingly enough, he was the great grandson of one of those who labored with Dan Oatman in the long ago to create this High Bridge that would "last a hundred years and more."

By that year of 1969, however, the sign at the entrance of Chiselville Bridge had been slightly re-worded to meet changing traffic conditions. Daniel Oatman's had originally warned: "One Dollar Fine for Horses Faster Than a Walk." Oatman knew that a *rapid* rhythmic beat of heavy hoofs upon the planks could create a destructive vibration in the structure.

About 1900, the sign was changed to: "One Dollar Fine for Crossing This Bridge Faster than a Walk". That would cover cars as well as horses. Some men argued that it covered them and their cattle also. Therefore, the sign currently states: "One Dollar Fine for Driving Faster Than a Walk ON THIS BRIDGE." That prohibited any *partial* crossing by drag racing, also.

Another possible deterrent to fast driving on this bridge for some years may have been the carved communications upon the interior beams. Some of the most distinct announced: "D.E. loves W.H.", "Kiss Me Baby Nothing — Makes Me Sick," and "Patty's Measurements 38 - 42 - 46—Wow!"

These bits of jack-knife art were all that remained, until recent repairs, of the many colorful messages that have appeared upon Chiselville Bridge. In its earlier days, large white characters painted upon its sides admonished the less religious ones of that era: "Sinner, repent," and "Prepare to meet your Maker." So far as is recorded, no one has yet met his Maker by accident at this bridge.

Vivid posters extolling the virtues of various patent medicines frequently adorned the interior until 1883. That year the State Legislature passed a law which prohibited the use of a bridge or fence as a billboard. Reluctantly, many local patrons henceforth saw only bare timbers where they had previously read reassurance in "AYER'S HAIR VIGOR", "NO-AL CORN CURE", "UNION LEADER CHEWING TOBACCO", "CARTER'S LIVER MEDICINE", "DR. PIERCE'S PINK PILLS FOR PALE PEOPLE", and "LYDIA PINKHAM'S COMPOUND."

Today innumerable tourists come annually to visit Chiselville Bridge, to tread its worn plank floor, to "wish" beneath its roof according to tradition, to gaze at the Branch water pouring over the boulders forty feet below, and to photograph the framed red timbers standing solidly amidst the surrounding hills. Many of these visitors have another objective also—

they have come to shop at Candle Mill Village, the center of which is Remember Baker's pre-Revolution Mill, a mile or so from the bridge.

Those who have the time pause, too, to listen with awe to the tale of the Great Test and Proof of Dan Oatman's Bridge. According to one of the oldest residents of the area, on November 4th, 1927, following a day and night of flooding rain, the Battenkill rose to unprecedented height, spreading destruction throughout its valley. Creeks overflowed their banks along the western slopes of the Green Mountains, and thus, fed by hundreds of swollen streams, the Roaring Branch and the Battenkill sent a sheet of turbulent water through yards, cellars, streets, and fields for scores of miles along their banks. Practically every town in the county was in distress. For three days, oil lamps, candles, and wood fires provided the only light and heat. Railway service and mail delivery were washed out. As in 1869, flocks and herds were sucked into the raging current of the 'Kill.

Other bridges, including some covered ones, were swept away in piles of mangled timbers, part of which were hurled against a high rock bank several miles away. Dams were torn out and mills shattered. At one site, 300 tons of coal piled in the yardshed, were catapulted into the ravaging river, along with dam, shed, and mill.

"We all suffered great loss—some never recovered," the old gentleman reminisced. "But the High Bridge stood safe and sound through it all. And when the hurricanes of 1938 and 1950 destroyed hundreds of other covered bridges all through New England, that old Roaring Branch Bridge stood as solid as Noah's Ark."

Yes, we agreed, Daniel Oatman kept his word. He built "a bridge there" that never has washed out. "Taken care of" by Sunderland townspeople, as it long has been, and no doubt long will be, it well may stand another "hundred years and more", continuing to serve in its small way in the development of a still evolving nation.

10

WITH DORSET MOUNTAIN MARBLE

"First Marble Quarry
Oldest Quarry in United States, 1785
Westerly near Mt. Aeolus"

This Historic Site Marker on U.S. Route 7, a few miles north of Manchester, Vermont, points toward that first quarry pit, which is actually in South Dorset, four miles or so west of the marker.

For nearly two centuries, Mount Aeolus, another name for Dorset Mountain, has been yielding stone for building and beautifying America. At one time or another, 28 quarries have belched their dust and thunder from man-gouged caverns in the mountain sides. Currently, Danby Tunnel at the northeast end of Mount Aeolus is the only one in operation. One of its present contracts is for stone to construct a major addition to the United States Senate Office Building.

The original quarry opening is now a public swimming pool, 90 feet deep, 150 feet long, and 125 feet wide. Great blocks of discarded marble, half hidden among the maples, pines, and birches, are reflected in the spring-fed depths of the abandoned quarry pit. Against their backdrop of blue sky or grey, of spring and summer green, of autumn red and gold, or of winter's shadowed white, these rough-hewn giants bear silent witness to man's sundering of the mountain to meet construction need.

According to *The Geological Survey* by Edward Hitchcock and Albert Hager in the 1860s, "The fine mountain in Dorset contains the most remarkable display of white and grey limestone in New England—perhaps in the United States; the strata here piled upon one another to the height of 1800 feet —These layers vary in thickness from one to six or eight feet, and they usually run horizontally from the surface back into the mountain, the greater their depth, the finer their quality. From five to twenty of them may occur together, resting one above the other, with seams between. Each keeps its own peculiar characteristics of color, thickness, texture, and markings."

It was believed by the surveyors that marble output from this mountain would be limited only by the amount of capital and labor available for quarrying operations there.

Geologists have explained that this crystallized limestone was formed from countless trillions of tiny animalcules called rhizopods that took the lime from the water of an arm of the ocean that reached up through this Vermont valley 480 or so million years ago. During one of the oscillations of the unstable earth crust, the waters became turbulent and muddy, so the small lime gatherers were destroyed. Their calcerous shell remains, reaching a tremendous depth, were laid down in a horizontal position, which, under "monstrous compression", became hard limestone rock. A great crustal movement followed, bending the limestone beds into gigantic folds and lifting them high above the water. This mighty twisting and bending during the mountain building period generated powerful heat by which the limestone beds were transformed through long ages into marble, a dense composition of calcium carbonate. Chemical impurities caused occasional shadings of light grey and white, as well as some variety of textural patterns, in the metamorphosed stone.

During the following ages, including the Ice Age, some erosion of the land crests exposed marble surfaces.

Like all the other great marble beds of the world, the Dorset ones were produced in a mountainous area, Dorset Mountain being a part of the range known as The Taconics. Rising approximately 3,000 feet above the valley floor, it extends eight miles from Dorset Hollow on the west to the town of Danby on the east.

History reports that Abraham Underhill and other 1768 first settlers of Dorset Township took particular interest in the great white blotches, resembling snowbanks, amid their hillside forests. Grey lichens and green moss followed porous ridges along the exposed surface of this otherwise unyielding rock. These stout-muscled men were seized with a mania to dig for the hidden treasure which they were convinced that the wooded mountain held locked up within itself.

Marble beds, they had read, followed a continuous vein deep in the earth. This surface stone might well lead to a valuable deposit. A more immediate demand, however, was the clearing of land to establish homes, so it was 17 years before any real quarrying of marble was begun in Dorset.

In 1785, Isaac Underhill set to work splitting out and shaping grave markers and fireplace stones from a marble ledge at the base of the Mountain in South Dorset. Here was heard the clink of hammer on chisel for tapping this wealth of the ages, and here the first "raise" was made. This came to be known as the "Valley Quarry" and was the first marble quarry ever opened in what is now the United States, though Dorset was then in the Independent Republic of Vermont. Within a few decades, the quarry was nationally famous.

The fire jambs, hearths, chimney-backs, and lintels, that Underhill produced here, were so much more beautiful than the slate and fieldstone ones for the great houses being built that people came long distances, sometimes 100 miles, to purchase them. Soon there was also a demand for marble sinks and doorstones.

As young Underhill was unable to keep up with his orders, his neighbors John Manley and Reuben Bloomer joined in the enterprise. The latter's family of 13 sons and daughters, "all husky", proved most valuable assistants in the quarry labor.

For 20 years after Isaac Underhill opened "The Valley", the workers labored there under great disadvantages. They were compelled to seek out the ledges where the strata were seamy or subdivided, as only these could be hewn to the desired size, shape and smoothness by mallet and chisel. The more compact and consequently better marble, two to five feet in thickness, could not be shaped with a chisel, so they made no attempt to raise it.

Then, in 1804, Eben W. Judd Esq. of Middlebury, 60 miles or so to the north, adopted the plan of the marble workers who lived in the days of Pliny. As early as 350 B.C., Judd had learned, hand saws without teeth, fed with sand and water, had been used to cut marble. Also in 1480 A.D., Leonardo DaVinci had designed a marble-sawing machine with two blades, which likewise employed sand and water as an assistant cutting agent. Esquire Judd laboriously devised a method which similarly utilized a smooth strip of iron tightly stretched on a moving frame, assisted by a mixture of sand and water which was poured upon the block to be cut. The method came into use at the Valley Quarry about 1812. This first marble mill consisted of a gang (or group) of saws driven by an undershot water wheel about three feet in diameter. The sand was dried on a slab of marble over a log fire and then placed in a hopper over the gang of saws. The sand and water were then run upon a grooved board to a point where the stream diverged to feed each of the saws. Once "wound up", this contrivance would run for a long time with little attention.

Although the form of the machine was changed and improved during the next century and a half, this main instrumentality, sand, or some other abrasive, and water moved by the iron saw, has continued to be the basic method used.

Almost immediately after the introduction of the mill, the sale of marble for building blocks and for grave markers rapidly increased at Dorset. In 1812, the Vermont Congressman, Ezra Meech, contracted to supply a quantity of the Dorset Mountain marble for a government building in Charleston, South Carolina. Tremendous challenge though it was, the zealous men of the township bent to the task. Day after day, regardless of weather, the hills echoed with the cracking blows of hammer and wedge, with the screech of the saw, and with the creak of heavy wagons or sleds as the great blocks of stone were heaved upon them. Six-horse teams hauled the five-ton loads up over the rugged steep of Rupert Mountain and thence along the 50-mile turnpike to Troy. There the marble was put aboard a sailing vessel bound for Charleston by way of the Hudson River and Atlantic Ocean.

Another fine contract came in 1837, this time for what was later known as "The Old Custom House" in Erie, Pennsylvania. Again brawny arms swung long reverberating hours to the rhythm of chisel and sledge. At the nearby finishing shed the blocks were shaped and smoothed. But this time, horses and oxen hauled the marble 30 or so miles northwest to Whitehall or to Comstock Landing whence it was shipped by barges on the Champlain and Hudson Canal southward to the Erie Canal. Thence it went west to Buffalo, New York, and on, by Lake Erie, to its destination.

The Erie, Pennsylvania, *Observer* for August 5, 1837, carried a news item, which Brazil Ladd, who drove team for the quarry, used to recall that the Dorset quarrymen, cutters, and teamsters all eagerly read. "The United States Bank is about commencing a bank house, which we are informed will be of white marble and built at a cost of not less than $20,000 (an astounding sum in those days) and will be one of the richest specimens of architecture in the western country. It will be located in State, one of the most delightful streets in our Borough, and will be a splendid ornament to our place. The contract for furnishing the marble will be taken by Messrs. Underhill and Strong, who are already beautifying our country with the rarest and richest specimens of marble from the Vermont Quarry."

Between 1840 and 1860, Dorset marble found a vigorous sale in Buffalo, Cleveland, New York, and Philadelphia. For building stone and tombstones, it was likewise in demand in every state in the Union and in many parts of Canada. To meet this increasing demand, several quarry openings were hewn out of the mountainside to supplement "The Valley" output.

Production was greatly facilitated in 1841 by the introduction of hand channeling. This new cutting tool was a round bar six to nine feet long, each end carrying a steel chisel which was used to cut a groove one to two inches wide along the length and width of the block to be raised.

Again Brazil Ladd used to reminisce regarding this operation: "It was a great sight to see 100 men in a row, striking their drills in o a channel cut."

Aseph Memsel, Solomon Weed, and some other experienced workmen could each channel between five and ten square feet per day at 28 cents per channel foot, that is, a groove one foot long and one foot deep.

As the quarrymen prepared to strike their long drills into the channel cut, they hung coarse cotton sheets on high wooden racks above the channeling. These shaded the cuts and so enabled the driller to see better what he was doing as well as protected his eyes from the glare of sunlight on the white surface.

After the block was channeled, wedges were inserted in the strata seam at its base and other accessible points, and the stone was cleaved from its bed by the powerful arms of the workmen. Until 1848, the blocks were also raised by hand, but in that year a man-operated derrick was installed, thus greatly implementing the fulfillment of the rapidly increasing contracts.

By 1861, a million square feet of marble from Dorset Mountain were being cut annually by the 90 gangs (multiple blades set in movable frames) of saws in the several mills. Three hundred eighty-five quarrymen, sawyers, and stonecutters, ranging in age from 12 years to 80, were riving, tending saws, or cutting letters and designs on those nearly 19,000 tons of stone.

One of the 12-year-olds, who began as errand-runner, was soon promoted to lettering tombstones for the Valley Quarry in 1848. A large number of these were produced in the quarry mills. They were then loaded on horse-drawn wagons and peddled throughout Vermont and neighboring states.

As this boy, Truman Bartlett, a native of Dorset Hollow, labored at his lettering, he longed to create figures of his own from this fine, hard white stone.

Leaving Dorset in 1855, after securing a loan of $10, he finally got a job in New York at $3.50 a week. There he obtained from night school sufficient training in sculpture to enable him to go to Paris in 1867, taking with him his wife and small son Paul.

During the succeeding years, both Truman Bartlett and his son became internationally famous sculptors. The father sometimes observed, "Man's destiny is often determined by the physical characteristics of the land where he is born and raised. Mine was early shaped by Dorset Mountain and its quarry."

Throughout the first three quarters century of its operation, Dorset Quarry was producing a quantity of unmarketable trimmings, as well as its vast output of salable stone. Slabs of the waste were given to anyone who spoke for them, and their uses were varied.

Great-Great-Grandmother and her neighbors, as well as several succeeding generations of homemakers, always kept a foot-square slab or a 6-by-18-inch one to heat at their hearths on wintry nights and then tuck into their feather beds.

Uncle Liurendus and Aunt Relief maintained that no other stone could equal the broken bits of marble that they set as a protective wall around the ox-cart wheel-boundary of their herb bed. Marble they declared, assured the most even temperature so essential for the effective growth of their basil, thyme, mint, and marjoram.

Innumerable slabs went into the township kitchens, too, for baking the buckwheat "pannie-cakes". The customary "receit" instructed: "Mix sufficient buttermilk and buckwheat flour with a working batter (yeasty mixture) from the previous setting. Put into a large vessel and set in a warm corner by the fireplace. This runs over, so stir down often. Bake on a hot marble slab." What delicious aroma and what countless tender brown pancakes came from those hot marble slabs from Dorset Quarry!

From 1840 to 1900, much of the lesser quality stone was being used for sidewalks in neighboring villages. In 1890, approximately four miles of the sidewalks in the resort town of Manchester were of marble, the first of which had been laid about 1840, in front of the home of Levi Orvis, now a part of the famous Equinox House. Legend states that Mary Todd Lincoln, wife of the "Great Emancipator", was especially impressed by the marble sidewalks there when she stayed at the Equinox during Civil War days for a short "refreshment" for herself and two sons. Many of those miles of marble sidewalks throughout Bennington County are still in use. What an eventful record of daily living has been tapped out upon their enduring surfaces!

It was during the mid-1800s business boom among the Dorset quarries that the mountain of marble received its name of Mount Aeolus. On Saturday morning, October 13th, 1860, about 30 members of the senior class of Amherst College, piloted by their professor of geology, Dr. Charles H. Hitchcock, visited Green Peak, a spur of Dorset Mountain. The purpose of the excursion was to study the geological strata. An appreciation of the scenic beauty of the area inspired the young men to make the event a dramatic as well as a scientific one. After exploring the operations among the quarries, the class arrived at a huge cave near the top of the Peak. It was rumored that the windings of this great dark cavern penetrated the very bowels of the earth. Local natives dared to spelunk only a few rods into the cold, bat-inhabited interior, but they loved to picnic on a ledge near its tree-shaded entrance and listen to the wind sing among the pines. The valley below, with its picturesque white houses, fertile fields, pastures, and orchards, presented a panorama of pastoral serenity. The young men from Amherst must have been doubly delighted that October day, when the hills and valleys were brilliantly decked in their glorious autumn foliage.

Following a classical pageant symbolic of the mythological Aeolus, god of the winds, presented by the students, Dr. Hitchcock ceremoniously poured a bottle of water from the Valley Quarry over the earth at the cave entrance. As he did so, he announced that henceforth Dorset Mountain would bear the name Mount Aeolus.

Frederick Field, Esquire, representing the citizens of Dorset, welcomed the class. He then accepted the name "bestowed upon our hoary mountain to which all look up with so much love and reverence" adding that the name was an appropriate one, "because the Greek god of the winds Aeolus did dwell in a cave. Besides," said he, "this is a region of winds, and this lofty mountain greatly affects their direction and power in the neighboring valleys."

Mr. Field then pointed out that the natural resources of this mountain had, from the original opening of the marble quarry at its base, been characterized by beauty as well as by utility.

The coming of the steam-powered channeling-machine two or three years later revolutionized the Dorset industry. This large, clumsy jack-hammer, mounted on its short track and operated by a steam boiler fed by wood and water from the mountainside, could channel more marble in a day than 12 men could. Because this machine threw many hand drillers out of work, it could not be operated except in daylight. Under cover of darkness, the displaced workmen would lurk at the edge of the quarry and throw stones at the night operators.

Bernis Kinnie, generally known as "D", who lived out his 90-odd years near the mountain, spent most of his working life at the quarries. He used to reminisce about one Patrick O'Keefe who migrated to Dorset from Ireland, along with scores of others, after the Potato Famine in the 1840s. O'Keefe was particularly bitter over the loss of his job. Hurling a rock at the channeling-machine one night, he growled acrimoniously into the dark pit, 'Take that, ye damned old steam engine, cheating an honest man out of his work! But one thing, bejabers, ye can't vote."

In spite of its inability to vote, the "damned old steam engine" continued to power the channeling of greater and greater blocks of marble from the mountainside during the next half century.

Although from 1853 on, the Rutland Railroad was carrying most of the Dorset marble output from Manchester Depot to far markets, teamsters were still hauling the stone from the quarry mouth to mill and depot. One of the most noted of these was John Stockwell. After his retirement from quarry teaming, he drove the Manchester village stage until he was well into his 80s. In those years, he frequently entertained his passengers with stories of his quarry days.

"I began driving for the quarries when I was about 17. That was in the late 1860s, around the time that 10,000 markers for the nameless dead in Gettysburg Cemetery were taken out of the Upper Prince opening. It used to take six horses and a team of oxen to haul the block wagon up the mountain, and to cart the blocks down. We had to have good stout brakes, too. Sometimes we hitched a tree on behind to act as an extra brake. On the highest pitches we had to chain the wheels.

"One day, just as I was ready to start down with a big block, the quarry foreman, Deacon Lonson Gray, shouted to me, 'Wait! Wait! There's a bad thunderstorm blowing up!' The sky was as black as your hat, and it was rumbling heavy in the northwest, but I gave back to the Deacon what he was always saying, 'In God we trust', and with that I yelled to the horses to get going, and off we started.

"Just a little ways down the hill, right on the steepest pitch, that storm struck us. I was never out in its like before. We had to go 'round all the corners just so, or we'd tip over and land in Kingdom Come. But my horses knew the way just as well as I did. Mebbe better. Between claps of thunder, I talked to them same's I always did, and they worked their way down without a single botch. I can see 'em yet, swinging 'round all those curves and down all those pitches just right.

"When we got down to the mill the storm was about over, but the road had washed out right behind us."

Mr. Stockwell would often spread out his powerful hands to show their huge joints. "That ain't rheumatiz." He would grin at his wide-eyed listeners. "I got all that swelling from hanging onto the lines so tight for more than forty years when I was teaming. Took most all the strength I had on some of those pulls."

Foreman Gray was mightily relieved to know that Teamster Stockwell had not been washed down the mountainside along with the road during the storm. However, the Deacon was also a man of stern action when occasion demanded. His two supreme interests were the church and the marble quarry, and to each he gave his staunch Calvinistic devotion. Again, John Stockwell recalled an incident at the quarry.

One day, Foreman Gray's right middle finger was smashed by a stone that unexpectedly slid. Almost nothing was left beyond the middle joint.

"Cut it off for me," he ordered the workman next to him. Horrified, the man refused.

Looking down at the mangled flesh, in which dirt and stone dust were embedded, Deacon Gray solemnly pulled out his pocket knife and performed the operation himself. As the red blood gushed forth, cleansing the stump before he bandaged it, he no doubt inwardly observed John Stockwell's pronouncement as he set forth in the thunderstorm.

During the late 1800s, Dorset marble production steadily decreased. Fewer orders came because Rutland was producing improved stone at lower cost.

Suddenly, at the turn of the century, Dorset Quarry came into a business boom. Spafford West, who had been in Dorset marble for more than 30 years, and who was then quarry boss at Great Barrington, Massachusetts, had recently become a partner of Orlando W. Norcross, a noted contractor and builder of Worcester. To them, in 1901, came the great contract for the New York Public Library. The specifications called for nearly a half million cubic feet of cut stone similar to that in the Drexel Building on Wall Street, which had been constructed of Dorset marble.

"You find the money, and I'll find the marble," Spafford West promised his partner. West had long held the reputation for "having a nose for marble". In this instance, his instinct led him to the old Isaac Underhill quarry, which had been closed since 1876. Very much closed it was, for the east road from Manchester to Dorset Village a couple of miles to the north had been built over its top, where it had been filled in with limestone, other rocks, and trees left from clearing the ground for quarry operations farther up the mountainside. In that year of 1901, after West's coring (boring for a sample) had verified his intuition, workmen ripped up the road and built another, which today skirts the quarry pit swimming-pool.

Into the reopened Underhill quarry swarmed workmen and equipment. The 1785 clink of hammers on chisels was replaced by the roar of 20 Sullivan Channelers and a half dozen gadders.

"Those dark streaks you see up there on the pit walls," D. Kinnie used to point out, "were made by oil fumes and smoke from the engines West brought in. Those two-ton hammering machines were oiled by steam as they worked, and the pit was nasty with their grease. A quarryman would set his overalls up in a corner of the backroom when he went home from work, and they would stand there all night. Next morning he would put them on again to go back into the quarry hole. No use washing them. They'd be stiff again in no time. Bessie M— used to take her husband to work and home again every day in the carriage he bought for her. A neat turnout it was, too, shiny black with trim to match her buckskin mare. Bess always kept a big black oilcloth on his side of the seat so he wouldn't grime up the cream-colored corduroy. A man got $1.50 a day for regular labor swinging a sledge hammer to drive in the wedges. Some of them thought they had a fortune when they had laid up three or four hundred dollars."

D. went on to tell of the quarry process. After the coarse surface marble or overburden was cut and drilled out to a depth of 16 feet or so, the bellowing, smoke-spouting channeler went to work on the first layer of fine-grained, slightly streaked "commercial white" stone for the New York Library. The five pointed steel drills, clamped together, were rapidly lowered, raised, and re-lowered, tattooing a long channel, an inch wide, and six to ten feet deep, in the marble bed. When a series of these channels had outlined the length and width of the desired sections, men drove in wedges at the bottom, horizontally, to split off the blocks to be raised by the derricks.

"A wedge would 'sing'," D. recalled, "when it could go no further. Then the boss would say, 'Hold up, boys, let it draw.' After being thus split three or four times, when the block was ready to let go, it would loosen.

"Those drills had to be sharpened often at the blacksmith shop," D. added. "The smith tempered them in oil and knew by the exact color when the right degree was reached. They had to be exactly right, too. No guesswork or the bits wouldn't bore.

"As the channeler cut down the first two feet, a workman removed the stone dust from the groove by a thin scoop. His face, hands, and garments would be covered by the dust that he steadily scooped out. As the steam chopper bit deeper, its pump, drawing water from the hillside springs, flushed out the dust. In winter, ice formed in the channels, so the men had to pick it out with crowbars.

"The derrick chain would break if it was snaked across the bare quarry floor, so we used to keep the pit bottom covered with unsplit elm cord wood (4-foot logs) six inches or so in diameter. Once, when the chain did break, it took 12 men walking as close together as they could to lug it to the blacksmith to have it repaired.

"Big Tom McCormick was quarry boss. Spaff West brought him here from Ireland, and everybody liked him. He treated everybody the same, but everybody had to do what Big Tom said or there'd be tarnation to pay. He was a big, stout, red-faced fellow, so nobody fooled around much. A good thing, for he knew marble! All the blocks had to be sorted and stacked by type—plain white, mottled white, grey, and so on, and they had to be stacked exactly straight.

"One day a couple of the 16-year-olds, Mike and Fred, put marble chunks between the layers instead of the elm logs, 8 or 10 inches in diameter, that they were supposed to use, to keep the blocks apart so we could jerk the cable out from between them as they were loaded by the derrick. The marble props were waste stuff and they crushed. The whole pile, five or six blocks high, tipped and came tumbling down. The boys jumped, but Mike was right in line with all that falling stone. Lucky for him he fell head first and rolled so he was caught only by one arm. But the bone was broken, and somebody had to run and get Tom who had gone home to supper.

"What a fracas came up then. Tom's wife was sick and couldn't milk their cow as she always did. The old Jersey wouldn't give down her milk to a man, so Tom had put on his wife's red caliker skirt to fool her. When Fred went bellering to Tom about Mike's being hurt bad, Tom came a-running. He was hanging onto the empty milk pail with one fist and had his wife's skirt wopsed up around him with the other. I thought we'd die laughing.

"And then we pretty near did die cleaning up that mess before dark. Big Tom never said a word about the skirt nor about our laughing. But he got Mike to the doctor in a hurry, and he sure did set us to work!"

For the next ten years or so, through sometimes scorching heat or below-zero cold, the days of the quarryman's year revolved. Amidst the hiss and shriek of the engine, the clank of hammers and crash of stone, shrouded with dust and steam, and blackened with grease, he toiled. Rivers of sweat poured down his heaving body; frost whitened his whiskers and eyebrows; but his brawny arms and horny fists swung on, rending the stone to build and beautify his country and to shape his own future.

Until 1904, teams hauled the huge blocks from the quarry to Norcross and West's splendid 16-gang mill at Manchester Depot. There in the sprawling one-story building, 20 by 150 feet, the blocks were shaped, planed, rubbed, and cut to design by several hundred workmen. This mill, which was in use only a dozen years or so, cost approximately a quarter million.

Another $135,000 went into the construction of the single-track standard-gauge railroad which in 1904 replaced teams in hauling marble from quarry to mill. Chartered as the Manchester, Dorset and Granville, in order to secure the right of way, it never extended beyond the quarry. Its initials and its surroundings led to its being termed locally the Mud, Dirt, and Gravel.

A hundred and fifty Italian immigrants and blacks assisted Dorset workmen in laying ties and tracks for the M. D. & G. and in fencing it from fields and road. Tiny, one-room wooden shanties with tar paper roofs sheltered most of these laborers. Others were lodged in a big farmhouse, where bunks were hastily built as close as they could stand in every room. Any man or boy who came asking for work was hired if he could drive a pick or swing an axe or shovel.

In July of 1904, 10 flat cars, a passenger coach, and the locomotive began rolling on the M. D. and G., shuttling four times daily between quarry shed, passenger station in South Dorset, and Manchester Depot. Often, a thousand tons of marble a day thundered along the resounding rails, with Kirk Adams at the controls. The locomotive pushed passenger coach and flat cars to South Dorset, where it left the cars for loading, while it pulled the coach and loaded cars to Manchester. In order to retain its charter, the company had to maintain its scheduled passenger service.

Tragedy was barely averted on the Mud, Dirt, and Gravel one July day in 1906. Three flat cars had been anchored together on the Upper Quarry siding where the sharp grade had prodigiously taxed the locomotive to push them up. Two cars were to be loaded with marble, the other with wood from the adjacent woodpile for refueling the locomotive at the engine yard. A railroad tie blocked the lower wheels of each car. The middle car had been loaded with two 25-ton blocks, after which its brake was released, and it was eased part way down the hill in order to bring the uppermost car within loading range of the derrick. One of the men, supposing the brakes would hold, kicked the ties away from the wheels. A 30-ton block was on the last car, and the boom was hoisting a 20-ton block also aboard, when to their horror the men saw that the wheels were beginning to roll. The derrick engineer tried to crash the great stone onto the car, thus jamming it against the rails to prevent all three cars from moving. Hoarsely shouting to the quarrymen to get out of the way, he was compelled to slow the drop of the block, to avoid hitting them, to such an extent that his crashing attempt was futile.

Down the incline crawled the three cars, picking up speed as they descended. Minutes before, the locomotive and passenger coach must have left the station on its 11 o'clock run, carrying a full load of passengers.

Frantically, the derrick hand, who was on the rear car for its loading, tugged at the brake, but to no avail. Faster and faster the wheels spun down the grade. After a mile-long struggle, he leaped off. Nothing could be accomplished by a suicidal ride to the Depot.

Shaking so that he could barely crank the telephone on the shanty wall back at the quarry, the foreman called the mill. Then, weak with relief, he learned that the passenger coach had arrived five minutes earlier, unloaded, and was standing on the siding. The engine was safe in the roundhouse.

By the time the runaways thundered into Manchester, at 30 miles an hour, the rail switch had been pulled, so they catapulted against only the passenger car. The impact tore the coach from its wheels and hurled it upon the foremost empty flat car. A considerably different load from the wood it had been assigned to carry.

A few months later, when the New York Library was nearly completed, Spafford West died. His son Ernest, a graduate engineer, then assumed the quarry responsibilities.

About this time, it was becoming difficult to secure the white marble designated in the Library contract. The fine sound grey stone appearing at the lower depth of the Valley-and-Plateau Quarry was assigned to the building of the United States Rubber Company in New York, and the surplus was given by Norcross and West to the re-building of Dorset Church that had been destroyed by fire a few months before. Because of this gift, the new edifice, erected by the same contractors, cost the parishioners only $15,400 when it was completed in 1910.

Searching the mountain, Norcross and West finally found the desired white marble at a point where an intermittent stream flowed over the snowy outcropping. This area they purchased and opened as the Whitestone Brook Quarry. From it they took the rest of the Library stone.

Every Dorset man, who had swung a sledge to rive the marble from its ancient bed or who had performed any other labor toward building the Library, felt a surge of pride when the construction was completed. Eagerly they all read of its gala opening to the public on May 23, 1911, in the presence of President William Howard Taft, Governor John A. Dix, Mayor William J. Gaynor, and approximately 600 other invited guests.

Proudly, too, they read the caption beneath a photograph of the new Library, which appeared in *The Times* of that approximate date: "ITS MARBLE WHITENESS proclaims a new note in the life of New York."

Further details in the article stated that the Modern Renaissance building, 390 feet long and 270 feet deep, with its five floors built around two inner courts, had been named in the *Architectural Record* of the preceding September as "the one building which American architects in good standing consider embodies most of what is good in contemporary architecture."

No doubt Architects Carrere and Hastings of New York, who in 1897 had won the stiff competition for designing the building, also felt a surge of pride for their part in creating this "Marble Whiteness" which proclaimed "a new note in the life" of their city. So, too, perhaps most of all, did Norcross and West.

Those who had known Truman Bartlett, the Dorset Hollow boy who had become a famous sculptor and who was then a professor at Massachusetts Institute of Technology, were likewise proud to learn about another detail of the building. The sculptor, who created from Dorset marble the six figures representing History, Drama, Poetry, Religion, Romance, and Philosophy to stand above the main entrance, was Truman Bartlett's son Paul. Both men had shown a special interest in the erection and adornment of this Library, constructed from marble that had been rived from the older sculptor's native mountain and from the quarry where he had worked as a boy.

From quarries in that same mountain went out also in the early 1900s the marble for the American Trust and Savings Bank in Chicago; for the Safe Deposit Trust Company Building, the Temple Israel, and the Tremont Building in Boston; for the John Hay Memorial Library at Brown University; and for the Harvard Medical School buildings. About the same time there went, too, the stone for the exterior of the United States Supreme

Court Building, for the Red Cross Building, and for The Daughters of the American Revolution Continental Hall at Washington, D.C.; for the monoliths of the Montreal Art Association Building, and for numerous banks, hotels, and other buildings erected by Norcross and West. Somewhat later, Dorset Mountain supplied the stone for the United States Senate Office Building, and then for its major addition.

By 1917, the Norcross and West quarries were closed. No contracts during the World War I years required marble from the Valley, the Plateau, and the Whitestone. The Manchester mill was razed, and the rails of the M. D. & G. were sold for scrap iron.

The Vermont Marble Company who by then were the owners of the Dorset Mountain quarries continued operations at the Danby Tunnel and adjacent area. Famous for its production of particularly fine crystalline stone, the Tunnel supplied the marble for the Jefferson Memorial on the bank of the Potomac, as one of the structures of which the quarrymen were particularly proud.

In the early 1900s, the Tunnel sent out its biggest single block. This 93-ton giant was shipped to Salem, Oregon, where it was used to create the covered wagon in the Historical Group Statuary of the Capitol.

Another of the largest blocks from the Tunnel, weighing 83 tons, went to form the eagle, carved in relief, on the Veterans' Memorial Building at Detroit, Michigan.

By the late 1960s, the 105 workmen in Danby Tunnel were laboring in comparative comfort. Roy Webster, who had been the quarry superintendent for nearly a quarter century, estimated that the year-around temperature is 47°, and humidity is never uncomfortably high. In this dark interior, electric lights produce no hampering glare as did sunshine in the open pits of earlier quarries. There is no need here to hang cotton sheets on wooden racks above the channeling as did the pitmen a century ago.

The white haze of dust and vapor does still cloud the air and coat men and machines just as in olden days. Since the calcium carbonate is not considered harmful, no one complains. The workers do wear special earmuffs to protect their ear-drums from the still harsh shriek of the machines.

Today's saw is much different from the one introduced at the Valley Quarry in 1811. The one in current use is a huge twisted wire of carbon steel, 2200 feet long, welded to work as a belt. Operating on the principle established in the time of Pliny, its abrasive used with water is composed of corundum and aluminum oxide. This effectively cuts through the several types of stone, all extremely hard, found in the ten variously marked layers of the Tunnel stratification.

Until 1967, the annual output of 45,000 to 60,000 tons from this quarry was brought out of the cavern and down the quarter mile of steep mountainside to U. S. Route 7 by means of gravity-powered cars on a standard gauge railroad. More recently, the 10 huge blocks per day are carried by cable car to the quarry entrance only. There they are loaded onto specially constructed trucks which transport the massive stones directly to their destination. Quite a contrast they are, indeed, to John Stockwell's horse-and-ox-drawn block wagon, with a big maple dragging at the rear for brake-support.

The quarrying operation, even so, is still a match of might. Machines roar, men strain, and the stone finally breaks from its bed, but only to the tremendous power pitted against it.

One of the several-generations-Vermonters who was profoundly impressed by the Dorset Mountain quarrying was Mark Whalon, the local rural mail carrier. His daily rounds for many years took him past the Valley Quarry and the Danby Tunnel. Gazing up at the caverns in the wooded mountainside, he often meditated upon the beauty and the grandeur of quarry, earth, and sky; upon the boundless wonders of the universe; and upon the oneness of them all with humans, their Creator, and their building. Some of these contemplations he expressed in a poem, later published by The Tuttle Company of Rutland, in *Rural Peace*, by Mark Whalon.

"QUARRY VOICE"

"Hiss of steam and shriek of power,
    Grinding gear and creaking crane,
Moan of rock torn from the strata
    Where for ages it has lain.

Angelo saw beauty prisoned
    In each stone unhewn, I know,
Some there are who glimpse the vision
    Further back than Angelo;
See the prisoner deep earth-hidden
    And in freeing him rejoice,
Love the struggle as the triumph,
    Love the strident quarry voice."

For nearly two centuries now, Dorset marble has been bringing fulfillment to vision. Through University and Art Gallery; through libraries housing countless volumes for diversion and research; through memorials to human sacrifice; through the highest court of justice, church, and capitol; through pillar, hearth, and lintel; and through miles of village sidewalk. All these support the structure of human "struggle" and its "triumph" in stone rived from Dorset Mountain, "Where for ages it has lain."

11

ABOUT MEMORIALS
FROM MOUNT AEOLUS

"When death and everlasting things
Approach and strike the sight,
The soul unfolds itself and brings
Its hidden thoughts to light."

Those words carved on the marble tombstone: "In memory of/ Asa
Farwell/ who departed this/ Life June 16 A.D.C. 1815/ in the 59 year of/ his
age" are especially appropriate for marking the grave of one who helped to
open the quarry that supplied this very stone and that was also the first one
ever opened in the United States.

As a 12-year-old, Asa Farwell had come, among the first settlers, to
Dorset in the Benning Wentworth Grants, and as a 20-year-old, he had
enlisted in the Continental Army to serve in the Revolution. Uppermost in
the "hidden thoughts" of his "soul" from childhood until the time of his

death was the desire to help build a strong Independent Republic here in his Green Mountain State and subsequently in his United States. Uppermost, too, was his desire to achieve a good life as "neighbor, husband, father, friend." The tributes from all who knew him eloquently testified to his achievement.

Little did he realize, as he toiled at the Underhill Quarry during the late 1700s, in his spare time from work on his valley farm, that he was helping to record national history. Yet, the blocks that he assisted in hewing from the quarry have provided a stone-carved chronicle of his country's philosophical and religious thought, of its industry, of its genealogy, and of many of its historical events.

Certainly he and Isaac Underhill, Reuben Bloomer, and all the rest of those whose mallets drove the chisels to open Dorset marble, never dreamed that stone from this mountain would, within less than two centuries, provide memorials for innumerable ones of the nation's dead, from the most obscure to the most renowned, throughout America.

Even before that first quarry at the foot of Mount Aeolus was opened, an occasional marker for a loved one's grave was hewn from the marble outcropping on the hillside. Great-Great-Grandfather Zechariah was one of those who first noticed the rock that "resembled a big snowbank", when he was on his way from Bennington to Rupert to visit some of his former neighbors, in the late 1760s.

From this deposit on a friend's holding, soon thereafter young Zach split out a slab about two feet square and somewhat less than three inches thick to mark his mother's grave. A stonecutter, Roger Booth from Massachusetts, with hammer and chisel then shaped a scroll, adorned with a simple rosette design, symbol of "loving memory", at one end to form the top of the marker. After somewhat smoothing the decorated side, he lettered thereon: "In Memory of/ Mrs. Bridget/ the wife of/ Mr. Benjamin Harwood/ who departed this Life/ November 10th, 1762/ in the 48 Year of her Age."

This small, rough headstone for the first woman to arrive in the Bennington Grants and the first to be buried there in the churchyard, has weathered its more than two centuries of service without any noticeable deterioration.

Countless other gravestones from Mount Aeolus have likewise kept their vigil through the years. Not far from Bridget Harwood's is the marker for another early settler who helped to establish the Bennington colony. A winged skull at its top and a primitive design of leaves and flowers were crudely sculptured into the stone. Below was lettered: "In memory of/ Mr.

John Pratt/ he died May ye 16th, 1768/ In the 77th Year/ of his Age." This design was characteristic of those done by Zerubabel Collins, who arrived in Bennington from Connecticut in 1778.

Nearby, a small memory stone set for an infant of old Bennington, has a cherub's head chiseled at the top. Beneath this frequently used design, the inscription stoically tells of a double bereavement. Set in place in the 1780s, by a young widow, it states: "To the memory of the only child of Mr. Archelaus Tupper (who fell by an enemy scout October 23, 1781, aged 29 years), and Mrs. Submit, his wife, who died March 16th, 1777, aged 5 weeks and 2 days."

For the rest of her life, that memory stone brought some measure of comfort to her who had been so chastened by grief.

Soon after Isaac Underhill opened the first marble quarry in 1785, the headstone business was giving work to many of his townsmen. In a short time, they had learned from Zerubabel Collins to carve the symbolic saints' heads, winged skulls, cherubs, and other expressive designs and to letter the eloquent epitaphs then in vogue. The limited facilities for labor and the Puritan taste of the craftsmen in those early days set the standards of simplicity, which mainly prevailed, and which made the cemeteries richer and more picturesque as a result. It is noteworthy that a similar simplicity of line and an even greater simplicity of adornment prevail in this twentieth century when there is no such limitation of labor.

In 1790, Jonas Stewart came to Dorset from Claremont, New Hampshire, where he had been producing slate and granite tombstones. The intrinsic beauty of the marble challenged him, and he was inspired to create increasingly elaborate designs and epitaphs. The urn of flowers denoting loving memory; the weeping willow expressing tears of grief as well as representing the first growth to put forth leaves in spring and the last to shed them each fall; the sheaf of grain symbolizing God's harvesting "fullness of days"; the vine bearing grapes and the oak branch with acorns, denoting death before the allotted 70 years; the lamb, symbolic of an infant's being taken home to its Master; the draperies half drawn across a window to portray the half-vision of life-after-death; and the hour glass, emblem of the passing of one's earthly days, all were among the designs credited to Jonas Stewart and his peers, many of whom he taught.

The now quaint, but often beautiful, verses which long ago enabled the mourner to pour out his grief and which today are often copied by hordes of visitors to our old cemeteries, were also frequently the product of the combined efforts of Jonas Stewart and those who worked with him at one time or another. So flourishing was the business that many throughout the area were soon learning from Stewart the art of carving and lettering the stones. Among those whose work was in great demand was Josiah Manning, an itinerant stonecutter.

One of his masterpieces was placed upon the grave of the first pastor of the first Congregational Church in Bennington. This approximately three-by-four-foot marble slab was elaborately carved with the head of a saint in ministerial garb, above a heart set in branches of laurel. A horn-of-plenty scroll denoting the pastor's abundant contribution to life, bordered the rest of the stone. Its epitaph poignantly proclaimed: "In Memory of the Revd Mr/ Jedediah Dewey, First Pastor of the/ Church in Bennington, who after/ a Laborious Life in the Gospel/ Ministry, Resigned his Office in/ God's temple for the Sublime/ Employment of Immortality. / Decmbr 21st 1778/ In the 65th year of his Age/ Of Comfort no Man Speak/ Let's talk of Graves and worms and Epitaphs/ Make dust our/ Paper and with Rainy Eyes/ Write sorrow in the bosom/ of the Earth".

The hour glass was the design that the even more proficient Zerubabel Collins chose for embellishing a neighboring tombstone. Beneath it, he inscribed: "November 14th 1787 about/ three o'clock p.m., departed/ this life Mrs. Jennet/ Henderson, the amiable Consort of Mr. Thomas/ Henderson, aged 41 years, / 2 months & 16 days/ Behold the Glass, improve the time/ For mine is run, and so must thine/ I have found Godliness great gain/ So run till you the Prize obtain."

"Mementomory" ("Remember death") was Collins' admonition, carved above the likeness of a boy's head in a scroll-bordered panel that topped the burying-ground piece, set near this, for a youth, in the 1790s. Lettered below was: "To the memory of Leiurendus/ Belina Smith, the Only Son of / Doct. Gaius Smith who / Departed this life on the 10th of / December, 1794 in the 17th/ Year of his Age. / Look fellow youth/ behold and See/ What havock Death hath made on me./ Between these Stones in Death I lie/ You are mortal as well as I. / When God Jehovah Gives the Call/ These Bones must rise, these Stones must fall."

Least ornamented but most impressive was the stone that Collins lettered to place near the entrance of the first Bennington churchyard. It marked an empty grave but paid well-earned tribute to one who was entombed in England. It proclaimed: "IN MEMORY OF/ CAPT. SAMUEL ROBINSON/ The Pioneer in the Settle/ Ment of Bennington/ He was born in Cambridge, Mass. / in 1705, married to Marcy Leonard / and removed to Hardwick, Mass. in 1728/ became a Captain in the King's forces and/ served as such in the vicinity of Lake / George during the French war that resulted/ in the conquest of Canada by the English/ On his return from

Lake George mistaking / the Walloomsac for the Hoosic river, he came / to this place and encamped with his soldiers/ Pleased with the country which he called / The Promised Land, he applied to Gov. Wentworth/ secured the township, sought for settlers/ and commenced its settlement in 1761/ Capt. Robinson was the acknowledged leader of / the settlers of the New Hampshire grants in/ their trying controversy with New York/ and in Oct., 1766, at a convention of the town's/ was appointed agent to represent their case to the/ King. He immediately repaired to London where by/ his exertions he obtained the well known order/ of the King to council dated July 24, 1767, pro/ hibiting the Governor of New York from making/ other grants of the lands in controversy./ He died in London Oct. 27, 1767, and was buried in/ the church yard of the Rev. Mr. Whitfield."

Beside that tablet which records the beginning of the Green Mountain State stands a much smaller marble slab, which Collins also created, to mark the grave of Robinson's widow. At its top, he chiseled the design of an urn of weeping willow. Below this, he inscribed: "In memory of/ Marcy Robinson/ relicks of/ Samuel Robinson Esq., who died on the 3d of June/ 1795, in the 83d year of her age/ in the hope of a blessed immortality/

"Farewell world I must be gone
This is no house or home for me,
I'll take my staff & travel on,
Till I a better world can see."

According to Bennington history, Marcy Robinson might well hope for a better world. Most of her years on earth she had had to struggle against the hardships and hazards of pioneer life. The story was told that she had helped with her own hands to build the log cabin in which she, her husband, and eight of their ten children began the settlement of the Grants. When her husband went to London, she and her three youngest children, David, Jonathan, and Anna, aged 12, 10, and 7 years respectively, remained alone in the cabin.

One wild winter night early in 1767 a pack of hungry wolves came clawing at the door and windows to gain entrance. Courageous Marcy Robinson pounded with her bake kettle on the heavy plank door and set the children screaming at the windows. As soon as the animals had cringed back a short distance, she seized in both hands firebrands from the hearth, had the boys open the door, and waved the fiery chunks almost in the faces of the howling beasts. Terrified by what no doubt seemed to them the onslaught of a forest fire and of some screaming animal seeking to escape it or to attack them, the savage pack fled, never to return. That was only one of the many occurrences that challenged this pioneer mother, both as a wife and as a widow. No wonder that her children and Zerubabel Collins chose for her stone "the hope of a blessed immortality" in a "better world" that she could see.

A similar hope was expressed on numerous other stones inscribed by Collins and his co-workers. "He died with calm but manly resolution....in the 63d year of his age, with confident submissive hope of future life and glory" appeared on one, embellished by the weeping willow.

For another, "in the 28 year of her age", he lettered among vines loaded with grapes:

> "Farewell bright Soul a short Farewell
> Till we shall meet again above,
> In the Sweet Groves Where pleasures dwell
> And Trees of life bear fruits of love."

About the same time, in the early 1790s, according to legend, another Vermont carver, Samuel Dwight was also employed to provide the tombstone for one who had helped in the 1800s to "lay out the First Division" in Rupert and some of the other townships of Bennington Grants. Later, he had served as a Loyalist in the Revolution and had died on his way to asylum in Canada. His grave in the Arlington Cemetery had remained unmarked for nearly two decades. The "Mementomori" that Dwight created in 1792 shows a winged skull in military uniform, surrounded by flowers and foliage. Underneath this elaborate design, we read: "IN MEMORY OF/ Captain Jehiel Hawley of/ Arlington in Shelburne county of/ Chittenden this Man died November/ The 2d A Don 1777 Aged 66 Years/

> "Death reigns Triumphant
> 'This man has ceast he speaks no more
> His Troubles are past his fears are ore
> Then speak no ill Ye men of Spite
> For God's a God that Judgeth right.
> Let him that standeth
> Take heed lest he fall."

As the stone indicates, "this man" had been a controversial figure. Several of us, who came upon this marker, did some research regarding him whose "Troubles are past his fears are ore." In a *Churchman's Magazine*, published about the time that the grave marker was set, we read that Jehiel Hawley had "commenced the worship of the church at Arlington" upon his settling there in 1764. It stated further that he had come from Stratford,

Connecticut, where he was born in 1712, and where he had been "annually chosen Reader of the Episcopal Church in Roxbury, for the space of twelve years. With the blessing of God upon his unremitting and pious labours, he so spread the doctrines of the Church, that until the time of the Revolution, almost the whole town (of Arlington) consisted of Episcopalians....

"For the heinous crime of loyalty to his sovereign, he was apprehended and committed to Litchfield jail, from which, through the mediation of his friends and the fairness of his character, having obtained his liberty, and not knowing of any asylum where he could be safe, necessity obliged him to join the army of General Burgoyne, who was then on this (the Vermont) side of Lake Champlain, and who appointed him president of a Board of Examiners to ascertain who were and who were not loyalists among his prisoners. Before this Board persons frequently were brought who were not loyalists, to whom Mr. Hawley was always wont to show every indulgence compatible with his office, even when his coadjutors were of a different opinion. His language used to be, 'Man is a free agent. The question between America and the mother country is not decided. Each party has the right of thinking as he pleases. Today these men are in our power, tomorrow we may be in theirs. That mercy we would receive from our enemies is certainly due to such as are in our hands. Let it be known that we are Christians, whose duty it is to be merciful and to forgive our enemies.'

"Such had been his conduct that after the capture of Burgoyne (one of the articles of the capitulation being that those who had not taken up arms might go to Canada), those very people who had so much abused and persecuted him, now invited him to return to Arlington. But firm to his purpose, he undertook the journey to Canada, but he died on his way at Shelburne, Vermont.

"Thus ended the life of this truly great and good man."

The marble marker, set in memory of Jehiel Hawley in the graveyard of the Green Mountain village that he helped to establish, has inspired numerous other visitors there to read the story behind the stone. Often both youth and the older tourists remark about their "new perspective" regarding the deeds and attitudes of the early builders of our nations, and about their appreciation of finding such records of America's steps through the years engraved upon the Mementomori stones from Mount Aeolus.

A five foot by two foot slab of pure white marble from the Valley Quarry was set at Zerubabel Collins' own grave within a decade after he began his work with Jonas Stewart. Legend credits this stone also to the folk art of Samuel Dwight, but records show that it was carved by Benjamin Dyer, one of the apprentices to Collins. The folk art of the period seemed to follow a similar pattern among the carvers of that time. Like the other gravestones of that era, it is only two inches or so in thickness. The usual chisel marks appear at its back, too, as only the front surface of a marker was smoothed. Across its top, ornamented by an urn of weeping willow, the stone bears the arresting inscription: "Your Fathers, where are they?/ And the Prophets, do they live forever?/ In/ Memory/ of/ Zerubabel Collins/ who/ died Dec. 22 1797/ In the/ 64 Year of his/ Age.

> "When you my friends are passing by
> And this informs you where I lie
> Remember you ere long must have
> Like me a mansion in the grave."

Certainly his "mansion in the grave" is among surroundings that would please him. Tall oaks shade the upjutting, lichened grey rocks that companion it beside the old Baptist church in Shaftsbury. And the Taconic Mountains shadow the sunset there just as they did the Valley Quarry where Zerubabel Collins spent his most creative years.

Hopestill Armstrong was another Bennington County man who promoted the headstone business from Dorset Mountain. For forty years or so, he and several others periodically loaded as many of these burial ground pieces as a wagon would hold and traveled long miles up and down Vermont and over into New York State, peddling from door to door. Epitaphs and embellishing designs had been carved on the stones in advance by Collins, Dyer, Manning and others. Names and dates would be lettered in at the time of sale. The State Geologist, George H. Perkins, nearly a century later observed that "almost all the headstones standing in the Bennington to Burlington Cemeteries 1788 to 1830 came from this old quarry and are still in good condition. They were marked, cut and tooled by hand from practically surface marble in the Underhill Quarry, then 150 by 125 by 16 feet."

This system of preparing tombstones in advance for peddling resulted in a great similarity of sculptured design and sentiment throughout the area. Some of the most frequent repetitions appearing under the traditional designs of cherub, hourglass, or nature symbols were: "We all do fade as a leaf"; "She wears the crown without the cross"; "Though He slay me, yet will I trust in Him"; "The gift of God is eternal life"; and "Love can never lose its own."

Numerous children's graves were marked by stones bearing the inscription: "Weep not mourning mother that the flower be plucked so soon/ God hath taken it from earth in paradise to bloom."

Another favorite was:
> "Sleep, gentle babe, thy spirit's gone
> To that bright world above,
> Where pain and sorrow never come
> Where all is joy and love."

Most frequently appearing on an infant's gravestone was:
> "We loved her (or him), yes, no tongue can tell
> How much we loved her and how well.
> God loved her, too, and he thought best
> To take her home to be at rest."

By contrast, there appears a uniquely intellectual verse upon a child's grave marker in the Salem, New York, Cemetery: "Sheldon/ son of/ Moses S. & Susan/ Curtis/ died June 25th/ A.D. 1808/ in the 4 year/ of his/ age Each moment has its/ sickel emulous/ Oftimes enormous sythe/ whose ample sweep/ Strikes empires from the root;/ Each moment plays/ His little weapon in the narrow sphere/ Of sweet domestic comfort/ and cuts down/ The fairest bloom of sublina/ ry bliss."

A mother's gravestone was often inscribed with:
> "Beneath the cold and silent clod
> Here lies our mother dear;
> Her soul has fled to meet her God;
> Tread softly, a mother is sleeping here."

Many of the bereaved chose, or composed, their own sentiments which they requested to be inscribed on the loved one's memorial. One of the most eloquent of these appeared in the Old Cemetery at West Rupert: "In memory of/ Molley L. Brown/ the wife of William/ Brown who died Dec. 24th, / 1803, in the 40th Year of Her Age/

> "To rise again, the Sun goes down,
> And in the Furrows, Grain is sown.
> Beauties that Sleep through Winter's Reign
> When Spring returns, revive again.

Shall then the Friend, for whom we mourn
Never to life again return?
Great source of Life! Light! Love & joy!
Let no such tho't our Hope destroy.

Our lively Hope that some time Since
Through the Redeemer's Influence
In whom she plac'd her hope & Trust,
Shall burst this Tomb, shake off her Dust,
Ascend to where God holds His Throne
And Immortality put on."

Another epitaph for a wife and mother indicated much more than the words actually said. It appeared in the North Rupert Cemetery: "Erected to the memory/ of/ Mrs. Margaret Sheldon/ wife of Capt. Moses Sheldon/ who died at Rupert 27 Oct./ 1816/ AEt.60years/ A 4th Husband & the Children of three families lament her loss. She possessed an amiable and placid disposition & an intelligent & elevated mind exemplifying in her life the law of Christian kindness & charity.

"Joyful to dust I now resign
These weary mouldring limbs of mine."

A rather more earthy reassurance may be read on the gravestone placed some years later in the Rupert churchyard for the town blacksmith, who was often spoken of as "poor but honest". "Preserved Wright, December 11, 1823, age 52."

"Though greedy worms devour my skin
And gnaw my wasting flesh,
When God shall build my bones again
He'll clothe them all afresh."

The Wright family were staunch believers in physical and spiritual reincarnation, as were a majority of the townspeople of the early 1800s.

One of the most aptly applied of the headstone engravings that appeared in a local cemetery about this time was the "EPITAPH ON A GLAZIER". The community glass-cutter died in 1807, and on his grave marker were inscribed the words:

"Precarious dealer! Death, alas
Has cut in two life's brittle glass.
Keen was thy di'mond on the pane,
And well thy putty stops the rain;

"But all the arts were weak through life,
Death cut more certain with his scythe;
And thou, safe from a rainy day,
Are puttied up in mother clay."

When a western Vermont man and his wife were killed by a runaway team in a blinding blizzard a few years later, the marble memorial set upon their double grave was a single stone. It announced:

"Ezra King/ died/	Mary/ Consort to/ Ezra King
February 6th	died/ Febr. 6th, 1813
1813	aged
aged 51 years	47 years

"One we were in life and death
Together sleep in dust;
But God has given diviner breath
That we may live among the just."

Nearly a half century later, a 10-foot obelisk was taken from Dorset Mountain to mark the graves of a beloved Bennington physician and his wife. The inscriptions thereon are among those most frequently copied by tourists in the old Bennington churchyard. On one side was lettered: "Dr. Noadiah Swift, M.D., died March 21st, 1860, in the 84th year of his age.

"Now peace for war is needless,
And rest, for storm is past,
And goal from finished labor,
And anchorage at last."

On the opposite side was inscribed: "Jennett Henderson, wife of Noadiah Swift, born January 24, 1779; died February 10, 1853.

"Death is the crown of life.
Were death denied
To live would not be life."

"Even the most beautiful verse utterly fails to express the beauty of human love," Aunt Delight Clark once commented. She was remembering what her parents had said when her brother was killed during the Civil War. By then, gravestones were being taken from the recently opened Upper Prince Quarry on a steep slope of Dorset Mountain known as Owl's Head. This was located about 700 feet above the Valley Quarry, which had fallen into disuse. Upon a tablet of this white stone banded with grey, the grieving parents chose to use their own inscription instead of a "bought verse". Their son's grave was therefore marked by: "A dear and only son/ John M./ son of Calvin & Delight/ Gookins/ a member of Co. G. I Vt. Cav./ died at Winchester, Va./ Oct. 29, 1864/ AE 20 yrs. 4 mos. 19 ds./ We miss him."

Sadly, indeed, they did miss him. Life lost much of its radiance for Aunt Delight and her parents after John was gone. How well they remembered the day that he had joined the other enlistees at Rupert Depot to set forth to the national capital. The boys all looked so young and yet so gallant with the sprigs of evergreen in their caps, as the badge of their enlistment. And how their strong clear voices had sent "Hail to Liberty" and "Battle Hymn of the Republic" echoing and re-echoing among the wooded hills and along the ringing railroad tracks as the rumbling coaches bore them out of sight. Parents and sister had thought that John seemed the most eager-eyed of the whole dozen boys going forth that morning to defend the Union. And the handsomest! Yes, they would "miss him" always.

On the other side of the mountain, a few months later, a stone was set in memory of a Dorset "boy in blue", who was also killed in the War between the States. At its top was carved a replica of the Union flag floating in the breeze. Beneath it were inscribed the words: "Medad Peck/ Co. G. 11 Vt./ Was wounded in the taking/ of Petersburg, Va./ Apr. 2 and died in/ Hospital at Washington, Apr. 17, 1865/ Ae 47 years." The now half obliterated lettering at the base reminded the passerby that Peck gave his life defending his country for the cause of liberty and to "save our lives."

According to legend, the people of Dorset held a day of mourning in their village church in late April of 1865. It was a service to honor both their assassinated President and their native son, Medad Peck, who had been fatally wounded in the final, decisive battle of The War.

A few years later, 10,000 headstones for the unidentified boys, who fell on Gettysburg Battlefield, went also out of the Upper Prince opening in Dorset Mountain. White, white banded with grey, or white with a bluish sheen, the 6-inch square markers stand in as unyielding lines as the unknown heroes they commemorate once stood, on the vast Pennsylvania field, known as the National Cemetery, today. Of the thousands of brave boys, who fell on that Battlefield July 1, 2, and 3 in 1863, the burial places of the "nameless volunteers" are marked only by these small marble shafts. Yet each stone bears witness to the history, the philosophy, and the sacrifice voiced by President Lincoln as he stood only a few feet from where the markers now stand at the dedication of this Cemetery on November 19, 1863. Poignant reminders they are, indeed, of the words that have rung down the years: "....a new nation, conceived in liberty and dedicated to the proposition that all men are created equal..as a final resting-place for those who here gave their lives that that nation might live..that from these honored dead we take increased devotion..that government of the people, by the people, for the people shall not perish from the earth."

Two other openings in Dorset Mountain, the Whitestone Quarry and the Danby Tunnel, provided the fine, hard, white marble for the Arlington Memorial Amphitheatre. Could the strata of Mount Aeolus speak, would Gettysburg and Arlington converse about the nation's martyred heroes whose deeds they commemorate? Certainly their supreme sacrifice inspires in all who gaze upon their memorials a solemn reverence for their patriotism and for the ideals that they defended .

In 1906, Spafford West, who was in charge of supplying the marble for the half finished New York Library, died. Believing that the great structures which he had helped to build throughout America would always be monuments to his memory, Ernest West had no adornment nor sentiment inscribed on his father's grave marker. For this, he directed the excavation of a 20-ton block of marble from the re-opened Valley Quarry, where his father had spent so many of his days. It required twelve heavy work horses with their drivers to haul the five feet wide, five feet deep, and nine feet tall finished marker to the Dorset Cemetery. There it rests, a sturdy giant among the elms and evergreens, symbolic of a great quarryman, contractor, and builder. The simple inscription upon it states: "West/ Spafford Holley West/ Born April 8, 1846/ Died Dec. 15, 1906."

During World War II, the Danby Imperial marble from the Tunnel Quarry on the other side of Mount Aeolus went forth to construct the Thomas Jefferson Shrine, memorial to the writer of the original draft of the

Declaration of Independence and the third president of the United States, at the nation's capital.

Shortly thereafter, a simple headstone of the Imperial was also quarried in the Tunnel to mark the grave of Franklin D. Roosevelt the only four-term president of the United States. The stone's smooth whiteness there in the midst of the rose garden at Hyde Park again resembles "a great snowbank", as it perpetuates the name of another builder of his country.

Still another president's final resting place is guarded by "the gold-veined white Imperial" from Danby Tunnel. In 1965, this marble was chosen for part of the John F. Kennedy graveside memorial. The stone for the ten steps leading to the eternal flame, as well as the terrace immediately surrounding it, was taken from the same section of the Mountain as was the marble for the Arlington Memorial. Now companion stones in the National Cemetery, each was once a part of the others, deep in Dorset Mountain.

Like all the other memorials hewn from Mount Aeolus, they represent the search for solace for human grief as each one strives to fulfill the demands of destiny.

12

IN MOUNTAIN GROVE SANCTUARY

"This must be the most peaceful place in the whole world, and the most beautiful."

Two of us were on one of our favorite hikes up a southwestern Vermont hill trail one glorious afternoon last August when we were thus greeted by a young man and woman, each with a knapsack and a New York accent.

All four of us had arrived simultaneously at the beech-shaded bank of the brook that babbles down the glen at the west side of several wooded acres locally known as the Mountain Grove.

As we gazed down through the cathedral-like arches of trees at the vista of wooded slopes, shimmering ponds, rolling farmlands, and the village church spire against a backdrop of distant mountain ranges, we agreed.

Thrushes flitted and piped among the branches that cast cool shadows on the sun-drenched grass at our feet. The rustling pines scented the air with pungent fragrance.

As the elixir compounded of all the natural elements here filled our beings with the joy of living, the young man continued. "Our marriage had just about fallen apart when we finally decided to see a counselor. He had vacationed down there in the village, so he told us to come up here and "spend two or three days like gypsies. THEN see what you want to do."

We waited for him to tell us more, but he was looking happily at his wife.

"We found ourselves and each other and a wonderful new meaning to life by just being here alone together in all this quiet beauty," she said simply.

They smiled at each other, spoke a brief farewell to us, and walked hand in hand down the trail.

We lingered, entranced by the white cascade from the spring among the rocks above us. As it swirled over the mauve and green pebbles in the pool beside us, its force was calmed into a tranquil stream of silver that flowed on, singing, down the hillside toward its journey's end in the far sea. Standing there on the grassy bank, we felt a oneness with the gliding water. And with the grove around us.

For centuries, now, this mountainside grove has been providing sanctuary for man and animal and bird. Its initial survey stated: "Bounded by..a Beech staddle (group of young trees) & Stones the S.E. Corner of Sd Harmon's 60 acre Lot....then W. 10° N to a Maple marked G.S. then S 10°—4 rods to a black Spruce Tree, then N. to a black Birch Staddle at the foot of the ledge; then W. by a Walnut 40 rods to a Bass tree marked P.S. and G.S., thence 14 rods to a White Ash tree then to the bounds begun at 6 ch. & 25 links, Eleazer Baldwin Surveyor.

"I have hereunto set my hand & seal in this 14th day of July in the Sixth Year of his Majesty's reign, 1766.   Sam'l Robinson"

Thus, "For and in consideration of" 100 pounds, Barnabus Barnum received title to "10 Rights of a sidehill," which he later deeded to his neighbors. About 35 acres of it were considered untillable and were left as a grove, bordered by rocks, a grassy clearing, and a brook.

"The ledge" was a towering rock formation that afforded a safe, protective shelter from rough winds and storms. According to legend, the Indian runners of the Five Nations sometimes camped here when they were en route from a lodge on the Connecticut River to one on the Hudson. In our childhood, the ledge was called Indian Rock.

At the western boundary of the Birch Staddle a never-failing spring still sends its overflow cascading down the slope. Nearby is a large, comparatively flat open space which has been the scene of numerous community gatherings.

As soon as the two pioneer women, Hepzibah Barnum and Elizabeth Eastman, had "set up" in their log houses a mile and a half apart, in the late

1760s, they began meeting at the Beech Staddle for occasional woman's-need visits. Here they exchanged recipes for cooking the wild game and directions for making their men's deerskin clothing and their babies' knitted garments. Here they gathered the nuts for food and the leaves from a nearby birch for a tonic tea. Here, too, they shared their tears and laughter, as well as nostalgic memories of their former homes in the Bennington Grants.

Sometimes, when the two young matrons were so pressed by household duties that they could not meet, they left messages for each other in the crevice of one big beech trunk. On strips of white birch bark they scrawled with bits of charcoal: "Mattie and the babe do well"; "Flax-breaking next Monday"; "Potash-toting Wednesday"; "Plots darken"; "Try cherry bark for your cough"; and "Barna-bas says we can't stay the winter."

"Barnabas says we can't stay the winter" was the last note that Hepzibah left in the tree. Because of her prolonged illness, she and her husband returned to her parents' home in Bennington a few days later. Although they hoped to return to their log house on the mountain the following spring, the hope was never realized.

Upon the death of his wife shortly after their leaving the mountain, Barnabus returned to visit the Eastmans, and to them he sold his Rupert holdings. That afternoon he climbed to the grove that had once been his. As he strode along a familiar trail, the serenity of woods and water gradually eased his pain over the loss of his Hepzibah.

"The strength of the hills is his also", held new meaning for Barnabas as he emerged from the grove. His friends noted that a ray of peace shone in his face.

But the peace of the hill settlers was soon shattered. Following the Battles of Lexington and Concord, Josiah Cass declared himself a Tory. So did a group of other settlers in White Creek Meadow at the western end of the township. The Eastmans, Harmons, and several others were equally outspoken for American rights and freedoms. The Propriety was fast dividing against itself.

In the meantime, the Curtises and Harmons had offered winter storage space in their barns to some recently arrived settlers. The newcomers had found time only to build their log houses and crop their few cleared acres, so they gladly accepted the offer. The three big log barns were packed with a goodly harvest, enough to insure all the families' wintering well.

Suddenly, one night each barn burst into a wall of flame. Dark figures skulked away from the conflagration into the darker woods. The richly kerneled wheat sheaves crackled and blazed, "making the neighborhood as light as day," an old diary stated. Helpless, their faces white and drawn with despair, the hill dwellers watched the greedy flames devour their entire harvest. Nevertheless, by the next morning they were voicing their determination to remain on their Grants and crop again.

Then came the pounding of a hard-ridden horse's hoofs, and Jonathan Eastman's lathered roan raced from door to door. 'The Tories are coming. Get to Bennington!" the rider shouted hoarsely and thundered on.

Lucy Hodge and her three small children could not join the exodus. Her husband Daniel was on a potash journey to Albany, taking their only horse. Clutching her little ones, she fled to the shelter of the grove. Here among the trees and underbrush they crouched throughout the Tories' plundering of the other barns and folds. All that fiend-filled night, Lucy leaned against the great beech tree and prayed. And when her husband came frantically calling through the staddle two days later, he thanked God for finding his wife and children here, unharmed, and with their hunger staved-off by the beechnuts, their thirst quenched by the spring.

During the next several years, only the deer and raccoon, the porcupine, rabbit, and squirrel trod paths through the grove. The beat of mallet and axe no longer mingled with the drum of woodpecker, partridge, and bounding stag. Only the notes of the crow and bluejay, of the lark, the thrush, and the warbler, of blackbird and snowbird, each in its season, echoed where the voices of humans had called to one another. The Tories, after driving their freedom-seeking neighbors to their stronghold in Bennington, had themselves fled to Canada in fear of retribution.

The fall of 1780, several of the Proprietors returned to their rights. Among them were the Hodges. All labored together to restore their fields, their stock, and their homes.

Pausing to rest at the stile in their line fence by the grove one December twilight, Daniel and Lucy gazed toward the West. The setting sun blazed red in a jagged mass of smoke black clouds, portending storm. Memory gripped Lucy, memory of the flames that had consumed both hope and harvest here on this mountain five years before. Then, as man and wife lingered to re-lay a portion of the wall, where it had been tumbled by weather or some animal, they saw the full moon rise, white, serene, and radiant, above the mountains to the East. Their weary spirits lifted.

Just so, Lucy reflected, fortunes and passions change, bringing peace from conflict. Now she and Daniel and their three sons were working for a fine new home here on their promising acres. Tenderly she touched the silver bark of the big beech that had been a refuge for her and her children.

A few years later, the Hodges' oldest son Enoch was one of the several young people, who, during the succeeding scores of years have done their courting on long walks in the grove. Although Enoch and the girl of his choice, Janie, were married the winter after they started "keeping company", another courtship here in the late 1700s was not destined for such a happy culmination as theirs.

Hope Barnes and Luke Elwell began walking up the hill together the spring that they were eighteen. With them walked Hope's older brother David and his betrothed, seventeen-year-old Nancy Holmes. Often, one to a half dozen unpaired brothers, sisters, or cousins accompanied them. Together, the young people searched out the fragrant pink trailing arbutus in its covert of leathery brown leaves and April snow high on one sheltered slope. Later, in the lower glades, they gathered the sweet wild strawberries and raspberries now and then on a Sunday afternoon, heaping the birchbark baskets, that they fashioned from a nearby tree, with the juicy crimson fruit. Gleefully, they were well aware that if they were caught by the tything-men they would be arrested and fined for breaking the Sabbath with such profaning activity. But no tything-men ever invaded their highland sanctum.

Often, too, a half dozen of those who were "sparking" would rendezvous by the spring, in the dewy, moonlit grove at the end of a hot day in the hayfield and the cheese room.

By late summer, all the hill residents were expecting that Hope and Luke would soon be "setting up" for themselves. Some, however, voiced their disapproval.

"She pokes fun at him because he squints," one irate neighbor commented.

"She makes eyes at other fellows right under your very nose," Luke's grandmother told him. "Then she turns around and makes up to you just because she knows you're so good-natured and that your father has the biggest house and the most land of anybody around here."

In spite of criticism by others, Luke could see only bewitching charms in Hope. Her long silky black hair, her plump white neck. and her parting of her full red lips when she laughed, even at him, enchanted him. And every time he lifted her slim, round body over the wall at the edge of the grove, his whole six feet tingled with delight at her clinging to his strength. Then one early September evening came heartbreak.

Luke had invited David, Nancy, and two of Nancy's cousins, Peter and Martha Holmes, who were visiting her from their "city home" in Albany, to join him and Hope at the grove spring for a feast on the season's first watermelon from his father's garden. That garden was noted for the fine flavor of its melons. Filled with pleasant anticipation, the three couples hurried to the appointed place beneath the beech trees as soon as the moon rose.

There in the cold dark water bobbed the big melon, which Luke had cut from the vine before daybreak and brought here to chill. Peter held the great dripping green ball on a flat-topped stump while Luke deftly halved it with one clean stroke of his hunting-knife, brightly burnished for this occasion. Then stunned with disbelief, Luke's ruddy face went ashen. Chagrin turned his genial smile to a distressed grimace. Six pairs of incredulous eyes stared at what lay on the stump before them.

Instead of the anticipated juicy red flesh inviting the beholders to partake of its lusciousness, there lay a pale hard mass, grinning diabolically in the moonlight.

"Gosh-almighty, ye cut yerself a green punkin!" David bellowed, doubling up with laughter.

A shrill whinny from Hope cut Luke as though it were another knife. "Squinty can't tell a punkin from a watermelon! Hee-hee-hee!" Hope's hand clung to Peter's arm as she jeered at Luke.

It was Martha who picked up his knife when Luke fl ng the offending fruit into the dark underbrush. And it was Martha who saw Luke climb drearily back up to the grove later that evening after bidding his guests a brief goodnight at Hope's door.

Here, Luke flung himself face down on the mossy turf beside the spring. Shattered and numbed by his broken image of Hope, he lay long hours in the dark. At last, the glow of daybreak, the murmur of the brook, and the chorus of waking birds pulled him to his feet. Shortly after dawn, Martha saw him return from the staddle.

Perhaps it was because she also had silky black hair and skin like wild plum blossoms, or perhaps it was because she ached so deeply for Luke's cruel hurt and humiliation. Whatever the reason, it was Martha who set up a home with Luke within sight of the grove the following spring.

For the next half century, the trails among the hillside trees provided them, their children, and their grandchildren with many an unforgettable excursion for wild flowers, berries, nuts, or just the joy of walking.

For many years during the 1800s, patriotic groups annually assembled in the grove to celebrate Independence Day on the Fourth of July and Bennington Battle Day on the 16th of August. A description of one of these events may still be read in a Bennington newspaper of the early 1800s.

"Agreeable to notice given by a committee of arrangement, a respectable number of the citizens of Dorset, Manchester, Rupert and Pawlet convened at Jenks' Inn in Rupert where the flag of union was suspended from a lofty flag staff. About ten o'clock in the morning, on July 4th, 1809, the procession formed under the direction of Col. Stephen Martindale, marshal of the day, and James Moore 2nd, his assistant. In front marched the infantry, artillery, and martial music in their order, followed by the authority, clergy, aged gentlemen, ladies, and others. The procession moved to the grove previously prepared, and formed a hollow square around the ceremonial setting.

"Here the flag of the United States was hoisted and suspended on the tall flag staff erected in the center front of the bowery. On one side was represented an eagle bearing in its beak an olive branch, in the act of descending to drop the emblem in the midst of the assembled throng of Freemen; on the opposite side was represented a form from Heaven, the Goddess of Liberty, at full length, with bare feet, flowing robes, and loose ringlets—her left hand supported a wand, on the top of which she had placed her cap; she stood in an attitude of solicitation, calculated to win the patriots to her standard and to show to the Republican Freemen assembled that her banner over them was love.

"When all were assembled, 18 young ladies dressed in white advanced carrying spruce boughs, and bearing a replica of the cap of liberty, which the leader gracefully delivered to John Shumway Esq., the Chairman. They then took their proper places, equally spaced around the square, and each unfurled a banner that she was carrying. These were arranged from north to south, in conformity with their geographical situation—on each of the rectangles of white homespun linen the name of a State and its motto were worked in cross-stitch in the colors of the State it was designed to represent, and Louisiana.

'The effect of the whole was striking; it was not only ornamental but expressively emblematic and sentimental. It made every Freeman feel the importance and dignity of his station......It awakened in prospective to the reflecting mind the exalted destiny that awaited them, if social intercourse was cherished & harmony preserved.

"Col. Robert Cochran, aged 72, and Lieut. Jonathan Farrar, both of whom had served in the Revolution, then came in, bearing the United States and Vermont flags, and followed by a number of other aged and venerable heroes who were in the Revolution as soldiers and officers. Seventeen of these bore each another flag in honor to the States and Louisiana. They solemnized and gave much credit to the day. Several were near 80 years of age among the 150 or so.

"The Rev. Mr. Chamberlin of Manchester opened the exercises by prayer.

"Perez Harwood, acting as toastmaster, proposed the following:

"1.Republican Liberty—May it be enjoyed for ages to come, in the same degree as within eight years past. (This Republican Party was formed by Thomas Jefferson in 1801.)

"2.The President of the United States: the bold stand that he has taken in defense of the honor of the Government increases our confidence in his rare abilities to make a grateful people happy.

"3.Jonas Galusha, Governor of the State of Vermont: a plain farmer, an eminent statesman; may his virtue, patriotism, and wisdom be the governing planet for the proud disorganizers of our republic.

"4.George Washington: the father of his country; his name will be revered as long as there remains a republic on earth.

"5.Liberty, Equality, Unity, and Peace: the grand pillars of our government; may they stand fair until the last shock of time shall bury this globe in ruins.

"6.The Constitution of the United States: under the inspiration of wisdom, it drew order out of chaos, gave vigor to industry, and stability to liberty.' "

There followed a toast to Education, to The Plough, to Agriculture and Commerce, to The Heroes of the Revolution, and to The People, respectively. The last one, to "The People" added: "the rightful Governors of the Union– Let their servants be faithful if they expect further employment."

The newspaper article noted: "A salute of three guns was scheduled to be fired following each toast except the one to George Washington. That was to be drunk with no gun, all standing uncovered. However, Captain Roberts, with his company and piece of artillery, after saluting the assembly, withdrew on account of expressions of approbation and confidence in the President of the United States and some other toasts agreed to be drank. (Captain Roberts opposed the Republican Party). This unexpected withdrawing of the artillery produced however no disorder.

" 'Col. Martindale then read an editorial from a county newspaper: 'Money is with propriety considered as the VITAL PRINCIPLE of the body politic' says the editor of *The Washingtonian*. What an affront to the principles of the Revolution, and to the memories of our fathers who perished in that glorious storm! What do the maxims of Washington inculcate?

That money is the vital principle of the commonwealth? No! they tell us that public virtue is the soul of the republic; and that without this vital principle, liberty cannot endure; and yet a detestable hypocrite, whose sordid soul is a standard of mercantile patriotism, has the impudence to make the name of Washington a post-horse to give currency to such an infamous sentiment.' "

Everyone, from the bannered girls in white to the flag-bearing, aged veterans in buff and blue, applauded the Colonel's reading.

The newspaper account continued: "Band music soothed the asperities, lessened the fatigues, and increased and tempered the hilarity of the day. All joined in singing 'Past, Present, and Future', 'Independence', 'Liberty Tree' and 'Yankee Doodle'.

"The scene was closed in season by The Rev. Mr. Chamberlin with the text 'All the law of liberty is fulfilled in one word, even in this: thou shalt love thy neighbor as thyself. But if ye bite and devour one another, take heed that ye be not consumed one of another! "

An old diary commented: "The gathering of citizens from miles distant, on foot and on horseback, was, indeed, a simultaneous expression of gratitude for our country. Order and decorum were preserved; no noise or riot disturbed the solemnities; no disputes interrupted or checked the temperate festivities of the day. They whose hearts were not with us scattered abroad."

The two hundred or so who remained gathered around the plank-and-log tables set up among the trees. One of the women observed later: "The tables were loaded with Ham, Roast Chickens, Baked Pig, Pies, Tarts, Cakes, Cheese, Raisins, Nuts, &c, &c. After dinner, there were running races: pipe, potato, sack, and wheelbarrow. John Turner caught the greased pig, said to be worth $10. He earned it!"

Some target practice, dancing of the Virginia Reel, playing hide-and-seek among the trees, and personal recollections of bygone days passed the afternoon, as all grouped themselves according to their individual interests.

The day closed with everyone's singing "Hail Columbia" and "America". One of the flag-bearers recalled, "Our music was sweet—composed of two or three German flutes, clarinets, one hautboy, a key bugle, and a violin.

Great-Grandfather's cousin, Benjamin, was one of those who heartily disapproved of the Republican Party, but since his wife and young son wished to attend the festivities, he brought them to the Inn and walked with them to the grove. There he withdrew from the throng and sat himself down on the bank of the brook spilling out from the grove spring.

Baiting his hook, he cast his line into the stream and spent a day of serenity in fishing. Asked later why he had lunched on only bread and cheese, washed down with cider, when a table of tempting victuals was spread a few rods away, he replied testily, "I wouldn't care to sit down at a Republican table on Independence Day with a gag in my mouth." Like his co-thinkers, he judged it best to "scatter abroad" when his ideas were completely irreconcilable with those of the controlling party. As ever, the tranquility of the grove had promoted peace.

Meditation alone in the grove likewise eased the mental turmoil of numerous others. One of these was Benjamin's son, who signed himself "H.H." According to his diary in April, 1813, he went into the grove one clear, cool Sunday morning and laid himself on the ground on the south side of a stump. Here he remorsefully read his journal pertaining to his enlistment in the army on Training Day, June 3, 1812.

His entries included: "Sept., 1812: Received orders to march on the 10th inst. for a six months campaign..Gratitude forbids me ever to forget the kind assistance I received from my Mother, my oldest sister, cousin Ruth, and all my relatives and friends, especially my father....on this occasion.... I avoided shaking hands or looking others in the face after Grandfather said 'It is not likely you will ever see me again.' Struggled with all my might against a torrent of suppressed tears, but ran off as fast as I could and rode away in a waggon with my father."

The clear ringing of a church bell in the valley now told H.H. that the afternoon service was about to begin. That same bell had rung farewell to him and the other militiamen the morning that they set forth for Plattsburg. Its musical tones had carried a message of encouragement for several miles along the route toward battle. Now the reassuring notes pealed only an echo of shame for him as they resounded among the rocks and trees of the grove. H.H. writhed in painful recollection as he resumed his reading.

For the next four days and nights the journal told of "dinners of bread, butter, crackers & cheese with cider, or bread & milk." The men "cooked supper in borrowed utensils over fires struck up in the highway." They slept in barns on haymows or loads of hay and were "given plums, apples, cucumbers, fryed apples for sauce" at Sudbury, Hubbardton, Whiting, and Cornwall. As they marched, they "sang patriotic songs and the new Canadian hymn."

"Sept. 17th, Thurs. - Marched into Burlington at sunset. Being dismissed, marched to quarters in the Barracks & deposited Knapsack. Companies separated at Burlington College. Mess usually bread and fresh beef.

"Sept. 21 - Men washed clothes in the Lake. Discontent haunted us. Militia assembled N. W. of Burlington....I did not march with the music but carried a sick man's gun..Later lost out as fifer to other one who could not carry a musket....Visited my Uncle Ebenezer on Montpelier Turnpike & lost my camp gloom. Pitied my poor comrades in their cold wet tents.

"Oct. 1st - Continued drill. Increasingly uneasy. Wrote my father to procure a substitute for me."

The bell of the other village church was now mingling its deep throated tones with the music of the warblers and bluebirds in the grove. Every note increased the bitter remorse within H.H. as he read on.

"Lieutenant Lacy returning to Bennington in order to bring on delinquents, by him I wrote a billet to Mr. Elijah Ballard in N.W. part of town to go to my father and make a bargain with him about taking my place. (The fee later agreed upon was $20.)

"Oct. 10th - John Crawford of Bennington, an elderly gentleman serving here in son's stead, came in with Capt. Hawkins of Rupert, Capt. of Artillery, and Lieutenant Lacy bringing in the delinquents of Col. Martindale's Regiment.

"Oct. 13th - 1st Rgt (the writer's) began to be struck about 6 in the morning but bad blizzard halted operations.

"Next day - 1st Regt went on board the Steam Boat & Sloop Champlain via Batteaux—too windy for others to reach wharf. Half the men on board puking at the same time, there being scarcely 10 men on board who were not seized with vomiting more or less violent. Lake too rough to land at Plattsburg. I and a great many more descended into the hold and piled ourselves on heaps of tents, chests, and other camp equipage, and although indisposed, obtained a few hours repose amidst singing, hallooing, groaning, dog-barking, and cock-crowing.

"Next morning - Seasick, I left my knapsack on deck last night...lost it & clothes worth $12; a good flute & *The Fifer's Companion* - $4 value. Sent home for more and again solicited my father to send on a substitute."

H.H. buried his face in his arms. The April sunshine poured its warmth upon his bowed head. In a nearby pool the peepers piped their joy in release from winter. After a while he turned to his notation for December 6th: "feeling melancholy and remorseful for not sticking out my enlistment– a wound that never will heal. Dread to meet any I know but must if I would perform the duty of an independent citizen."

As H.H. perused his journal here in the grove that April day, he was torn by remorse for his own termination of army service, through the service of another, and by distress for the universal suffering caused by national conflict. Thoughts of the recent Bonaparte Campaigns mingled with those of the "War to the North". Deeply depressed, he observed in his journal that the endless battles of the world were actually the "effect of commercial avarice" or grand ambitious views on the part of the extraordinary Man" who wields the destiny of a nation or an empire.

"It incites in me the most melancholy reflections to picture to myself such mighty masses of men collected from all parts of a great country for no other business than most cruelly destroying each other in cold blood in order to decide who among a few great ones hall rule," he concluded.

Above him, the white birches were misted with the green of new leaf buds. High in the blue, the rhythmic honk of a flying black wedge told him that the wild geese were winging their way to their nesting place in the North. The North! Scene of battle for men, and yet a biding-place for new homes, new families, new hopes for these wild ones. Deep in the grove, a partridge drummed for its mate. Amidst melting snow and thawing leaf mold, the trout lilies were spreading their carpet of gold. Stretching away to the horizon, freshly plowed fields lay richly dark upon the breast of the burgeoning land. All around him, the sunshine was warming the winter-chilled earth to its renewal of beauty and substance. His little dog, Keeper, trotted close, licked his hand and snuggled down beside him.

By slow degrees, H.H. was filled with a sense of his own renewal. Surely the mysterious Force that governed eternal life in Nature must also govern eternal life in Man. From these meditations, he gradually derived the fortitude to "perform the duty of an independent citizen."

Many local farm and village boys tramped through this Grove on the eve of their departures for service in the Union Army some years later. And here they, too, found a fortifying power in the serenity and the eternity of the trees.

From the late 1860s till the end of the century, Memorial Day observance superseded the earlier patriotic celebrations in the Grove. Here, in the early 1880s, the Oration for one of these observances was Will Carleton's "The Festival of Memory; a Converse with the Slain" which had been published in *Farm Festivals* by Harper and Brothers in 1881. This long commemorative poem had been read at the National Cemetery on the Custis Farm, Arlington Heights, Virginia, on Decoration Day, 1877.

Since Will Carleton's poetry was much read and greatly enjoyed in the countryside. this grove meeting was especially well attended. Among those, who found greatest comfort from the Memorial Day reading here, was a mother who had lost her only son in the War for the Union. When the report had come from Gettysburg that "The order was given to put the

Vermonters in front and keep the column well closed up," she had felt some pride in knowing that her David was one of those chosen for the front ranks because of their staunch courage under fire. Nevertheless, grief had remained her constant companion and burden through the years ever since. On this Day, however, as she listened to the message of Will Carleton's "Converse with the Slain", mingled with the windsong and the birdsong of the grove, the stanzas brought her healing.

> "Our heads droop on the world's broad breast,
> Our work is done, and we have gone to rest.

> White faces sunk into the grave—
> Black faces, too - and all were brave.

> To cringe and toil and bleed,
> Your sires and you were born,
> You grew in the ground of greed,
> You throve in the frost of scorn!
> But now as your fireless ashes
> Feed Liberty's fruitful tree,
> The black race proudly flashes
> The star-words 'We are free!'

> "From our dead foemen comes no chiding forth;
> We lie at peace; Heaven has no South or North.
> With roots of tree and flower and fern and heather
> God reaches down and clasps our hands together."

The drums and fifes struck up "Battle Hymn of the Republic", and the assemblage, led by the Civil War veterans of the township, filed down the trail. Baseball games. parades, and other attractions in the villages by then superseded many of the former activities in the grove. A few years later, the grove provided a refuge for the son of the one who gave that Memorial Day reading. One June day in the late 1800s, ten-year-old Adam was swept up in a disastrous tornado that roared along the ridge. Hurled several rods through the air like a bounding baseball, he landed on a mound of moss at the foot of a sturdy old hickory tree. Here he clung with all his might to the rough trunk and one gnarled root that projected above the ground, until the force of the wind and rain was spent.

Although during the tornado, several barns, cattle and sheep were destroyed, and two men injured so they died, the boy survived without even a scar.

A few years later, one of his friends, Roswell Flower, recalled that story of the ridge tornado and of Adam's refuge, with particular interest. Young Flower was about to take up a homestead at Humboldt, near Fort Dodge, Iowa. His cousins, who had already settled there, reported that there was "not a stick of timber" on his new land. Roswell, having himself experienced the force of numerous winds and remembering the tragedy of the local tornado, resolved to make provision for a windbreak for his new home on the Western prairies. Turning to the grove where he had so often roamed as a boy, he selected two poplar saplings, noted for their toughness of fiber and rapidity of growth. These he carefully dug out of the earth, both well fortified with a generous supply of their native dirt clinging to their roots, and bound them in wet hemp sacking. When Roswell Flower's ox-cart rolled through Fort Dodge several weeks later, his pioneer load was topped by the pair of saplings. Today, nearly a century since, two tall cottonwoods (another name for this kind of poplar), that sprouted on the Vermont hillside, stand at the center of the protective grove for Roswell Flower's great-grandson's home at Humboldt.

Near the brook-bordered, rock-sheltered clearing, beside which both Adam's hickory and the pioneer poplars sent down their seedling roots, a Forest Festival was celebrated one September day in the 1950s. Because this was also United Nations Day, and because a recent U.N. monthly bulletin had cited a valley in the same county as "A Picture of Peace", the chairman of the Festival was inspired to include in the program the reading of a part of the United Nations Economic, Scientific and Cultural Organization Charter. The whisper of the wind in the pines mingled with the cadence of the words of the Preamble: "Since wars begin in the minds of men, in the minds of men the defenses of peace must be constructed." The bugle notes of "The Star Spangled Banner" and of "America" accompanied a lusty chorus. Up and down the mountainside echoed the words, "Sweet land of liberty",.."I love thy rocks and rills, thy woods and templed hills", .."Long may our land be bright With Freedom's holy light"

Peace that day pervaded the nation, and peace pervaded the grove. The arching elm and maple, birch and beech trees were aflame with their autumn glory of reds and golds amidst the greens of spruce and pine and hemlock. A pair of bluejays fluttered among the scarlet leaves of a nearby dogwood, feasting on its berries. The red and blue silhouette against a white birch trunk repeated the hues of the national flag, billowing on the light breeze from its staff set in a crevice of the grey-lichened rock beside the picnic table. The flutelike notes of a wood thrush gave the grove's response to "in the minds of men the defenses of peace must be constructed." Were the spirits of "H.H." and Will Carleton hovering near that September day? Whether they were or not, those who met here to promote the conservation of American forests, were likewise preserving the long time sanctuary.

A part of the forestry program which they sponsored was the managed cutting of timber in the adjacent woodland. One morning, shortly after the Fall Festival, when some loggers drove up from their homes in the village to start the day's work, they saw two dogs slink away from the tool shack as their truck approached. Nearby they found a young doe lying in a pool of blood. Her great soft eyes painfully begged for help. From their first aid kits, the men applied ointment, after which they sutured and bandaged the trembling but trusting wild body. They then bedded the deer on a blanket in their shanty.

For days, they shared their lunches with her, petted her, and tended her wounds. As soon as she was able to hobble, Bitsy, as her benefactors called her, began to nose open their lunch boxes and help herself to sandwiches, cake, cheese, pickles, tomatoes, and whatever else they contained. Although this pursuit was soon terminated by the men's putting their lunch boxes on a high shelf beyond her reach, Bitsy continued to linger near her two-footed friends.

When the logging job was finished in late October, she gazed wistfully after the departing trucks. Although she trotted after them a short way down the trail, at the edge of the grove she turned back to the sheltering trees.

The following June the loggers, returning to their work in the woodland beyond the grove, again saw Bitsy. To their astonishment, they now discovered that she had a snow white fawn with her. Though she paused and gazed at them from afar as if greeting them, she would not let them go near her. Her motherhood made her wary even of those who had once saved her life.

"Who'd ever believe that such a mangled body as hers could bear such healthy young?" they marveled. "And such a rare one at that!"

Soon, groups of people from all over the county were congregating near the staddle each evening to catch a glimpse of the white wonder fawn. Only occasionally, however, did they remain far enough away and sufficiently quiet to be rewarded, throughout the summer.

Early one morning in late August, the crippled son of one of the loggers rode up to the grove, when his father went to work, to watch for the famous doe and fawn. Nineteen-year-old Nathan had been permanently injured in an automobile accident a year before, just as he was about to enter aviation college. For months he had lain completely dependent upon others. Then, when his cast was removed, he faced the shattering realization that every career requiring physical soundness would be forever closed to him. Before him lay only helplessness, hopelessness, and a wasteland of dreams.

In mental torment as well as physical, he alighted on the flat bordering the brook at the edge of the grove that summer dawn. Leaning his crutches against the towering beech, and clutching its trunk, he painfully lowered himself to the mossy rock beneath.

A cardinal flashed among the birches. A pair of chewinks bugled to each other from deep among the trees. Chipmunks scolded and scampered across the flat, their jowls bulging with hazelnuts, their beady eyes distrustingly watchful of this strange being hunched against their own nut tree. A red fox leaped down from the ledge and whisked into his burrow beneath. How full of life and energy was every creature in the grove except himself, Nathan thought bitterly.

A rustle among the fallen leaves startled him to attention. It was only Old Stumpy, the raccoon that had gnawed off both forefeet when caught in a trap several winters ago. Nathan had sometimes seen him before, valiantly humping along the trails of the grove. Now the grizzled ring-face plunged into the brook, drank, snorted, cleaned himself, and clawed his way out again. Shaking himself free of the glistening drops, he prowled away in search of his breakfast. Nathan felt a twinge of identifying pity at the sight of his clumsy maneuvers. Suddenly, it was replaced by a surge of admiration for the resourceful old hero.

The next instant, light footsteps pattered near. Nathan tensed. Out of the thicket came Bitsy and her fawn. The mother paused, head high, ears forward, looking and listening intently. Nathan sat motionless, barely breathing, grey garbed against the grey tree trunk. Reassured, the doe and her little one lowered their noses into the cool depth of the pool from which the brook flowed past the boy. Sunlight sifting down through the leaves of the bordering beeches dappled the tawny hide of the mother and the velvety white coat of the fawn.

Delight mingled with shock as Nathan stared past the fawn at the doe. Her flanks were deeply furrowed with scars, one hip was hunched and misshapen, and her left hind foot dragged as she walked. Yet she was a valiant mother, capably and tenderly caring for her young, fulfilling her precarious role against all the predators of the woodland.

Having drunk deeply, doe and fawn sniffed among the fallen leaves at the brink of the water. Their forefeet dug in the rustling pile in search of nuts and tender roots. On these, they browsed briefly until the raucous cry of a bluejay swooping near sent them bounding away into the underbrush.

Nathan lingered, musing soberly. Even here in the seeming tranquility of the grove, life held its perils. Here the wild creatures, too, were maimed. Like himself, they must cope with their injuries, must overcome, or must endure. So many times his grandfather, who had often brought him to this grove as a child, had told him of his forebears, who had owned this hill. Hardship had been their challenge, Gramp had pointed out; ingenuity, faith, perseverance, and courage had spelled their survival, both in body and in spirit.

As the boy gazed up through the branches, leaf-laced and nut-lined against the blue, and as he listened to the lilt of the brook below, memory brought him the words of the Psalm that he and Gramp had often repeated here: "...And he shall be like a tree planted by the streams of water that bringeth forth its fruit in its season; whose leaf also doth not wither, and whatsoever he doeth shall prosper."

"That bringeth forth its fruit in its season...whatsoever he doeth shall prosper..whatsoever he *Doeth*."

Nathan's mind at last was at peace. Hope now diminished his despair. He reached for his crutches and dragged himself to his feet. Then, with the glow of renewed purpose, he resolutely worked his way down the hill from the grove toward whatever life would surely permit him to do.

Like all the others, who have walked these trails, his footprints lay fresh upon the earth for a moment. Then they vanished, to become a part of all that had been here and all that would be, an infinitesimal but infinite element in the process of Creation.

INDEX